For Maria Lough

Staging the Easter Rising

Staging the Easter Rising

1916 as Theatre

JAMES MORAN

CORK **cup** UNIVERSITY PRESS

First published in 2005 by
Cork University Press
Youngline Industrial Estate
Pouladuff Road, Togher
Cork, Ireland

© James Moran 2005

British Library Cataloguing in Publication Data
A CIP catalogue record for this book is available from the British Library

ISBN 1 85918 401 4

Typeset by Tower Books, Ballincollig, Co. Cork
Printed by ColourBooks Ltd, Baldoyle, Dublin

www.corkuniversitypress.com

'To take as a headquarters the most prominent target in the whole city,' said a man in a middle-aged growl, 'what a ridiculous strategy.'

Old George Roberts took the tumbler from his little full lips and stroked his beard. 'But what taste – what impeccable taste,' said he.*

---
* Brendan Behan, 'The family was in the Rising', in *The Dubbalin Man: A New Selection of his Irish Press Columns* (Dublin: A & A Farmar, 1997), pp. 75–8 (p. 75).

Contents

Acknowledgements

This book owes thanks to a number of people. First and foremost I would like to express my gratitude to Maud Ellmann. Her excellent academic guidance, sense of humour, and numerous editorial suggestions have provided the backbone to my writing and have made studying the history and theatre of Ireland a true pleasure. Other sharp-eyed readers have guided me through this project since it began life as a PhD thesis, and I remain particularly indebted to Jean Chothia, Tom Dunne, Luke Gibbons, and Drew Milne. I am also thankful to Joe Cleary, Seamus Deane, Jeff Dudgeon, Declan Kiberd, John Paul McCarthy, Medbh McGuckian, Angus Mitchell, Cathy Phillips, Roger Sawyer, Marcus Tomlin, Kevin Whelan, and my colleagues in the School of English at Nottingham University, who have been generous with their time and advice.

Further thanks must be extended to my own students at Cambridge and Nottingham who have frequently indulged and helped to clarify my ideas about the theatre; to those at Downing College who helped provide me with the space, time, and funding to write much of this book; and to the staff at an assortment of libraries, museums, and archives. I am especially grateful to Mairead Delaney of the Abbey Theatre, Sunniva O'Flynn at the Film Institute of Ireland, Kathleen Dickson of the British Film Institute, Jo Wheatley at RTÉ, and the staff of the Irish Traditional Music Archive in Dublin. Thanks also go to John Kirk for permission to reproduce sections of this book that have appeared in *To the Other Shore: Crosscurrents in Irish and Scottish Studies*, ed. by Neal Alexander, Shane Murphy, and Ann Oakman (Belfast: Cló Ollscoil na Banríona, 2004), pp.128-36.

I am also indebted to Margaret Cahill for allowing her house to become my Dublin B&B, and for giving me the benefit of her encyclopaedic knowledge about many decades of the city's life. In addition, I would like to acknowledge my gratitude to my first and best critic, Ed Purcell, and my inspirational grandparents; particularly the late Paddy Cahill, a garrulous and good-natured Dub who never forgave Éamon de Valera for allegedly swiping a bicycle from the family garage in Donnybrook.

Finally I would like to thank my mother, my father, Thérèse, Angela, and Maria. Without their unwavering encouragement and support this book would never have been written.

The following institutions and individuals have kindly given permission to quote from unpublished or copyright materials: the National Library of Ireland, the British Library, the National Archives of Ireland, Muireann O Briain for the Estate of Roger McHugh, A.P. Watt Ltd on behalf of Michael B. Yeats, John Countryman, Felicity Ashbee, Colin Smythe for the Estate of Oliver St John Gogarty, the Estate of Sean O'Casey, the British Board of Film Censors, Pat Cooke of the Pearse Museum, Garret Fitzgerald, the Society of Authors on behalf of the Bernard Shaw Estate, and the Society of Authors as the Literary Representative of the Estate of Alfred Noyes.

Abbreviations

BBC	British Broadcasting Corporation
BL	British Library, London
GPO	General Post Office, Dublin
IRA	Irish Republican Army
IRB	Irish Republican Brotherhood
NAI	National Archives of Ireland, Dublin
NLI	National Library of Ireland, Dublin
RTÉ	Radio Telefís Éireann

Introduction

They shall be speaking for ever,
The people shall hear them for ever.[1]

We have had our brains washed, as Pearse intended, by the para-theatre of
the 1916 Proclamation.[2]

Reprising the Rising

The Easter Rising of 1916 was something of a military non-event. It was
crushed in less than a week by the British, involved only 1,500 rebels, and
occurred at a time when the eyes of the world were focused not on a street
battle in Dublin but on the carnage of the Western Front. Yet the Rising would
prove, retrospectively, to be one of the most talismanic moments in Irish history,
and exerted a mesmerising effect in the modern Irish state whose very existence
it had helped bring about. People have repeatedly returned to 1916 during the
twentieth century, describing it with a kind of impulse that can be likened to
the Freudian trauma; relating the story over and over again yet never being able
to feel that it has been formulated adequately in a final, definitive form.

When the Rising is re-told it is not necessarily the same event that is
remembered each time. Ever since Pearse led his troops out on that bright
April morning the meaning of the rebellion has constantly been shifting and
evolving. The anthropologist Gearóid Ó Crualaoich's question about the
reality and significance of the insurgence, 'When was 1916?', is not therefore
such a self-evident absurdity as it might at first appear.[3] During the twentieth
century various competing factions invoked the names and ideals of the dead
rebels in support of often mutually exclusive ideas. The Easter Rising means
something different to residents of Dublin today than it did to their counterparts in 1966, and to those living in the city in the spring of 1916. Part of the
brilliance of W.B. Yeats's most famous poem about the rebellion, 'Easter 1916',
lies in the writer's fundamental uncertainty, in his recognition of the equivocal
and mutable nature of the event. Prompted by Yeats's poem, this book seeks
to understand what the uprising has signified at different times in Ireland
since 1916.

When Walter Benjamin described his library he commented that authors
tend to write books 'because they are dissatisfied with the books which they

1

could buy but do not like', and this is largely the reason why I came to write this study about Easter week.[4] Several years ago I started an essay about the way that W.B. Yeats had influenced Ireland's changing attitudes towards the insurgency of 1916. However, as I worked my way through my university library, I grew increasingly frustrated. I was unable to examine the way that Yeats had affected the evolving interpretations of the Rising because very little had been written about the cultural significance of the Easter insurrection at all. A great deal had been published on Yeats, but it was hard to find anything about the continuing impact of 1916 upon Ireland and the Irish. To me, this absence of discussion seemed very strange, because, in my own experience, I had heard tales of the rebellion recounted many times: in the pub, on the television, or in the rousing anthems that my uncles sang at an assortment of family get-togethers. Yet, as soon as I arrived in the library, I discovered that the impact of the insurrection had virtually disappeared from academic discussion, and that those recent books which did deal with the Rising were, in the main, unremittingly hostile to its participants.

As I continued my research I found that my suspicions about the Rising were shared by others. At the beginning of 1991, the superintendent of the Pearse Museum in Rathfarnham asked two academics, Máirín Ní Dhonnchadha and Theo Dorgan, for assistance in organising a conference on '1916 and its interpretations'. But the idea failed to attract official support and had to be abandoned.[5] Across Ireland, official commemorations of the seventy-fifth anniversary of the rebellion remembered the Rising in a similarly subdued and half-hearted way. One member of the committee coordinating a nationwide series of commemorative events reported on 'commitments reneged on, grants withdrawn, projects rejected', and the Dublin Promotions Organisation Ltd, the company charged with managing 'Dublin 1991: European City of Culture', decided against funding a street extravaganza to commemorate the Rising.[6] Apparently the promotions company felt that 1916 failed to 'fire the imagination'.[7]

Three years later, in 1994, the journalist John Waters announced:

> If you had a pound for every time in the past 20 years that an Irish politician invoked the name of one of the 1916 leaders, you would be in need of the services of St Vincent de Paul [. . .] This goes far beyond politics. It afflicts the entire edifice of Irish public discussion. We no longer talk, as a society, about 1916. The whole thing is all a bit embarrassing.[8]

Similarly, at the dawn of the new millennium, the theatre director Ben Barnes spoke about the 1916 proclamation to a group of actors who gaped back at him with an utter lack of comprehension. Their reaction made him realise that 'the proclamation has been bled out of the Irish education system'.[9]

Even those who hold views inimical to Irish nationalism have noted this discursive silence about the uprising. In 1995 Conor Cruise O'Brien observed that the memory of 1916 had become 'something hesitant and mostly subliminal, tinged with apprehension and with guilt', and concurred that 'the official commemoration, in 1991, of the seventy-fifth anniversary of the 1916 rising was much more muted than that of the fiftieth anniversary'.[10]

Máirín Ní Dhonnchadha and Theo Dorgan, who had seen their conference about Easter week fail to attract support at the start of 1991, were anxious that the idea behind their failed symposium should live on, and edited a multi-authored volume, *Revising the Rising*, later in the year. In their introduction they noted that, 'outside the realms of embattled historiography, open and general discussion [of 1916] has been curiously muted, not to say inhibited. There are those of us who feel that, as a reaction, amnesia – private or communal – is both unhealthy and dangerous'.[11]

Yet this amnesia about the uprising was a relatively modern problem. During the Lemass boom years of the 1960s, roughly between the important publications of F.X. Martin's study of the countermanding order and Maureen Wall's analysis of Clarke and MacDermott's deception of the IRB, popular and scholarly interest in the Rising had proliferated.[12] Only in the following years, once the embers of sectarian hatred had been fanned into full conflagration in the North of Ireland, did the Rising appear a less appetising subject, thanks largely to the O'Brienite thesis that the modern IRA was descended from the Easter rebellion.[13]

However, this perceived connection between the Rising and the situation in the North has not been the only problem deterring scholarly enthusiasm for the revolt. Another difficulty is the sheer scale of 1916. By contrast with the reticence of the political and academic community to chart the meanings and implications of the Easter Rising, in popular culture retellings of the rebellion have multiplied and proliferated. 1916 is consequently an unwieldy and expansive topic, and Sisyphus himself would baulk at tracing every individual instance of the conflict's reappearance. The insurrection has been the subject of a relentless number of jokes, letters to newspapers, provincial memorial ceremonies, popular ballads, decorative tea towels, novelty mugs, and a bewildering array of other flotsam and jetsam. Quite aside from the vast scale of 1916, dealing with Easter week also leads into some of the more problematic areas of Irish cultural debate – such as revisionism, the legacy of de Valera, and the history of Irish socialism – all of which have their own guardians and their own pitfalls, making it perhaps easier to comment upon only one tightly delineated part in the chronology of the Rising rather than developing a way of discussing the broader impact and meaning of the rebellion. Consequently, the uprising is a common and clichéd but widely unexamined referent, something Paul Bew notes when he says in Ireland 'people talk of the Easter Rising without considering the real problems involved'.[14]

1916 in the theatre

Fortunately, the Irish playhouse provides a site where a number of disparate views about the insurrection have been distilled. As Martin Esslin has asserted, the theatre is 'the place where a nation thinks in public in front of itself'.[15]

When judging cultural and political interaction the ability of a play to generate a shared response, which can be historicised, gives it an advantage over the dissemination and reception of poems, books, or any of the other multitudinous forms in which the Easter Rising has been depicted.

Raymond Williams observes that playwrights have the advantage of speaking directly to their constituency, and it is this theatrical immediacy, together with the unusual fecundity of the Irish stage during the opening decades of the twentieth century, that provides an incisive way of investigating the evolving significance of the Easter rebellion.[16] Some of the best scholars of Irish studies have written philosophical reflections upon ideas of state formation and national identity, but, although informed by this work, my book focuses instead upon theatrical productions within particular historical contexts.[17] By analysing the original plays and performances given by different groups, and examining contemporaneous accounts of nationalist activities and attitudes, this book offers an analysis of certain moments at which Ireland has needed to repeat or reappraise its foundational cultural myth according to different and mutually antagonistic political agendas.

In 1916 Irish playwrights were gripped by the events in Dublin, and presciently recognised the consequences of the rebellion. G.B. Shaw declared it 'absolutely impossible to slaughter a man in this position without making him a martyr and a hero, even though the day before the rising he may have been only a minor poet. The shot Irishmen will now take their places beside Emmet and the Manchester martyrs in Ireland'.[18] Lady Gregory reported that Yeats 'spoke against the executions, said England was stupid as usual and ought not, in her own interest, to have "allowed them to make their own ballads"'.[19] Pádraic Colum quoted from *Cathleen ni Houlihan* in his observation, 'An Irishman knows well how those who met their deaths will be regarded –. "They shall be remembered for ever; they shall be speaking for ever; the people shall hear them for ever"'.[20]

Yet in the following years some commentators became convinced that Ireland's playwrights had relinquished the Rising. In 1966 the *Irish Independent* stated that the 'greatness of the Easter Rising has not been reflected to any commensurate degree in dramatic literature. O'Casey apart, it has not inspired any writer to works of powerful stature or enduring fame'.[21] Eight years earlier, Denis Johnston had written his play *The Scythe and the Sunset*, and asserted that as far as he was aware 'only one other play about 1916 was performed prior to my own'.[22] However, I am concerned to recover the other performances of the rebellion that Johnston had forgotten, and argue that far from having forsaken the revolt as a topic, those who strove to dramatise the Rising in the period immediately after 1916 helped to influence the way that the insurrection was viewed for the rest of the twentieth century.

As with many scholars of Irish theatre, my work owes much to *The Modern Irish Drama* edited by Robert Hogan and others, Robert Welch's history of the Abbey Theatre, and Cheryl Herr and Stephen Watt's work on the importance of melodrama in the Irish theatrical tradition.[23] I also owe a debt to Declan

Kiberd's impressive study, *Inventing Ireland*, which has worked to heal that long-standing scholarly estrangement between the spheres of political history and literary examination.[24] Recent biographies of Synge by W.J. McCormack and of Yeats by R.F. Foster have further demonstrated the importance of using politics as a key to understanding some of Ireland's best-known theatre writings.[25]

In addition, it has been exhilarating whilst writing this book to find that, perhaps partially facilitated by the IRA ceasefires of the mid-1990s, a fresh crop of superb critical works operating on the interstices of politics and theatre studies has emerged. Christopher Murray, Nicholas Grene, Lionel Pilkington, Christopher Morash, and Ben Levitas have all published recent works charting the interaction of the stage and the state in Ireland, helping to dismantle the dominant critical belief that the playhouse provides a purely aesthetic forum which is able to transcend the contradictions of the political world through some strange sort of 'rough magic'.[26]

The rebellion and its re-enactment

My work owes a debt to the erudition of previous theatre historians, but unlike its antecedents *Staging the Easter Rising* examines how dramatic representations of the Dublin revolt often converge around the issues of sex, gender, and reproduction: issues that have been relentlessly replayed in performance because they were part of a series of unresolved tensions that were an inherent part of the original rebellion itself.

In 1916 the insurrection contained a number of contradictions. For instance, the rebellion's main nationalist thrust as expressed by Pádraic Pearse was an awkward blend of diverse influences. Pearse continually evoked the Roman Catholic religion, and, in particular, was concerned with thoughts of the martyred Christ. But Pearse also drew on the Gaelic Revival's ideas about the pagan warrior-prince Cuchulainn, a character popularised by Standish O'Grady as being willing to sacrifice himself for an originating Gaelic nation.

The contradictions in Pearse's thought were reflected in the opinions of others who fought in the rebellion. On the one hand, some of the rebels saw the conflict as a chance to recreate the old Gaelic, sovereign land whose citizens held all their possessions in common. This view followed the thinking of labour leaders such as W.P. Ryan and James Larkin, who felt that Gaelic Ireland could be remade in the form of socialist Ireland. But on the other hand, many nationalists demonstrably said the rosary during the fighting of Easter week, felt that their rebellion would preserve or reinforce existing social structures, and actively sought approval from the Catholic Church. Indeed, parts of the rebellion took on such a Catholic character that even avowed atheists ended up receiving the last rites.[27]

It is therefore more appropriate to speak not of the coherent nationalism of the Rising but of a conjunction of diverse and often contradictory nationalisms. And amongst these disparate and competing ideologies there existed a strongly theatrical and an avowedly radical element, with a significant number of the nationalists of 1916 having been associated with the Irish playhouse, a place that was dominated by powerful women and which had staged controversial plays to challenge traditional female roles. Some of the most important leaders of the rebellion encountered a kind of proto-feminism through their intimate involvement with the Irish theatre, and went on to write dramas about gender and rebellion before mobilising their ragtag republican army in 1916. In particular, Thomas MacDonagh and James Connolly rehearsed the rebellion on the Irish stage before they led troops into the streets of Dublin, and their plays envisage an Irish nationalist battle being fought for political independence and for female suffrage as well. As scholars like Margaret Ward and Ruth Taillon have pointed out, during the revolutionary period many women were important and enthusiastic supporters of the nationalist movement, and although the rebel men often displayed downright hostility towards them, a number of female helpers turned out during the insurrection.[28]

Writers such as Jeff Dudgeon and Susan Cannon Harris have also emphasised that some of the most prominent rebels of 1916 may have been homosexual.[29] This is not to say that there was any affirmative homoerotic ideology underlying the rebellion; indeed, overt homosexuality would have been utterly repugnant to most Dubliners at this time. However, when Pádraic Pearse wrote a play that rehearsed the rebellion prior to Easter week he did include strong homoerotic currents in his text. Consequently, although we tend to remember the religious and social orthodoxy of the Rising, it is apparent that a number of its participants held, or were at least closely associated with, a range of attitudes that were far from recidivist or reactionary.

With such a variety of nationalisms being involved in the insurgency of 1916, then at the time of the rebellion there were a number of potential readings inherent in the original event. Yet, in the years following the insurrection, some of these readings vanished from the historical narrative. In particular, after 1921 the independent Irish Free State ditched the parts of the rebellion that had been associated with female suffrage, in a wearyingly familiar postcolonial manoeuvre. Ashis Nandy has suggested that the colonial relation is inevitably a profoundly gendered one, as the occupying power justifies its presence as civilising and paternal towards the 'underdeveloped' subjugated people, who are figured as feminised to make them seem passive and unthreatening.[30] Of course, colonialisms vary from place to place, but Nandy's suggestion that indigenous peoples can be feminised resonates with imperial discourse about Ireland. Matthew Arnold, for instance, described the Irish as perennially defeated and 'feminine' to distinguish them from the British self-image, and Margaret Thatcher later justified her policy towards the hunger strikers in the Maze by suggesting that the 'men of violence' were trying to 'prove their virility'.[31] Indeed, Horace Plunkett, the Dublin unionist, showed how the imperial stereotype of the feminised Celt could be internalised by Irishmen themselves when he said, 'this impression is not merely the cheap attribution of racial inferiority by the alien critic with which we are familiar, it is our feeling about ourselves'.[32]

After independence the nationalist response to the colonial caricature of the feminised Celt was to insist on Irish masculinity. When the machinery of the independent state remembered the uprising of 1916 all hints of female involvement and women's rights were erased. On the Irish stage, works about 1916 written by Daniel Corkery and Maurice Dalton showed no female participation in the insurrection other than that of the passive sacrificial mother who was linked with traditional depictions of Ireland as the Shan Van Vocht (the 'Poor Old Woman') and with the Catholic iconography of the Virgin Mary. The gun-toting female fighters of 1916 were ignored, as women were portrayed as hyper-feminine and men as hyper-masculine. In recent years a growing body of feminist scholarship has explored the consequences, both for Irish women and for Irish national politics, of the imposition of such a reactionary gender model.[33] Susan Cannon Harris and Éibhear Walshe, for instance, have fruitfully examined the way that Irish heterosexist and dominant political systems might collude with one another.[34] Influenced by such insights, *Staging the Easter Rising* examines how the plays of Corkery and Dalton, as well as official government depictions of the Easter Rising, portrayed a conservative family and sexual identity as a cardinal part of being Irish, nationalist, and patriotic.

However, in some quarters the private lives of the main protagonists of the Rising continued to be scrutinised in the years following the executions. Suspicions about Pádraic Pearse's pederasty, the homosexual activities of Roger Casement, Éamon de Valera's illegitimate birth and his affair with Kathleen O'Connell, and Michael Collins's philandering and bisexuality have all been fond topics for feverish if largely speculative gossip.[35] Whilst little is written by many academic historians about such subjects, it is still common to overhear conversations or joking about the sexual predilections of the famous (or infamous) when in Ireland. In fact, Lucy McDiarmid suggests that discourse about the enigmatic sexual lives of public figures is a distinct Irish speech genre that corresponds with Luke Gibbons's analysis of rumour as an important counterbalance to 'official' information in the country's public life.[36] But rumours about the sexuality of the Easter rebels have not only been raised in the scurrilous gossip of the alehouse. In the playhouse too 1916 has been associated with sex by writers such as Sean O'Casey and W.B. Yeats, who contested the sanitised version of the insurrection promulgated by the Irish government.

O'Casey and Yeats

O'Casey and Yeats are often considered to have held completely divergent views about the Easter Rising. Whereas O'Casey is remembered by Tim Pat Coogan as one of the few writers who 'kicked their country's most cherished beliefs so firmly in the national testicles', Yeats is celebrated as a decolonising poet in an influential analysis by Edward Said.[37] In consequence, Declan Kiberd's *Inventing Ireland* directly contrasts 'Easter 1916' with *The Plough and the Stars*:

> Whilst Yeats lists the names of the warrior dead, O'Casey worries about the nameless civilian casualties. Where Yeats salutes the heroism of the rebels –

while, of course, questioning its necessity – O'Casey goes farther and questions the whole idea of a hero.[38]

Kiberd's textual analysis is sound, but the rhetorical construction that sees Yeats and O'Casey as necessarily antithetical is misleading. In actual fact, O'Casey was not always a revisionist yin to Yeats's nationalist yang.

Indeed, O'Casey had once venerated nationalist shibboleths. Before 1916 he was a member of the IRB, and wrote doggerel that solemnly declared, 'Now Fenian proud, lift high your head', 'green and white and orange hue/Shall signal death to England's crew'.[39] Even O'Casey's cynical view of nationalism in *The Plough and the Stars* betrays his former enthusiasms. Fluther Good describes the Rising as a 'few hundhred scrawls o' chaps with a couple o' guns an' rosary beads, again' a hundhred thousand thrained men with horse, fut, an' artillery [. . .] D'ye want us to come out in our skins an' throw stones?'[40]

Said's Fanonian case for Yeats, although seductive, is also apt to be overstated. Indeed, Said himself subsequently drew back from his earlier views about the Irishman.[41] The issue of Yeats's political identity is a vexed one, as Daniel Corkery indicated as early as 1931.[42] More recently, Lionel Pilkington has argued that the national theatre movement, over which Yeats exerted such a powerful influence, owed more to the 'constructive' unionist tradition than to political nationalism.[43] An example of how Yeats is erroneously accorded a central position in the revolutionary nationalism of 1916 appears in Allan Wade's edition of *The Letters of W.B. Yeats*. Wade includes Yeats's advice to George Russell in January 1898, 'I think you will yet out sing us all and sing in the ears of generations to come. Absorb Ireland and her tragedy and you will be the poet of a people, perhaps the poet of a new insurrection'.[44] This letter has been taken to imply that, more than eighteen years before the Easter Rising, Yeats realised that a revolt might be on its way and knew it would provide the opportunity to make a poetic reputation. As William Irwin Thompson asserts, in this letter Yeats 'bestowed upon his rival his own most cherished ambition'.[45] It can almost seem as though, in 1898, the zealously nationalist Yeats was already formulating the cross rhymes of 'Easter 1916'.

However, a crucial word in Wade's transcription is wrong. It is more likely that when Yeats scrawled this letter, in his usual sloppy and slapdash handwriting, he was instructing Russell to become 'the poet of a new inspiration' rather than the poet of a new 'insurrection'.[46] Despite having associated with the rebels, both Yeats and O'Casey were outside the IRB loop in 1916, and like most of their countrymen, were united in stupefaction at what had taken place.

Staging the Easter Rising examines the plays that Yeats and O'Casey wrote about 1916, *The Plough and the Stars* and *The Dreaming of the Bones*, in order to show that the works contradict each other far less than some have maintained. It is a scholarly commonplace to assert that Yeats's play is pro-1916 and that O'Casey's work is anti-1916, but by examining the way that the plays of Yeats and O'Casey were first realised in performance, rather than reading only the texts, the two pieces in fact reveal a common political aim. The issue is not so much whether these works were for or against the Easter Rising, but whether they were for or against what the Easter Rising had come to signify at the time that they were first performed.

In 1916 the Dublin insurrection was the rebellion of a small nationalist group convinced that a successful Irish revolution could happen when the British were fighting an international war. This rebellion was secretive and unpopular. Yet by the time that O'Casey and Yeats premiered their plays in 1926 and 1931 the Irish nation had steadily rallied behind the rebels through the protracted executions of the leaders and the election victory of the Sinn Féin ('We Ourselves') movement in 1918. The Rising became a national triumph rather than a covert and risible debacle, but during the transformation it had lost some of its contradictions and rough edges: the parts of the rebellion that had been socially radical were forgotten, and instead 1916 was commemorated as a straightforwardly Roman Catholic event.

The popularising of the Rising dismayed O'Casey and Yeats, both of whom had discovered a number of principles that they personally championed amongst the disparate nationalisms of 1916. By 1926 it was clear to Sean O'Casey, a fervent socialist, that the parts of the Rising he endorsed were being neglected. Ireland was following a path away from Russia's example and 1916 was not going to trigger a wider social revolution. O'Casey saw that the Easter uprising was being remembered incorrectly by posterity, and had become a traduced version of what a true rebellion should be. In *The Plough and the Stars* the disillusioned playwright therefore savaged the popular conceptions of the Easter Rising held in 1926, and included a particularly venomous attack on the way that the women of 1916 were commemorated. *The Plough and the Stars* criticises the nationalist tendency to celebrate powerless mothers, showing that the idea of a woman willingly encouraging her son to die for nationalism is obscene. More specifically, O'Casey turned his invective on an Irish mother who was held up as an exemplar by contemporary nationalism, Margaret Pearse. In *The Plough and the Stars* he denigrates the popularity of this mother and mocks the way that she wanted her son to be remembered. Consequently, during its first run *The Plough and the Stars* incensed an audience that included Margaret Pearse herself, and O'Casey later came to regret being so cruel about her.

At the other end of the political spectrum, in the 1930s W.B. Yeats was aligning himself with an authoritarianism that came close to fascism. Like O'Casey, Yeats disliked the way that posterity had appropriated the legacy of the Easter rebellion, and in 1931 the Abbey staged his work, *The Dreaming of the Bones*. In this play, as in *The Plough and the Stars*, a revolutionary from the GPO comes into contact with a woman who is far removed from the hallowed nationalist mother. The maternal figure in *The Dreaming of the Bones* is an adulterous traitor, and consequently the play's patriot frets about lineage and sexual pollution in the same way as the characters from Yeats's late plays *Purgatory* and *The Words upon the Window-Pane*. In Yeats's opinion, the 1916 rebels had tried to impose an elitist kind of government that was connected to eugenic ideas about breeding, and *The Dreaming of the Bones*, although written in 1917, was first staged in

1931 because Yeats was dismayed by the way that the 1916 rebellion had been hijacked by detestable mob democrats, who had not allowed the Rising to flourish into an aristocratic form of ruling administration. He was particularly alarmed by the success of those 'Warriors of Destiny', the Fianna Fáil party, and staged *The Dreaming of the Bones* during the preparations for Ireland's 1932 general election in order to contrast the Rising's original elitism with the contemptible populism which he now believed was endorsed by the 'Long Fellow', Éamon de Valera. The first performance of *The Dreaming of the Bones*, like *The Plough and the Stars*, used ideas about sex, gender, and reproduction in order to criticise the way that, long after Easter week, Pearse and his rebels were being remembered.

Fianna Fáil and the Easter Rising

The Fianna Fáil party was formed shortly after the Abbey Theatre produced O'Casey's play, and Yeats's work was staged at the same time as the election campaign that brought Fianna Fáil to government for the first time. In this way, both *The Plough and the Stars* and *The Dreaming of the Bones* clashed with Fianna Fáil's interpretation of 1916 at significant moments on de Valera's path to power. In the face of such challenges, members of Fianna Fáil decided to propagate their own dramatic version of the rebellion, but made use of the streets and cinemas of Dublin rather than the greasepaint and footlights of the city's theatres.

A familiar problem with Irish theatre studies is the enthusiasm of its scholars to examine only performances in Dublin or Belfast theatres at the expense of the amateur and community stage. My work is still biased towards Dublin because of the great number and variety of rebellion performances that appeared in the city that had been almost exclusively affected in the original military conflict.[47] But I am anxious to broaden the remit of dramatic analysis. Mary Trotter observes that studies of Irish theatrical practices conventionally focus on 'literary over non-literary dramas', and my book attempts to redress the balance by drawing on a wider array of non-literary and previously unexamined drama, investigating Fianna Fáil's exploitation of public mass spectacle and film.[48]

In 1935, members of de Valera's party gave a bullish assertion of their dominance over 1916 by re-enacting the storming of the GPO in the centre of Dublin. This commemoration portrayed de Valera as the most important figure of the insurrection, and deflected attention away from the divisions of the Civil War and the limitations of Fianna Fáil's domestic policies. Other vocal groups such as the IRA, the Fine Gael ('Irish Race') party, the Blueshirts, and Saor Éire ('Free Ireland') might have claimed to speak on behalf of the Irish people, but only Fianna Fáil was blessed with the legitimacy of 1916.

At the 1935 ceremony Fianna Fáil carefully expunged the rebellious women of 1916 and the statements about sexual equality made by the leaders of the insurrection. This omission was not part of an attempt to recreate the Easter-week

fighting with any kind of historical accuracy, but was instead a political necessity for de Valera's government. One group that had played an integral role in
1916, Cumann na mBan (the 'Women's Association'), had always been vocal in
its militancy and was supporting the modern IRA's violent attacks upon his
administration. Consequently, if de Valera reminded Dubliners of the significant part played by this women's organisation during the rebellion he risked
giving added credence to the IRA's campaign. De Valera was also being criticised by those who despised the financial support that his administration gave
to the Abbey Theatre, where O'Casey and Synge were widely seen to have
denigrated the purity of Ireland's women. In response, the organisers of the
1935 pageant ignored all of the progressive gender politics expressed in 1916,
and emphasised instead the parts of the rebellion that had reinforced traditional, Catholic models of passive womanhood, thus proving that both de
Valera's government and the Easter rebellion were as one in endorsing the
primacy of mothering in defining a woman's existence. This interpretation of
the Rising tallied with Fianna Fáil's new, anti-feminist constitution of 1937 and
with the government's renewed courtship of Rome. Although several of the
leaders of the original rebellion and many of the women involved in 1916 had
strived against creating a republic where women would be chained to the stove
and the sink, in 1935 the Fianna Fáil government was remaking the insurgency in its own image in order to demonstrate how de Valera's party bore the
true inheritance of the conflict.

Subsequent politicians in the north and south of Ireland have used mass
spectacle in a similarly cunning way. In recent years Bertie Ahern deflected
Dublin working-class support away from his electoral rivals Sinn Féin by
organising republican funerals to rebury patriots at Glasnevin, and David
Trimble secured his primacy over the Ulster Unionist Party after leading the
Orange march at Drumcree. Such moments of ritual are related to the theatre,
but it is important to discriminate between the two. In the first book-length
consideration of semiotics and theatre, *Littérature et spectacle* (1975), Tadeusz
Kowsan argues that dramatic literature, when presented, does overlap with
spectacle, but notes that, throughout history, dramatic literature has shown a
preference for known subjects, great myths, other literary works or historical
facts.[49] Whereas ritual retells the same story with the same conclusion over
and over again, the function of theatre is to offer a critique of pre-existing
stories and myths.

Yet even though the 1935 Fianna Fáil public commemoration of the Easter
Rising is recognisably distinct from the literary plays of O'Casey and Yeats, the
mass spectacle deserves examination alongside the more conventional performances and texts of the Irish theatre. Richard Schechner has defined
'performance' as 'the doing of an activity by an individual or group largely for
the pleasure of another individual or group', and Manfred Pfister writes that
therefore 'drama clearly belongs to this category as much as games with fixed
rules, sporting competition, ritual and unstructured forms of "play"'.[50] In the
years since Schechner and Pfister constructed their theories of drama there has

been a profusion of sociologically informed theoretical works on performance studies, but most commentators still accept the basic observation that other structurally related performance activities are partly connected to theatre by a series of progressive steps.[51] The 1935 mass spectacle was the direct forerunner of other more consciously theatrical pageants that commemorated the Rising, and many of the same people attended and acted in both Dublin's pageants and the city's plays. Drama critics have traditionally privileged texts over performances and high art over low culture, and so groups such as the Abbey or the Irish Literary Theatre have sometimes become the sole focus for scholarly examination. But the Abbey was not sealed off from the energy of other nationalist performances, and an analysis of mass spectacle gives a more complete picture of the Irish theatre's collaborations and confrontations over 1916.

The nation-building Warriors of Destiny were keen to downplay the proto-feminist aspects of the Rising, and Fianna Fáil also used dramatic performance to make sure that no connection with gay identity would be attached belatedly to the Rising. Homosexuality would continue to be taboo in the Irish state for many years, as the senator and gay-rights campaigner David Norris has written: 'There remained in the minds of many people until recently a doubt as to whether the terms [. . .] "Irish" and "Homosexual" were not mutually exclusive'.[52] Nearly twenty years after the rebellion, Fianna Fáil helped divorce Irishness from homosexuality by ensuring that the much-discussed gay identity of Roger Casement would be excluded from the narrative of 1916.

In 1934 and 1935 a Hollywood studio decided to make a film about Casement, and was confronted by the implacable opposition of Éamon de Valera. The Irish leader knew that a movie which probed the life of this particular rebel could be extremely detrimental to both the current government and the conservative version of the Easter Rising that Fianna Fáil promoted. The British film censor, who was also outraged by the prospective screen celebration of such an odious traitor, unwittingly rallied to de Valera's cause. The British and Irish opponents of the Casement film were then joined by an even more unlikely voice when G.B. Shaw stated his discomfort with Hollywood's project. Shaw had sympathised with Casement in 1916 and had tried to prevent the execution by writing a courtroom defence speech. However, Casement never delivered Shaw's oration, and the playwright's later hostility to Hollywood's endeavours stemmed from his distaste at the idea of seeing Casement directly represented by dramatists after the only script that really mattered had failed to have the slightest impact.

Shaw wanted Hollywood's producers to follow in his own footsteps, and to invoke Casement in an allusive fashion. Shaw's *Saint Joan* therefore refers to Roger Casement only indirectly, recycling the unused courtroom defence from 1916. Furthermore, *Saint Joan* also predicts that rebels who challenged sexual norms would prove difficult for nationalists like de Valera to assimilate, and Roger Casement indeed continued to be problematic for Fianna Fáil and for film producers alike after 1935.

Later representations of 1916

The final chapter of this book charts how the Rising was depicted after the mid-1930s. By 1935 the government version of 1916 was in the ascendant, and playwrights created depictions of an insurrection that cohered with the values promoted by Fianna Fáil. For a long time, Irish dramatists echoed de Valera's conservative sentiments about the Rising, and dissenting voices were raised almost exclusively in foreign countries. In Ireland the fiftieth anniversary of 1916 marked a particularly triumphant moment for Fianna Fáil's version of the Rising, celebrated with what David Trimble would later term 'an orgy of self-congratulation'.[53]

However, in the late 1960s and 1970s the North of Ireland spiralled into a depressing cycle of violence, and attitudes towards the insurgency changed. As scholars saw the IRA shedding fresh blood in the name of 1916, the number of academic publications about the Rising was reduced, and those works that were printed no longer adopted the hagiographic attitude towards the rebels that had once seemed a prerequisite. If books about the insurgents had previously born titles such as *The Story of a Success* they were now more likely to be called *The Triumph of Failure*.[54] Just as O'Casey had done in *The Plough and the Stars*, those who reassessed the Rising in the late 1960s and 1970s commonly focused on the sexual proclivities of the rebels, and viewed the insurrection not as messianic and glorious but as an outlet for the various personal frustrations and inadequacies of the bedroom. Playwrights and producers found O'Casey's writing freshly relevant, and in the heated climate of the late 1960s the brutality of the Northern conflict resurrected debates and arguments that had first been conducted between 1916 and 1935.

Later still in the twentieth century, the social attitudes of the 1937 constitution began to crumble, and homosexuals and militant women asserted their presence in the story of the rebellion. This brought its own problems, as in some quarters the apparent homosexuality of the newly fashionable Roger Casement and the direct autobiographical content of the homoerotic sections of Pearse's writings became the main focus of attention, even though Casement's sexual orientation is still debated, and the direct correlation between Pearse's real-life sexual peccadilloes and his creative writing ignores the broader Edwardian tendency to celebrate the beauty of athletic boyhood and the political purpose of contrasting heroic youth against a corrupting colonial parent state.[55]

Nevertheless, in the more liberal climate of the later twentieth century, playwrights were able to incorporate previously marginalised groups into their work, and in doing so looked back again to the earlier ideas expressed upon the Abbey stage. As the whirligig of time brought in its revenges, playwrights brought homosexuals and militant women to the stage by repeating the ways in which Sean O'Casey had depicted the Easter Rising, jarring with the views of those who believed that the insurrection should still be remembered in performances such as those orchestrated by Fianna Fáil between the 1930s and the

1960s. Despite all of the changes in Ireland, the conflicting nationalisms of 1916 had stubbornly refused to go away and still exerted a magnetic pull on playwrights at the start of the twenty-first century. Ever since the Rising of Easter week the original tensions that existed within the rebel ranks had remained unresolved, and were still being contested on the Irish stage many years after the gunfire had ceased.

1

The Rebellion
of 1916

But though one has admired this 'Celtic school' that has done so much for drama one has, not unreasonably been suspicious of its reality. Its two weaknesses have been so obvious, the 'drawing room touch' and the 'political twist'. How clearly this has come out in the rebellion, a rebellion partly in the clouds and partly on the roofs of the Dublin houses and that's why they made this last stand there poets and dreamers.[1]

A terrible beauty is born.[2]

The 'theatre of war'

When the Easter Rising began, some bystanders believed they were witnessing the opening of a play. As the orders for mobilisation were issued, an inquisitive member of the public meandered into the Liberty Hall, where the rebels were busily shifting grenades and ammunition. The building was well known for the dramatic productions staged there every Sunday night, and seeing the frenetic activity of the rebels, the unsuspecting visitor stopped Constance Markievicz to ask:

'Rehearsing, I presume?'
'Yes,' said Markievicz.
'Is it for children?'
'No,' said Markievicz, 'this is for grown-ups.'[3]

A similar blunder was made on Easter Monday when Dublin's ever-present playgoer Joseph Holloway noticed a hoarding displaying the 'Proclamation of the Irish Republic'. He noted the Gaelic heading and 'floridly worded' sentiments, and assumed that he was looking at an announcement for the Theatre of Ireland.[4]

In 1916 it was easy for Dubliners to mistake the Easter Rising for an Easter dramatising. They lived in a town of many theatres, where audiences were accustomed to watching noble patriots fighting valiantly against British enemies and impossible odds. The 1916 insurrection occurred near to, on top of, and inside these playhouses. Behind the GPO stood a brand new theatre, the Coliseum, which was completely demolished during the fighting whilst the rebels were attempting to burrow into it. Liberty Hall, where the rebellion began, was blown apart by artillery shells. Elsewhere a multitude of British troops mustered around the Abbey Theatre, where they found themselves disquietingly surrounded by playbills for *Cathleen ni Houlihan* and for a new work entitled *The Spancel of Death*.[5]

The visitor who mooched into Liberty Hall on the eve of the Rising was curious about Dublin's playhouses, and so may have known that Markievicz was a member of the Theatre of Ireland, or recognised her as the striking star of a production called *The Memory of the Dead* at the Abbey. When Joseph Holloway read the proclamation he was startled to find that an assortment of playwrights and producers had endorsed the document. He saw the names of Thomas MacDonagh, a writer whose productions had graced several of Dublin's stages; Joseph Plunkett, who worked with MacDonagh to establish the small, experimental Hardwicke Street Theatre in 1914; and James Connolly, who wrote a play that was performed at the Liberty Hall the previous month.

As Holloway studied the proclamation he also noticed the name of Pádraic Pearse, a schoolteacher from Rathfarnham. Pearse had, according to his sister, been fond of 'make believe' and 'dressing up' since he was a child (when he had a penchant for rambling around Dublin dressed as a girl), and as an adult he took to writing and producing acclaimed plays for schoolboys.[6] In 1909 Holloway had visited Pearse's school to watch the teacher's first production along with a glamorous guest list that included Edward Martyn, Pádraic Colum, Standish O'Grady, and W.B. Yeats.[7] Holloway was mesmerised, and called Pearse's show 'unique and inspiring'.[8] When the schoolboys subsequently came to perform Pearse's Gaelic passion play at the Abbey, Holloway made sure to attend and was again deeply moved. On Easter Monday, 1916, Holloway saw Pearse's name surrounded by the names of authors and organisers of the Irish stage, and understandably concluded that he was looking at a theatre announcement rather than a revolutionary manifesto.

If Joseph Holloway had seen a more extensive list of the rebellion's participants his conviction that the fracas was a theatrical event would have been reinforced. The Abbey's usherette, Nelly Bushell, the theatre's stagehand, Peadar Kearney, and its prompter, Barney Murphy, all joined the rebels. At the same time, one of the Abbey's main actors, Maire nic Shiubhlaigh, who often played the part of Cathleen ni Houlihan, made her way to Jacob's biscuit factory, where she was forbidden to leave the ground floor because of sniper fire, and spent a rather dull time cooking meals for the rebels. Others were far less fortunate. Helena Molony and Arthur Shields, both members of the Abbey company, were imprisoned after taking part in the fighting, and Francis Sheehy Skeffington, who had written a play called *The Prodigal Daughter* for the Women's Franchise League, was arrested whilst trying to prevent looting and then murdered by an insane British soldier. J. Crawford Neil, who had written and acted for the Theatre of Ireland and the Hardwicke Street Theatre, was also slain. In addition, Willie Pearse, who founded the Leinster Stage Society, and excited the notice of Joseph Holloway by playing the part of Pontius Pilate in the Gaelic passion play at the Abbey, fought alongside his older brother Pádraic during Easter week, and in the aftermath both brothers shared the same terrible fate.

Other members of Dublin's theatrical world also involved themselves in the Rising, but history has long forgotten them. In 1966 the Abbey Theatre produced a small plaque naming all the members of the company who had taken part in the insurrection, but the theatre ignored Edward Keegan, who had fought in the rebellion and had played a minor part in Yeats's *On Baile's Strand* and Lady Gregory's *The White Cockade*. To the annoyance of Keegan's wife, her husband was excluded from the commemorative list because he had been a part-time member of the Abbey company.[9] Still more unremembered participants in the revolt had literary and theatrical affinities, as evinced by an appeal that G.B. Shaw received shortly after the Rising. A woman whose husband had been locked in an English prison asked:

> Perhaps you and your colleagues in the Arts in England would try to secure for our people who have terms of Penal Servitude even though they may not serve them in full, that while they are in prison they may be allowed to write. So many of the men in prison have literary tastes of some sort, and to young poets and playwrights no matter how minor, the lack of writing materials is a real deprivation [. . .] there are a number of men who might be producing really good stuff.[10]

In the same vein, Helena Molony wrote from her jail cell, 'I wish you would write me a long gossipy letter about Abbey affairs. I am lost for inside news. Sometime I shall give way to a temptation I have long resisted, – in public anyhow – and take to play-writing'.[11] Extraordinarily, some of the rebels remained obsessed by the theatre even when they languished in prison, locked away from their homes and families, and facing a future of extreme uncertainty.

A number of years later W.B. Yeats celebrated the Rising in the following terms:

> Come gather round me players all:
> Come praise Nineteen-Sixteen,
> Those from the pit and gallery
> Or from the painted scene
> That fought in the Post Office
> Or round the City Hall,
> Praise every man that came again,
> Praise every man that fell.[12]

Yeats found the comparison between patriots and players particularly apposite because some of his militant acquaintances had died in ways that mirrored the scenes watched by Dublin's theatre audiences. In November 1915 Patrick Bourke's company performed *For the Land She Loved* at the Abbey, in which a rebel from 1798 faces an English firing squad and declares, 'do not bind my eyes; I am an Irishman and I am not afraid to die'.[13] When Maud Gonne's husband, John MacBride, was led into Kilmainham jail's yard to face the firing squad in 1916 he also 'requested not to be blindfolded [. . .] Turning slightly aside, he said [. . .] "I've often looked down their guns before"'.[14]

Seán Connolly's death owed even more than that of John MacBride's to the theatres of Dublin. Connolly was a young actor who appeared regularly at the Abbey, and was the first Irish soldier to die during the rebellion. His demise caused 'real grief' to Lady Gregory and prompted Yeats to proclaim him 'our only actor of subjective genius'.[15] The last time Seán Connolly was seen on the Abbey stage was on 7 March 1916, when he appeared in a version of Yeats's *Cathleen ni Houlihan*. Less than three weeks later the actor gave his final playhouse performance, in the part of McMahon in James Connolly's *Under Which Flag?*, a role that, according to Francis Sheehy Skeffington, 'produced a profound impression on the audience', and which involved Seán Connolly carrying a tricolour onto the stage and encouraging the Irish to give their lives for their country.[16] According to Peter de Rosa, whilst Seán Connolly was attempting to unfurl the very same tricolour during the Rising he was spotted by a British sniper and shot dead.[17] Like *Cathleen ni Houlihan*, *Under Which Flag?* gave its author good reason to ask, 'Did that play of mine send out/Certain men the English shot?'[18]

The fools, the fools

According to some historians, the dramatic fixation of the rebels demonstrates that the Rising was a crazed poetic folly. Ruth Dudley Edwards's *Patrick Pearse* and William Irwin Thompson's *The Imagination of an Insurrection* portray the leaders of the revolution as misty-eyed idealists who gloried in the symbolism of the stage world rather than the brutal realities of militarism and death. To die for the sake of an inane cause is the height of neurosis, and writers such as Dudley Edwards and Thompson emphasise the inanity of a military campaign that takes its cue from the playhouse, implying that the rebels' interest in the theatre led to stage a doomed rebellion that was obsessed by madcap fictional notions. Even in 1916 the theatrical proclivities of the rebels were censured. As Dublin lay in ruins the *Roscommon Herald* denounced the 'Poet's Rebellion with too much literature [about it]', and the *Hibernian Journal*, the official organ of the moderately nationalist Ancient Order of Hibernians, defended its organisation by saying:

> To those who sneeringly ask: 'What has the A.O.H. been doing?' It has done much; it has done it effectively, it has done it *sub rosa*. Its representatives have not been play-acting to the gallery. They have not sought the glaring publicity of the limelight.[19]

Michael Collins himself declared, 'Looking at it from the inside (I was in the GPO) it had the air of a Greek tragedy about it'.[20]

However, previous revolts had established the playhouse as the familiar stamping ground of revolutionaries, and showed that the stage could be invaluable to insurgency. In 1601 the Earl of Essex's attempted coup against England's Queen Elizabeth began with a special performance of *Richard II*, and in Istanbul in 1872 two performances of Namýk Kemal's drama about the Crimean war, *Vatan yakut Silistra* ('Fatherland or Silistria'), brought swarming crowds to call for holy war.[21] A company rehearsing Rossini's *Guillaume Tell* in France in 1830 found the cry of 'ou l'indépendence ou la mort!' so stirring that they rushed out into the street and joined the troupe that toppled Charles X. In the same year an audience in Brussels rushed from the *Théâtre de la Monnaie*'s production of Auber's *La muette de Portici* to storm the courthouse, and began the national revolution that established Belgian political independence.[22] Indeed, the British army's reaction to the Rising in 1916 was itself distinctly theatrical: one by one the rebels were dressed up and gunned down as a chilling example to the rest of the Irish nation.

Theatrical productions have customarily been organised and scripted by a small and exclusive hierarchy, whilst encouraging audiences to share collective emotion and popular feeling. As Yeats was fond of (mis)quoting, 'Victor Hugo has said that in the theatre the mob became a people', and, as the Easter Rising was opposed by most of those living in Ireland, its leaders knew that they had to shape the populace as if it were an audience in the theatre in order to attract popular support.[23] The rebels' interest in the stage arose not simply from vanity and foolishness, but from a pragmatic recognition of its importance to the rebellion. As Ben Levitas has shown, during the preparations for 1916 MacDonagh and Plunkett's Hardwicke Street Theatre provided a forum for strategic debate about the military tactics of the Irish Volunteers. Whilst some of MacDonagh and Plunkett's productions supported Eoin MacNeill's idea that the Volunteers should refrain from hostilities until they were attacked or until conscription turned public opinion in favour of revolutionary action, other plays performed in Hardwicke Street emphasised the success of the insurrectionary who acts without necessarily waiting for public validation.[24] A secret society like the IRB could hardly conduct an explicit public debate about their rebellion, and so the playhouse provided an alternative meeting place for ideological and tactical discussions.

One of the unresolved questions that was debated in dramatic performances but left unanswered by many nationalists at the time of the rebellion was the role that should be played by women in Irish society. A number of the leading rebels had a firm commitment to female suffrage, and envisaged the Easter rebellion being fought for both national and sexual equality. During the build-up to the revolt Pearse had delivered his 'Ireland unfree shall never be at peace' speech at O'Donovan Rossa's funeral, the biggest nationalist demonstration held before the fighting, where he had been thronged by such a large number of uniformed nationalist women that, rather unkindly, the Irish Women's Franchise League claimed most of the crowd believed they were attending a suffragette rally.[25] In 1916 Pearse spoke in front of another crowd, this time in Sackville Street, and was again soundly mocked, with the *Roscommon Herald*, for instance, condemning his declaration because it was 'drafted on Suffragette lines, and gives votes equally to men and women, and it also has a lot of other "crank" notions'.[26]

At various times since the revolt, feminists have celebrated the fact that 1916 was unique in being an event where men fighting for freedom voluntarily included women amongst their ranks. Many of the Dublin insurrectionists belonged to the Citizen Army, an organisation that eschewed class and sex distinctions, encouraged armed women to march side by side with men, and elected Constance Markievicz to its Army Council. Even the more conservative members of the IRB were affected by such ideas of equality, with the IRB newspaper *Irish Freedom* urging women to take up arms in 1913 and promising that 'in the days when Ireland is free, no one will have anything but admiration for the women who contributed in however great or small a degree, to the attainment of her freedom'.[27] Whilst Dublin burned, the female members of the Citizen Army tended to fight alongside the men, whilst the women of the IRB's sister-organisation Cumann na mBan were more likely to feed and nurse the soldiers, or carry dispatches, although this distinction between combatants and non-combatants was often blurred. Many of the women indeed felt that they were soldiers in their own right, and after the fighting had ceased these radicalised women played perhaps an even more important role, fundraising and organising protest meetings whilst the British kept the male rebels under lock and key. According to Kathleen Clarke, 'Pearse, addressing the women in the GPO on the Friday before the surrender, said that if it were not for the women, the fight could not have lasted so long, and that when the history of that week came to be written, the highest honour and credit should be given to the women'.[28]

However, there remained a solid block of male nationalist opinion that was unconvinced by female emancipation, and was unwilling to accept the political equality of women. The Easter proclamation itself reveals some of the tensions that existed within the rebel camp. This declaration did indeed guarantee 'equal rights and equal opportunities to all its citizens' at a time when most women in Europe were excluded from voting, and specifically addresses itself to both 'Irishmen and Irishwomen'.[29] Yet at other moments the proclamation serves to reinforce a rather more regressive and domesticated view of women. It speaks of an Ireland who 'summons her children to her flag and strikes for her freedom' and thus invokes the cult of Mother Éire, a figure primarily defined by her ability to raise offspring who would fight and die for the nation. This female version of Ireland frequently irks feminists who believe that it stereotypes women as passive and powerless. Elizabeth Cullingford, for example, writes, 'to gender it [the land] as female, therefore, is to confirm and reproduce the social arrangements which construct women as material possessions, not as speaking subjects'.[30] The Rising was, after all, orchestrated by the Irish Republican *Brotherhood*, and the Fenian movement's recruitment was traditionally connected to male activities like hurling, bowling, and drinking in the pub. In addition, the formation of the Irish Volunteers in 1913 was surrounded by assurances that recruits would 'realise themselves as citizens and as men'.[31] With the execution of some of the most radical minds of the rebellion at the end of the conflict, this kind of conservative thinking came to dominate the nationalist movement in the years after the revolt, leaving the women of Easter week pointing back in vain to the unfulfilled promises of equality that they had fought for, and that Pádraic Pearse had declared on the steps of the GPO.

Of all the rebels of 1916, those who had been in contact with the playhouses of Dublin were most likely to insist upon female emancipation at the same time that national independence was asserted. After all, by contrast with many other areas of Irish professional life, a relatively large proportion of the key personnel of the Irish stage was female. The founding patron of the Abbey was Annie Horniman, and her theatre depended on both a talented cast of female actors and the managerial skills of Lady Gregory. Alice Milligan wrote plays for the Irish Literary Theatre, as well as creating stories about revolutionary women and founding a number of nationalist women's committees in Ulster. In 1916 many rebels knew of Cathleen ni Houlihan's famous embodiment in Maud Gonne, who, away from the stage, was the imposing leader of a women's nationalist group, Inghinidhe na hÉireann ('Daughters of Ireland') whose members insisted that the chance to take up arms should not be denied to women. Amongst their other nationalist activities, Inghinidhe na hÉireann produced plays and tableaux, some of which were scripted by Milligan and starred the prominent actor Maire Nic Shiubhlaigh.[32]

Of course, melodramas with a regressive view of women remained popular in Dublin, but a number of contemporary plays and dramatic controversies in the city revolved around the unconventional status and behaviour of Irish women. In 1899 Yeats's *The Countess Cathleen* depicted a noblewoman saving a starving peasant community by bartering her highly-valued soul for food; Synge's 1903 play *In the Shadow of the Glen* presented an Ibsenite woman named Nora deciding to leave her husband for a wandering tramp; and most notoriously, in 1907 *The Playboy of the Western World* showed the women of Mayo being attracted to a man who brags of patricide. These plays caused great upset because, traditionally, Irishmen were depicted as idealistically and selflessly devoting themselves to the good of the wider community, whilst Irishwomen were portrayed as staying at home and keeping quiet about their personal desires. However, in the new and controversial plays of Dublin, such expectations had been turned on their head.

Certain of the 1916 leaders were particularly aware of the theatre's ability to challenge traditional views about women, and three of the most influential rebels, James Connolly, Thomas MacDonagh, and Pádraic Pearse, prepared for the Easter Rising by writing plays about violent rebellion that connected secretive and successful nationalist revolts to a reassessment of gender or sexual roles in Ireland.

James Connolly

Before he marched into the streets of Dublin at Easter 1916, James Connolly staged a play about fighting the British. His little-known work, *Under Which Flag?*, was set during the Fenian rebellion of 1867 and was performed immediately prior to the Easter Rising.[33] In Connolly's play the action revolves around the O'Donnell cottage, in which one of the sons of the house, Frank, is besotted with Mary O'Neill. Also living in their midst is a blind old man, McMahon, who participated in the 1848 rebellion and reminds the O'Donnell clan that Britain is still wronging Ireland. However, to McMahon's horror, Frank announces his wish to join the enemy army. In the next act Mary sees the Fenians drilling in secret, and considers telling the British about this until McMahon appears and warns her against it. When she returns to the cottage Frank pleads with her to dance with him but she refuses because of his pro-British sentiments. McMahon then enters and whispers to all the young men except Frank. Each man leaves to fight for Ireland, leaving only McMahon and Frank behind. Mary tells Frank that if he loves her he should go with the others, and so he straightens up and goes into battle for Ireland whilst McMahon kneels and prays for the rebels' success.

Under Which Flag? was first performed on 26 March 1916, in Liberty Hall where, just over three weeks later, the rebels would be stationed in real combat. Connolly's play was therefore a thinly disguised justification for the rebellion, a fiction in which there is no doubt that a secret revolutionary organisation might be misguided or wrong, or that it might fail to speak in the best interests of the majority of the nation. The revolutionists might be hidden, but, as evinced by the blind McMahon's faith in them, they are undoubtedly trustworthy. Accordingly, the play concludes by emphasising that fighting against Britain is divinely guided by 'God's blessing', and that the insurgents speak on behalf of all 'the land' (fol. 33).

Connolly also knew that previous Irish rebellions had been dogged by informers, and wanted to prevent details of his uprising being passed to the Castle. So in *Under Which Flag?* he uses McMahon to deliver a timely warning to potential Irish spies. Connolly would consequently have been pleased to find that, according to observers from James Stephens to Peter de Rosa, the Easter Rising was a rare example of an Irish insurgency that was unhindered by any moles within the ranks.[34] In fact, the British ignored the first reports of insurrection, thinking their information too fanciful.

Under Which Flag? also seeks to justify the kind of proto-feminism that its author was so enthusiastic about. Connolly felt a strong affinity with the women's suffrage movement, and he was adamant about including the pledge to equal rights and equal opportunities in the proclamation. He wrote that when 'justice is denied' women 'revolt, and revolt places women in comradeship and equality with all the finer souls whose life is given to warfare against established inequities'.[35] His daughter Nora later remarked:

> The more active part women took in a movement the greater his pleasure; by his advice and counsel he encouraged them; more, he gave them often that little push forward they needed. He saw nothing incongruous in a woman having a seat on an army council, or preferring to bear arms to winding bandages.[36]

In *Under Which Flag?* the main female character, Mary, might not at first appear to support the view of Connolly as a card-carrying feminist. Mary provides Frank with his sole motivation for fighting in the rebellion, and at the end of the play he realises that refusing to struggle for Ireland means foregoing his romantic desires. Consequently, he proves his love for Mary by facing the British bullets. In this way, by linking Frank's devotion to her with his devotion to the Irish nation, Mary evokes the common allegorical figure of Ireland as a woman that would recur in the Easter proclamation. Mary's name and her satisfaction with Frank's sacrifice for the common good of the nation also link her to that persistent image, deeply rooted in popular belief, of the mother of God who willingly offers her son to the pain of the cross. Some feminists have reacted with hostility against the Virgin Mary, seeing her as an icon whose function is to keep women in a straitjacket of purity and submissiveness. Elizabeth Cullingford, for example, suggests:

> Mary's role as the embodiment of maternity reinforces a biologistic insistence on woman's function as reproducer and nurturer, while adoration of her paradoxical virginity masks a hatred of the unclean female body and a denial of female desire. Mariolatry in Ireland must be understood as the deliberate identification of a conquered people with a cult which was anathema to their Protestant oppressors, yet its effects on Irishwomen have been repressive.[37]

However, in Connolly's play Mary is far from a symbol of feminine passivity, obedience, or domesticity. For one thing, she often flirts with Frank, prompting Frank's parents to worry that they may not be 'doing right to let you both in the one house together' (fol. 3). Whilst Mary's desire for Frank simmers throughout the play, she never allows herself to be dominated by him, and resists with determination when he tugs at her and insists 'come, Mary, dance, let us have this dance together' (fol. 30). Mary also contradicts conservative male expectations by disdaining housework: at the start of the play she proves uninterested in chores and is scolded for being unable to wind wool into a ball.

Mary recognises that Irishwomen face discrimination, and declares: '[I] Wish I was a man so that I could do something to make a stir in the world, and have people saying nice things about me, and bringing their friends to see me [. . .] Amn't I the strange girl [?]' (fols 15–16). Her decision to spy on the rebels is her most significant attempt to escape the usual powerlessness of the Irish female, even though she later comes to regret the fecklessness of this plan. Becoming an informer will bring 'all the people, high and low running to see me' (fol. 17), make her 'the great girl' (fol. 18), and grant her some redress for the humiliations that she has previously encountered as a result of her class and gender, such as the bullying that she has suffered at the hands of the local church warden. Whilst the figure of Ireland as a woman has been lambasted by present-day feminist critics, it is not always the case that this female character was necessarily passive and stoical before 1916.

By considering a career as a British informer Mary subverts the gender roles that had been popularised in ballads, cartoons, and melodramas, in which women encouraged men to fight but lacked the ability to affect a military struggle by their own unaided efforts. Nationalist women were often viewed in binary terms, being passive rather than active, domestic rather than labouring, and patriotically Irish rather than willing to help the British. Mary may not be able to fight at the end of the play, but at least she challenges the stereotype. It was little surprise that the staunch feminist Francis Sheehy Skeffington was enraptured by the play, exclaiming, 'at the present time nothing could be healthier for the youth of Ireland than the lesson it teaches'.[38]

Thomas MacDonagh

Like Connolly, Thomas MacDonagh was also concerned with gender equality. In 1913 the *Irish Citizen* labelled him 'one of the many poets and literary men who have publicly associated themselves with the women's movement'.[39] Before the Rising, MacDonagh also spent time writing a play, *When the Dawn is Come*, which connects the struggle for Irish liberation to a renewed scrutiny of female roles.

As with Connolly's play, MacDonagh's work was written to justify the clandestine tactics and organisation of the Easter Rising. *When the Dawn is Come* imagines a not-too-distant future in which the Irish army is in the field for the final showdown with England. The national struggle is coordinated by a small council of Ireland, and this council's leader, Thurlough, acts so secretively that his own colleagues mistake him for a traitor. However, he is vindicated at the end of the play when he rallies Ireland's troops to a decisive and comprehensive victory.

MacDonagh emphasises the importance of female thinking to nationalist insurgency. In *When the Dawn is Come* the commanding council of Ireland includes two women, one of whom, Ita, is also the most intelligent and trustworthy member of the group. Although Thurlough claims that she is emotional, he confides his covert activities to her alone, telling none of the other council members because he feels he will lose their support. When they learn of his furtive operations some of the members of the council do indeed condemn him, largely owing to old and illogical prejudices, but Ita maintains confidence in her leader and is proved correct at the play's conclusion.

When Thurlough is mortally wounded in the final conflict he rejoices in having devoted his life to Ireland, declaring 'My fate is kind'.[40] However, Ita's reaction is far more ambivalent. She adores Thurlough, and although she has encouraged his revolutionary activities she has also attempted to persuade him away from spying and secrecy by asking, 'You love to analyse your thoughts, and the thoughts of others – can you love aught else? You love to outwit the cunning – can you love aught else?'[41] At the end of the play, her repeated refusal to accept his death implies that his martyrdom for Ireland has made him an unforgettable hero, but equally indicates Ita's grief and shock at seeing Thurlough on his deathbed. She is not an incarnation of the sacrificial woman like Cathleen ni Houlihan who willingly sees her man die for the nation's communal benefit.

When the Dawn is Come was first performed in 1908, but MacDonagh was still revising it in 1914 or 1915.[42] As the bloodshed of the GPO drew closer

MacDonagh was obsessed by thoughts of secretive insurrection that would advance the national cause and might also help to advance the position of women in Irish society. He finished another play, *Pagans*, in time for performance in April 1915, in which a separated married couple decide to continue living apart, even though they still love one another. In *Pagans*, despite the husband's desire to live with his wife once more, she explains that married life constitutes an unacceptable infringement of her freedom: 'Your leaving me has not broken my heart. I have been happier alone here [. . .] I am not prepared to go into a different world from my own [. . .] I never explain or apologise no'.[43] Realising that she is adamant, he leaves at the end of the play with the cryptic intention of doing:

> Something worthwhile [. . .] sooner than you think, Frances, politics will be dropped here, and something better will take their place. I am now free to do something to bring the better thing [. . .] You will not know yourself in the Ireland that we shall make here.[44]

In *Pagans* MacDonagh showed that his interest in women's liberation remained undimmed as the secretive rebellion of 1916 approached, and that creating a new kind of Ireland involved rethinking the social relationships between the country's male and female inhabitants.

Pádraic Pearse

By contrast with Connolly and MacDonagh, Pádraic Pearse did not have any particular affinity with the cause of female suffrage. However, like the two other leaders Pearse did write a play towards the end of his life that proves anxious to emphasise the legitimacy of the forthcoming secret rebellion. Pearse wrote his play *The Singer* in the autumn of 1915 and originally intended to have it performed at St Enda's school in the week immediately before the Rising. However, after consulting with his brother and with MacDonagh, Pearse decided that an explicit depiction of insurrection might alert the British authorities to the real-life revolt that was about to occur, and so the performance was abandoned. Instead, the first production was given in the final weeks of 1916 at St Enda's by the same boys who had been earmarked by Pearse to act the piece before his death, and since then the play has been staged with some regularity by amateur and professional groups to celebrate the anniversary of the insurrection.[45]

The main character of *The Singer*, MacDara, has been in hiding for many years. The British want to kill him because he has composed popular songs containing revolutionary sentiments, but during the play he returns to the family home where his mother, brother, and adopted sister live. MacDara plans to launch a surprise attack on his enemy, and at the end of the play he leaves to fight the occupying army alone, declaring that 'One man can free a people as one Man redeemed the world'.[46]

The Singer is not full of the proto-feminism of *Under Which Flag?* or *When the Dawn is Come*, but is instead suffused with Catholic iconography. MacDara compares embracing his mother for the final time to Christ's embrace of Mary on the way of the cross, and both MacDara's mother and his adopted sister Sighle are sacrificial women of the Marian type who revel in the heroic death of their beloved son and brother. Yet *The Singer* was not entirely immune from the challenges to conventional male and female roles being posed by the Irish stage, and Pearse's play connects nationalist insurrection with a problematic realignment of erotic relationships.

When MacDara returns home he lusts after the same girl that his brother, Colm, wants to marry. Colm proposes to Sighle before his brother arrives, but she has long harboured a fondness for MacDara. Moreover, both brothers' desire for Sighle is quasi-incestuous, as she has been raised as MacDara and Colm's adopted sister. She came to their house when she was only a few years old and MacDara's mother repeatedly calls her 'child' and 'daughter' (pp. 3–5). Connolly's *Under Which Flag?* includes a similar relationship, as Mary has been raised in the same house as her beloved Frank, and their romance prompts her adoptive mother to declare: 'A sister, is it? 'Deed that's the quare kind of a sister [. . .] It is not with their own sister they [other people] danced with most or got in the dark corners with' (fol. 3). But in Pearse's play, Sighle and MacDara's love for one another is further complicated by overtones of paedophilia. Their erotic longing was first expressed years before, when he was an adolescent and she was a pre-pubescent girl. They kissed when she was eight years old and he was fifteen, at a time when she was 'only a weeshy child' but when he had 'strong, strong arms' (p. 6). MacDara goes on to explain that, 'sometimes in the street of a city when I have stopped to look at the white limbs of some beautiful child, and have felt the pain that the sight of great beauty brings, I have wished that I could blind my eyes so that I might shut out the sight of everything that tempted me' (pp. 26-7).

In addition, *The Singer* also includes hints of homosexuality. When MacDara returns from exile to live in the family home the two brothers compete for Sighle, and endure a tense and awkward fraternal relationship. As René Girard showed in *Deceit, Desire and the Novel*, the erotic bond that links two rivals can be as powerful and intense as the ligature between either of the adversaries and their beloved.[47] After Colm perishes in battle for Ireland MacDara decides that he must follow his brother to the grave, and opts to fight the British despite knowing that personal annihilation lies ahead. In an alternative ending that Pearse scripted, Sighle and Colm are in fact the last to kiss MacDara's hand before he goes out to die.[48]

It is tempting to get rather carried away by these erotic indications in Pearse's play, but in actual fact little evidence exists of Pearse himself having ever done anything remotely sexual in his entire life, and the subtext of this unperformed play certainly had small impact on either the conduct or the significance of the insurrection in April 1916. However, when writing his play about the forthcoming political revolution Pearse did expose the way, much like Connolly and MacDonagh did, that any such impending rebellion could be connected to a wider reappraisal of societal norms. Whatever about the reality of Pearse's own private life, *The Singer* reveals that breaking with British sovereignty could also mark a moment at which conventional sexual attitudes and orthodoxies would be re-examined and rethought.

The *mise-en-scène*

With the rebellion of Easter 1916 relying on the leadership of such men as Pearse, Connolly, and MacDonagh, it was little surprise that parts of the insurrection evinced the concerns of the playhouse. The nationalists were clad with an assortment of props and costumes. Some dressed up in kilts and decorative rings, whilst others, including Pearse, carried swords that were highly symbolic although of little practical use against British machine guns and shells. The rebels chose to fight in buildings such as the GPO that were hopelessly exposed to enemy assault on three sides but provided the ensuing carnage with an unforgettable scenic backdrop. The Liberty Hall was the workers' building that the *Irish Times* described as 'a thorn in the side of the Dublin Police and the Irish Government', and the newly refurbished GPO was the largest official site in the main thoroughfare of the national capital.[49] When flames licked across the timbers of these famous edifices Dubliners were suitably awe inspired. It must have appeared that the stage-world was spilling out into the streets of the city.

The concerns about the role of women that some of the leading rebels had encountered in the playhouse also affected the way that this theatrical Rising was conducted, and a recent study has recovered the names of almost two-hundred women who were involved in the insurrection.[50] However, there were comparatively few women amongst the celebrated prisoners of the rebellion because commanders such as MacDonagh sent the female participants home immediately before the surrender, fearing that the sight of captured women would demoralise the majority of already shell-shocked men.[51] Besides which, after the Germans had executed Edith Cavell the previous October the British had seen army recruitment double, and did not want to hand a similar propaganda coup to the Irish nationalists by treating the women involved in the Dublin Rising too harshly.

In the aftermath of the rebellion, with the execution of its leading thinkers, the nationalist movement gradually regrouped under a male leadership that was less amenable to the inclusion of women. If the rebellion had succeeded the Irish government would have founded the first welfare state in Europe and would have appointed Hanna Sheehy Skeffington as the first female government minister of any country in the world, a year before the Soviets named Alexandra Kollontai in 1917. Consequently, when the second session of the national assembly of Ireland ('Dáil Éireann') met in April 1919, de Valera was elected president and continued to abide by the principles of MacDonagh and Connolly by naming Constance Markievicz as the first woman Minister of Labour in the world. Yet Kathleen Clarke notes that Markievicz 'had to bully them' because 'the present leaders were not over-eager to put women into places of honour or power'.[52] In any case, Markievicz was demoted within two years. Similarly, after the executions, a new feeling of sympathy with the rebels swelled the membership of Sinn Féin, but at a local level women were almost entirely excluded from the Sinn Féin clubs.[53] Although women played an essential part in spreading the Sinn Féin doctrine whilst their male colleagues were interned after the rebellion, these women were to find themselves increasingly sidelined by the chauvinism of the post-1916 nationalist movement. The Sinn Féin convention in October 1917 welcomed 1,000 delegates, but only twelve were women.[54] Perhaps surprisingly, this convention decided anyway to pass a vote that acknowledged female equality with men in the nationalist movement, and during the debate about this motion the speakers argued about whether there would or would not have even been an Easter insurrection without the help and support of women.[55] The short-lived battle for Dublin may have been over, but the protracted battle about the rebellion's significance was only just beginning.

Guerrilla Theatre

Later in the twentieth century, performance theorists came to see that the political and social demonstrations of the 1960s were in some way connected to theatre productions. R.G. Davies describes symbolic public demonstrations as 'guerrilla theatre', and Richard Schechner argues that this form of theatre aims to 'make a swift action or image that gets to the heart of an issue or a feeling – to make people realize where they are living, and under what situation'.[56] Guerrilla theatre uses surprise, small groups of performers, and simple tactics to draw attention to previously silenced people or issues; and this theatrical form has been particularly associated with second-wave feminist groups bent on challenging conventional views about women. For instance, in 1968 a group interrupted the Miss America pageant in Atlantic City to crown a live sheep, and members of the New York WITCH organisation (Women's International Terrorist Campaign from Hell) confronted and cast spells upon bewildered commuters in the Wall Street area.[57] WITCH covens later sprang up all over the United States, and, even after the destruction of the World Trade Centre in 2001, feminist theatre that boasted of the desire 'to play with the fear of guerrilla warfare, to make people afraid of who we might be and where we would strike next' lived on into the first decade of the twenty-first century with the high-profile activities of New York's 'Guerrilla Girls', who demonstrated against the male domination of the art world and of Western culture at large.[58]

However, instances of radical guerrilla theatre can be open to accusations of hypocrisy, as the playwright and director Augusto Boal realised in the 1960s when touring with an agitational play to the poorest villages of northeast Brazil. Boal's show had encouraged the peasants to rise up and support a revolution against the landowners, but the cast was discomfited and humbled when the peasants then asked the actors to fight alongside them in a real revolt the following day.[59] By contrast, in 1916 an idealistic group of men and women, who also realised the power of the theatre, decided to practise what they had been preaching in the playhouse, and take control of the centre of Dublin. The rebels of 1916 were unlikely to win a military victory, but their Easter demonstration forced people to reconsider the political situation that existed between the two countries. Some of the rebels thought that they were seeking to preserve the current social order, and to rid it of an unwelcome imperialist intrusion. But, like the later guerrilla-theatre feminists, a number of the leading rebels of 1916 believed that their rebellion would also challenge the socially determined position of women. The opposition between these two viewpoints would remain unsettled in the conflict of 1916, and in the ensuing years would resound time and again upon the Irish stage.

2

*The Plough and
the Stars*

O Mother [. . .]
When men speak of me, in praise or in dispraise,
You will not heed, but treasure your own memory
Of your first son.[1]

I have only done what every Irish mother should do willingly as I did, give
their beloved ones for Ireland and for freedom.[2]

What stalked through the Abbey Theatre?

On Thursday 11 February 1926 W.B. Yeats rose to his feet to address the audience at the Abbey Theatre and declared, 'You have disgraced yourselves again'.
He continued:

> Is this going to be a recurring celebration of Irish genius? Synge first, and then O'Casey! The news of the happenings of the last few minutes here will flash from country to country. Dublin has once more rocked the cradle of a reputation. From such a scene in this theatre went forth the fame of Synge. Equally the fame of O'Casey is born here to-night. This is his apotheosis.[3]

Unfortunately for Yeats few people could hear what he was saying at this point because a sizeable part of the audience had gone completely berserk.[4] They had watched the Abbey's actors mocking the leader of the Easter Rising, brandishing the sacrosanct national flag inside a dingy pub, and portraying an Irish girl as a prostitute. Now the audience refused to watch any more. One gang stormed the stage whilst others smashed lamps and tried to burn the stage curtains: 'a silly thing to do', according to one observer, 'because most people used to know that the old Abbey curtain was rotten with the damp owing to a leak in the roof'.[5] Another faction was singing interminable nationalist songs and making loud speeches. Others booed and hissed. Meanwhile, a particularly frenzied thug walloped two of the female actors in their faces before being thumped from the stage by one of the company's men. When Yeats reached the front of the auditorium, it was so noisy that he decided to mime most of his speech. In response, somebody lobbed a shoe at his head.

Undeterred, the Abbey management decided that the play should complete its run, and pressed on with three more performances that week. There was again barracking during the second act, but the chaos of Thursday night was not repeated. Plain-clothes policemen packed the theatre, and audience members were encouraged to puff away on cigars throughout the performance to counteract the effect of stink bombs.

Elsewhere in Dublin, away from the now ordered but odorous theatre, three nervous gunmen attempted to kidnap one of the play's leading men. After tremulously knocking on his front door the gunmen were scared away by the actor's redoubtable mother, and so decided to nobble two of the female players instead.[6] The Abbey management realised that their cast members were in real danger of being abducted, and so locked all of the performers in the theatre until after the final show.

The company was struggling to stage Sean O'Casey's new play, *The Plough and the Stars*, a work that initially promised to be a runaway success. The Abbey box office had taken £179, £181, and £188 in the three previous weeks, but made more than £434 during the six days in which *The Plough and the Stars* was first produced.[7] When the play opened a long queue formed outside the theatre as those without tickets tried to squeeze into the back of the pit. At the end of the first show O'Casey received an ovation, and loud calls for 'Author!' brought him onto the stage. Lady Gregory declared that it was an 'overpowering play, I felt at the end of it as if I should never care to look at another; all others would seem so shadowy to the mind after this'.[8]

Yet the events of that opening week meant *The Plough and the Stars* became synonymous with theatrical chaos rather than with box-office triumph. By the end of its first run, as Yeats pointed out to the rioting audience, this work had provoked scenes reminiscent of the *Playboy* scrimmage nineteen years before. Just as the Abbey's spectators had previously disrupted Synge's portrayal of the Irish as lovers of violence by yelling 'Kill the Author!', so the livid audience of 1926 protested against O'Casey's depiction of the destructive carnage of the Easter Rising by leaping up to attack the players and raze the theatre.

Nationalism and socialism

In the early 1900s Sean O'Casey was a member of the IRB, the secret group that organised the Rising. He associated with Bulmer Hobson, a prominent republican who wrote manuals on guerrilla warfare, and with Tom Clarke, an old Fenian who was impatient with the timidity and caution of younger nationalists. However, O'Casey's friendship with the IRB's top men waned after he joined James Larkin's Irish Transport and General Workers' Union in 1911. The playwright now felt that reviving the Irish language and removing British rule must be welded to the philosophy of the labour movement. Rather than being content with an Irish republic he insisted upon an Irish 'Workers' Republic. O'Casey was filled with consternation by the IRB's failure to support the workers whose strike was brutally crushed by the police in 1913, and bitterly criticised the IRB leadership before abandoning the organisation.

O'Casey became involved instead with the Irish Citizen Army, a socialist group founded by James Larkin. In his enthusiasm for the organisation O'Casey designed the Citizen Army's membership card, its constitution and manifesto, and a number of its handbills and posters. In 1914 he was elected the army's secretary. However, O'Casey soon alienated himself again. Shortly after he became secretary he was asked to apologise for comments that he had made about Constance Markievicz, who was a member of both the Citizen Army and the more middle-class Irish National Volunteers. O'Casey felt that by joining both groups she had put herself in an untenable position and insisted that she sever her connection with either one or the other. This demand infuriated the leaders of James Larkin's organisation, and O'Casey resigned in a huff.[9] As a result he stayed at home and sulked when the IRB persuaded the Citizen Army and the Volunteers to fight in 1916.

Yet, although O'Casey had distanced himself from both the IRB and the Citizen Army, and was shocked by the rebellion, he retained his allegiance to the revolutionaries in the months after Easter week. He expressed sympathy with the aims of the rebels in a number of largely-overlooked ballads that were published by his Fenian friend Fergus O'Connor in 1918.[10] In the same year O'Casey articulated his pro-nationalist sentiments in *The Story of Thomas Ashe*, describing the 1916 insurgents as those who, because of 'the Hope that was in them', fought with 'the glow of enthusiasm lighting their hearts'; and although he criticised James Connolly when writing *The Story of the Irish Citizen Army* a few months later, O'Casey still avoided outright condemnation of the rebellion itself.[11]

At some point between 1918 and 1926, however, O'Casey decided to lambaste the Easter revolt in *The Plough and the Stars*. Scholars such as Desmond Greaves, Jack Mitchell, and Ronan McDonald disagree about exactly when and how O'Casey changed his position and switched from supporting the principles of the Rising to supporting communism.[12] Yet it is more appropriate to describe not only how O'Casey abandoned the Rising in the years following 1916, but also how the Rising turned away from him.

Before 1916 O'Casey saw the cause of labour and of nationalism as interdependent. He abortively tried to persuade a committee of the IRB to work with James Larkin's militant labour movement, and also helped Pearse to stage *The Cattle Raid at Cooley* by urging readers of Larkin's weekly newspaper the *Irish Worker* to attend the show. The IRB's betrayal of the labour movement in 1913 was a resounding blow to O'Casey's hopes of linking the two causes, but even after the 1916 rebellion O'Casey praised Thomas Ashe in the *Dublin Saturday Post* by saying:

> We all knew Thomas Aghas [Ashe] as the Gaelic Leaguer, the Commandant of Fianna Fail, but few realised that he was a true Republican and a firm and convinced advocate of the rights of Labour. It will be a surprise to many to hear that he loved the working classes as ardently and as fearlessly as he loved Ireland.[13]

When O'Casey later recommended communist revolution he endorsed the same organisational methods used by the IRB in 1916. He envisaged communism as being spearheaded by a small and intellectually select group, and claimed that Lady Dorothy, Lady Astor, and George Jean Nathan (who had a particular reputation for being a snob) were all essentially communists. O'Casey also told Harold Macmillan, 'When I talk to you, I am in the Revolution: & when you talk to others, you are in the Revolution. How? Because we are intelligent men; & intelligent men must ever be thinking of bringing about a change.'[14] After the rebellion O'Casey believed that the masses should be prompted into action by firm guidance from men and women of intellect and influence.

At the time of the Easter Rising, Pearse, Connolly, and MacDonagh acted much like the small, advanced leadership that O'Casey later desired for communism. After all, in 1916, the Irish revolutionaries were willing to put aside their democratic scruples and express contempt for the elected representatives of the Irish people, the Irish Parliamentary Party led by John Redmond. The rebels drew their legitimacy from the rightness of their political principles, ignoring the fact that they had absolutely no democratic mandate at the time. It was only through the dramaturgy of the deed that they eventually planned to generate a mass base of democratic support. But before the rebellion in 1916 the rebels saw little that indicated a forthcoming groundswell of support for their views, and so they were forced to take a gamble, taking action first, and then hoping that a popular mandate would be accorded to their rebellion in retrospect.

In the wake of the uprising, O'Casey hoped, as Lenin did, that a slender and able group might continue to direct the force unleashed by the Easter rebellion in the service of socialist revolution, regardless of what the bulk of the population actually thought at the time.[15] But these hopes were dashed at the end of the Civil War. Unlike the Bolshevik example, the Rising of 1916 had not been followed by an effort to overthrow the bourgeoisie and bring about a socialist regime. By 1926 it was clear to O'Casey that the Easter rebellion had become a grotesquely traduced version of the October Revolution, no longer owned and organised by a secretive cell of farsighted revolutionary thinkers, but by the bourgeois democrats who sat in the Dáil, in thrall to the opinions held by the bulk of the population at that time. The national movement and the workers' movement had parted company, and whilst O'Casey rehearsed *The Plough and the Stars* to denigrate the Rising he began working on a play to promote communism called *Red Star*.

In 1926 O'Casey looked with dismay at the way the insurgency was remembered as a triumphant popular event. At the time of the conflict, parts of Dublin had famously offered cups of tea to the Tommies and jeered at the captured rebels. But by Easter 1917 outward attitudes to the revolt were changing. On the first anniversary of the insurrection the British authorities feared that the Rising was attracting popular support and nervously forbade any public meeting or procession in Dublin, even banning innocuous events such as the Protestant Girls' Brigade drill display.[16] Of course, stopping the Girls' Brigade from marching was a little over-zealous, but the British were right to worry. The dead leaders were widely thought to be martyrs; during the Civil War both sides would jealously claim legitimacy from 1916; and when the Free State finally emerged the Easter rebels occupied a central position in Irish cultural life. In 1926, whilst O'Casey composed his cynical attack on 1916, the Cumann na nGaedheal ('Party of the Irish') government was reconstructing the shattered GPO, remaking the building in resplendent fashion but retaining the bullet holes that pock-marked its portico. At phenomenal cost, the rebellion's central image was fossilised in a permanent place at the heart of the national capital.

However, Ireland was remembering a different Easter Rising to that which had been seen in 1916. The IRB's rebellion was violent, secretive, and full of wild and contradictory ideas about religious retrenchment and radical social change. At Easter 1917 a group of Citizen Army women tried to remind people that parts of the rebellion were dedicated to female suffrage by reprinting the proclamation and pasting it around Dublin.[17] But these women were fighting a losing battle. The Catholic Church was proudly associating itself with the insurgency, in spite of the ambivalence that the organisation had displayed towards the rebels when the shells were raining down on Dublin. Songbooks publicised the fact that within three years of the rebellion Churchmen and women had written some of the best commemorative songs about it, with a nun having written the catchy ballad 'Who Fears to Speak of Easter Week?', and a parish priest from County Down having penned 'The Foggy Dew'.[18] In May 1916 the elderly Bishop of Limerick, Edward O'Dwyer, who had previously loathed Sinn Féin, refused a request from British General Maxwell to discipline two priests for their nationalist activities and told the general: 'your regime has been one of the worst and blackest chapters in the history of the misgovernment of this country'.[19] O'Dwyer's correspondence with Maxwell was celebrated in the Irish press, and balladeers wrote in honour of the cleric:

> 'Come, join me in my dirty work,'
> Wrote England's butcher bold;
> 'You've rebel priests within your See
> That love us not, I'm told'.[20]

The Bishop's portrait appeared in Dublin shop windows adorned with tricolour ribbons. Elsewhere, much of provincial Ireland remembered the Rising in the spring by holding special church services and marching to and from the local graveyard where a decade of the rosary was said in Irish. By contrast with their silence in 1916, the Irish bishops made a firm statement against British attempts to impose conscription in Ireland in 1918, with the Bishop of Down and Connor declaring that the bishops had to take a stand because 'no power has any moral right to coerce young Irishmen to fight in the alleged interest of freedom until they have been allowed to enjoy freedom for themselves'.[21] This put the Church in the same camp as Sinn Féin, and from 1924 onwards there was an annual, state-sponsored religious service at the Arbour Hill cemetery in Dublin, where the executed rebels had been buried. In consequence, by the time that O'Casey wrote his controversial play, most memorial ceremonies for 1916 incorporated the rituals of the Catholic Church, and the uprising enjoyed mass support as the bedrock of a conservative, institutional kind of nationalism.

In 1916 many of the rebels had been Roman Catholic, and the Church exerted a strong influence on the mindset of the leaders. But this had been only one part of the patchwork of nationalisms that made up the Rising. Pearse, for instance, had made the Eucharist central to his life, but had also felt that he was the successor to a series of pagan and Protestant heroes, and his philosophical ideas about sacrifice hardly dovetailed with Vatican social teachings about suicide and war. The rebellion was not exclusively Catholic or determinedly populist in 1916. In fact, before Easter week O'Casey had worked for the IRB when it was an undesirable revolutionary minority. But by 1926, less than a decade after the leaders were buried, this revolt was wrongly remembered to have unreservedly endorsed popular mass politics and the social attitudes of bishops and priests. Seeing this progression, Sean O'Casey decided to launch an attack on popular misconceptions about the Rising, and wrote *The Plough and the Stars*, a play that remains, as a text, permanently situated in the context of its first performance. Just as the author intended, *The Plough and the Stars* is still closely connected to the response provoked by its original staging, a gauge of the national mood in Ireland in February 1926. O'Casey strove to create a theatrical event rather than simply a play, an assault on popular pieties that would shock the audience members out of their complacency. Perhaps in homage to Synge, whose *Playboy* riot is described at length in the *Autobiographies*, O'Casey decided that *The Plough and the Stars* would invert the Roman Catholic notions that had become a pre-eminent part of the Rising by 1926.[22]

Maurice Dalton and Daniel Corkery

Today, *The Plough and the Stars* is one of the Abbey Theatre's best-known plays, and is an established part of the Irish school curriculum. Yet although *The Plough*'s success has utterly eclipsed its rivals, it was not the first play to have attempted to tell the Easter rebellion's story. Before 1926 other playwrights composed works that remembered the insurrection in a reactionary and conservative way, and, although history has largely forgotten these earlier plays about the uprising, they help to illuminate the reasons why the Abbey audience found *The Plough and the Stars* so insufferable.

In September 1918 Dubliners watched Maurice Dalton's *Sable and Gold* at the Abbey Theatre, and in 1924 an American theatre journal published Daniel Corkery's last English-language play, *Resurrection*.[23] Like O'Casey's play, these predecessors of *The Plough and the Stars* situate the Easter-week fighting offstage and show the effect of the violent political revolution upon particular family homes.[24] Another play by Corkery, *The Labour Leader*, was staged in Dublin in 1919 and also echoes O'Casey's work by offering a partially disguised portrayal of Pádraic Pearse. However, the most striking feature of the plays about Easter 1916 written before *The Plough and the Stars* is that they portray the maternal role of women in Irish society with a disarming degree of similarity.

In Maurice Dalton's *Sable and Gold* the two main male characters, Gregory and Paul, are friends who leave their Cork home to fight in Dublin. Gregory's father tries persuading his son to stay at home and find a wife, but Gregory's nationalism is fired by remembering the patriotic stories told by his mother. Gregory's sister, the cultural nationalist Eileen, also incites revolutionary sentiments in Paul. He realises that Eileen would despise anyone who fears warfare and so decides to go to Dublin with Gregory. At the end of the play Paul is butchered but Gregory sneaks away from the slaughter. When Gregory returns home he cannot tell his mother of his cowardice and she exults in his apparent bravery.

The women of *Sable and Gold* never ask whether they might themselves be able to leave the house and help with the revolution that they support. They are content with the domestic role assigned to them, powerless to influence national events unless through the actions conducted by their men. The first scene depicted as the curtain rises sets the tone for the rest of the play. Two men and two women play seven card tricks together, but the women are unable to win a single hand between them. In the political violence later in the play, men are again the lauded participants. The rebels are described at various points as 'Brave men', 'Righteous men' (p. 27), and 'brave lads' (p. 42). By contrast, those who turn from fighting are 'unman[ed]' (p. 38), and the women are discussed in relatively dismissive terms. At one moment Paul and Gregory joke:

> PAUL [. . .]   'Tis girls always set the fashion for our hypocrisy. Isn't it Gregory?
> GREGORY   No, we should not allow them to make us into hypocrites. (p. 7)

Later in the play Gregory's father asserts that it is 'quite natural for – girls to go to extremes; but Gregory – he ought to have better sense' (pp. 12–13).

Dalton's women are primarily defined by their role in sending men out to face the British guns. When the news of the Rising reaches their home Gregory's mother initially wants to keep the men away from fighting, but soon changes her mind. She declares 'as long as men think it worth while to die for her, there's no fear in Ireland' (p. 43) and when she realises that her own child is likely to be killed during the conflict she says coolly, 'I would *regret* it, John; but – I would never be ashamed of it' (p. 47). Meanwhile, as Paul goes to die he is inspired by the revolutionary mantra that he has been taught by Eileen, 'Fear goes in sable/Courage in gold' (p. 36).

Daniel Corkery's *Resurrection* gives a similar message about the way that gender roles operated during the Easter Rising. In Corkery's play the character of Terence attempts to dissuade his son, Shawn, from fighting in the Rising. Terence's other child, Michael, has already left home to play a doomed part in the revolt. Although Michael and Shawn's father was himself a Fenian rebel long ago, in 1916 he views the Volunteers' drilling and meetings as foolhardy and does not want his offspring to die. While Terence dissuades Shawn from taking up the gun, the matriarch of the house, Mary, encourages the boy to join the insurrection. She is Terence's mother and Shawn's grandmother, and tells them of the past wrongs inflicted by the British, reminding the men that their own ancestors were Irish rebels. Having persuaded Terence to revolt in 1867, she now, in turn, inspires his son Shawn to take up arms for Ireland. As Shawn leaves for Dublin a priest confirms the terrible news that his brother Michael is already slain.

In *Resurrection* Mary is a reincarnation of Cathleen ni Houlihan. She is '*an aged woman*', who is '*bent with age*' and walks '*very slowly*'.[25] Despite this physical frailty she has a mystical and otherworldly connection to the battles of Irish nationalism, and at the start of the Easter furore she rises from her bed knowing that the old times of rebellion have returned. When she hears phantasmal soldiers 'galloping on their horses' she realises that the men of her house will soon be involved in 'secret work', and at the end of the play her incessant and ghostly talk of past insurrections finally drives Shawn to join the latter-day patriots.[26]

Corkery also intended Mary to evoke the iconography of her predecessor, the Mother of God, who, in the years following 1916, became firmly associated with the rebellion through the praying of the Hail Mary at the culmination of anniversary marches across the country. Towards the end of *Resurrection* Corkery's Mary prays for the men of the rebellion, exclaiming, 'May the Lord have mercy on them and they going home in the darkness of this night – Amen.'[27] At this point Shawn bows at his grandmother's feet in recollection of the *pietà*, and when Michael dies the old woman glances towards a priest and leads the mourning. She has the same fixation with prayer, lack of sexuality, and tragic rejoicing in the sacrifice of her offspring that were commonly associated with the Catholic icon.

Corkery invoked the two figures associated with male sacrifice in Ireland, Cathleen ni Houlihan and the Virgin Mary, to give a relatively unenlightened view of the role of women. The only female character of *Resurrection* can hardly walk, let alone influence the rebellion by her own actions. She depends on what men can do on her behalf, and must be content with her life within the home and with the associated glory that she gleans from the sacrifice of her male offspring. Thus, Corkery dealt with the representation of gender in a different manner to the way in which Thomas MacDonagh and James Connolly had done before the insurrection.

However, it is unlikely that many people knew of *Resurrection* before *The Plough and the Stars*, as the British military censor refused to allow Corkery's incendiary play to be published in 1919 and the first production of *Resurrection* was delayed until 1936, when it was staged in Irish at the Peacock Theatre to mark the Rising's twentieth anniversary. The play was subsequently published in *The Capuchin Annual* and in a separate Talbot Press edition in 1942. However, Corkery also wrote a more coded work in praise of the revolution of 1916, and this was staged at the Abbey Theatre in October 1919. In this play, *The Labour Leader*, Corkery told the story of labour unrest in Cork and the struggle between a cautious strike committee whose members want to stay within the law, and their charismatic leader, who praises violence as the only way of shocking respectable people into action. Although *The Labour Leader* avoids dealing explicitly with the Easter Rising, Corkery's main character Davna is evidently based on Pearse. Davna is influenced by both the Bible and Cuchulainn, he remains unmarried so that he can devote himself more fully to his work, and in a series of bloodthirsty speeches he inspires his followers to take aggressive action. At the close of the play, Davna's idea of liberating violence is vindicated as a group of railwaymen strike in response to his rhetoric.

The central moment in *The Labour Leader* comes when Davna meets Mrs Tobin, an exhausted widow whose son has been jailed in the workers' revolt:

> DAV [. . .] Who's this?
>
> MUR   The mother of the man who is in jail for us.
>
> DAV   Ah! One of our Spartan mothers. I'll take your hand, Mrs Tobin (*she wipes her hand in her apron*). 'Tis clean, 'tis cleaner than my own. No fear of us while we have mothers like you. I'm glad to know you. (*They shake hands*)
>
> MRS. T   He's the only boy I have left, but take him, take him. I don't begrudge him at all.
>
> DAV   My Spartan mother, we accept him. Tell his father to raise up his head: his name will be honoured in the land.
>
> MRS. T   His father is dead fifteen years, sir.
>
> DAV   Then he honours his relics in the grave. And he honours your rearing.[28]

Mrs Tobin's willingness to see her son sacrificed echoes the role of Mary in *Resurrection*, and the mother-figure has a central part in both of Corkery's plays. Davna's meeting with Mrs Tobin is the turning point of *The Labour Leader*, as it is this moment that convinces him of the need for violent revolution. Although the revolutionary activities of the play are an exclusively male affair, Davna repeatedly cites the sacrificial mother's influence upon his thinking, claiming, 'Only for that Spartan mother I might never have felt that fiery thrill that – that *clanged* them all into one resounding word – violence!'[29] Once again, the Irish stage demonstrated that the role of Irish women was to remain passive whilst persuading the men of Ireland to engage in conflict, brutality, and bloodshed.

The young Sean O'Casey saw *The Labour Leader* at the Abbey, and told Joseph Holloway that he greatly admired it.[30] Some of the original audience found the committee scenes dull and Corkery's play has never enjoyed wider success, but it did have a determining influence upon O'Casey's later play about 1916. In *The Plough and the Stars* O'Casey would take the image of the orator preaching violence and divest him of his heroism, recycle the idea of the offstage public meeting, and literalise Corkery's idea that listening to passionate rhetoric was akin to being drunk on whiskey. Most controversial of all, however, was what O'Casey decided to do with the image of the revolutionary woman.

Both Daniel Corkery and Maurice Dalton presented versions of Irish rebellion on the Abbey stage that celebrated women only insofar as those women conformed to the old sacrificial female role. Nationalists had long used the metaphor of 'Mother Ireland' through the myth of the Shan Van Vocht in order to inspire patriotism. Typically, this poor old woman calls Ireland's men to rescue and revitalise her land by dying in battle for her. Such a sacrifice renews the youth and beauty of the Shan Van Vocht, but she remains unable to defend herself, much less to contribute actively to the rescue of the nation. This sacrificial women is popularly remembered in Tommy Makem's famous ballad, 'Four Green Fields', in which a mother sings of how her 'fine strong' sons have died in reclaiming her four fields from bondage, but who is full of hope because 'my sons have sons as brave as were their fathers,/And my four green fields will bloom once again said she'.[31] This woman relies on her sons to conduct the national struggle, and the prospect of a successful resolution comes only through the anticipation that she can nurture and encourage sufficient brave male offspring to continue fighting and dying for their country.

Corkery and Dalton's plays affirm that the place of Ireland's men is to bear arms for the country's glorious independence while it is the place of Ireland's women to stay at home and cheer from the sidelines. Hence, the more radical views about equality opined by some of the 1916 rebels are almost entirely neglected. In *The Labour Leader*, *Resurrection*, and *Sable and Gold*, Irish women are defined in terms of domesticity, the crowning glory of which consists in persuading a son to be slaughtered in the name of Ireland and freedom.

She doesn't like him even to get married

Sean O'Casey's *The Plough and the Stars* was not the first Abbey play to criticise a rebel of 1916. In 1918 Dalton's *Sable and Gold* had ended with the lily-livered Gregory fleeing from the GPO and then deceiving his proud mother about his shameful participation. But O'Casey was the first Irish playwright to denigrate the idea of sacrificial motherhood promulgated about the rebellion.

O'Casey thought that the idea of Irish mothers willingly sending their children to be massacred was repugnant. He wrote that the 'safety of her brood is the true mark of every woman. A mother does not like her son to be killed – she doesn't like him even to get married'.[32] In *The Plough and the Stars* O'Casey implied that the domestic realm was far preferable to the nationalist battlefield; he depicted women imploring their men not to fight; and thus he provoked a relatively well-organised protest led by the bereaved mothers and wives of 1916.

In fact, O'Casey had already written a play that connected the Easter Rising with a subversive view of the role of Irish women. In *Juno and the Paycock* the indolent Captain Boyle uses the rhetoric of the 1916 rebellion to boast about how he will superintend the behaviour of his wife, Juno. Boyle brags: 'Today, Joxer, there's goin' to be issued a proclamation be me, establishin' an independent Republic, an' Juno'll have to take an oath of allegiance.'[33] But a few moments later Juno appears and berates her terrified husband. The proclamation is comic in its utter futility. In *The Plough and the Stars*, The Covey repeats similar words to Boyle when describing the events at the GPO, and theatregoers with good memories might have realised that O'Casey was again mocking the Easter Rising and challenging male assumptions about the quiescence of Irishwomen.

In *Resurrection* and *Sable and Gold*, female absence from the Easter insurgency indicates womanly weakness. The female characters in the plays of Corkery and Dalton support the nationalist revolt but lack the capacity to join in. By contrast, the women of *The Plough and the Stars* refrain from insurrectionary activities out of choice, not because they are incapable of fighting. As Fluther exclaims: 'Women is terrible when they start to fight. There's no holdin' them back' (p. 207). The fearsome female characters described by Fluther steer clear of the Rising simply because revolutionary nationalism leaves them cold. When O'Casey's women bravely risk their lives in the streets during the conflict, they do so because they intend to protect their friends and families, and to furnish their homes with goods stolen from Dublin's abandoned shops. These women are unresponsive to the political aspects of the nationalist conflagration, and O'Casey's audience is encouraged to think that any right-minded person would share this indifference. In *The Plough and the Stars* the realm of hearth and home is always preferable to that of the bullet and the barricade.

Seamus Deane has noted that O'Casey encourages his audience to favour these apolitical women by using a kind of trickery.[34] In real life, being interested in people is not necessarily an antidote or an alternative to being interested in politics, yet this is the antagonism that O'Casey sets up in *The Plough and the Stars*. O'Casey's onstage women are more concerned with domestic security and the capacity for deep human feeling than with the dehumanised and illogical political activities with which his men are generally, although not always, obsessed. In broad terms, while the women speak a humanistic language that owes much to Boucicault and the Bible, the men speak a nonsensical jargon dissociated from the workaday concerns of Dublin's struggling slum-dwellers. When O'Casey contrasts the two, it is difficult to champion the excitable ideologue over the suffering woman who seeks to protect her home and family.

O'Casey's women are disdainful of nationalism, and the sacrificial mothers shown in Corkery and Dalton's plays have no place onstage in *The Plough and the Stars*. Instead, characters like Nora do all that they can to prevent the death of their men. In *Sable and Gold* Eileen fears that both her brother and her boyfriend may perish, but still insists: 'It would be a shameful thing, mother, if they had been with the boys all along, and then stood out when the time [of the Rising] came'.[35] Yet in *The Plough and the Stars* women espouse exactly the opposite opinion. Nora begs her husband to stay at home rather than join the rebels:

> No, I won't let you go . . . I want you to be thrue to me, Jack . . . I'm your dearest comrade; I'm your thruest comrade . . . They only want th' comfort of havin' you in th' same danger as themselves . . . Oh, Jack, I can't let you go! (p. 234)

The idealised woman of 1916 was supposedly eager to give her man for the sake of the common good. But in O'Casey's play Nora cannot care less about any esoteric nationalist notions so long as she can keep her husband safe from harm. By contrast with the sacrificial mother, Nora claims: 'there's no woman gives a son or a husband to be killed – if they say it, they're lyin', lyin', against God, Nature, an' against themselves!' (p. 220)

O'Casey, who had spent Easter week looking after his own bed-ridden mother, set about demolishing the image of the sacrificial woman with gusto. In particular, the women of *The Plough and the Stars* were supposed to act as an antidote to Pádraic Pearse's mother, who had become a kind of metonym for all the things O'Casey found unpalatable about contemporary nationalism. In response, this real-life woman, the most important emblem of the motherhood of 1916, came to participate in the protest against O'Casey's play, and in 1926 she greatly influenced the audience's reaction to his work.

Margaret Pearse

Pádraic Pearse was a Catholic Irishman obsessed with his role as a self-immolating victim, who orchestrated his own Rising at Easter. He was fixated on the sacrificial ideology embodied in the relationship of Christ and the Virgin Mary, and after the British captured him he was particularly taken by comparisons between his own mother and the Mother of God. From his prison cell he wrote the poem 'To My Mother', where he tells her that 'My gift to you hath been the gift of sorrow', and asks:

> For who hath had such faith as yours
> Since the old time, and what were my poor faith
> Without your strong belief to found upon?[36]

Pádraic Pearse warmed to his Marian theme as the firing squad beckoned. He dashed off another poem, 'A Mother Speaks', in which he adopted his mother's voice to implore the Virgin Mary to 'Receive my first-born son into thy arms,/Who also hath gone out to die for men'.[37]

After Easter week, popular support swung behind the rebellion and Pádraic Pearse's devotion to his mother became widely celebrated. By the autumn of 1916 the Dundalgan Press had published a picture of Margaret Pearse as the first page of its edition of Pádraic Pearse's *The Mother and Other Tales*, and Small, Maynard and Company produced a revised edition of *Poems of the Irish Revolutionary Brotherhood*, which now included Pádraic Pearse's poetry about his mother.[38] The 1917 *Collected Works* version of his plays, stories, and poems, which was in its sixth edition by 1924, anxiously tried to replace his interest in Cuchulainn with an edifying concern for Christian motherhood, stating in its introduction, 'Those who look in these pages for a vision of Pagan Ireland, with its pre-Christian gods and heroes, will be disappointed [. . .] everything is overshadowed by the Christian concept, and the religion that is found here centres in Christ and Mary'.[39]

In the same year as O'Casey's play was performed at the Abbey, *Irish Freedom* printed Nora Ni Chathain's short story 'The Old Woman of the House', in which a nameless old widow prays the rosary and celebrates the death of her children for the nationalist cause by repeating 'I never grudged *them*'.[40] Ni Chathain's widow thus echoes Pearse's poem 'The Mother', with its resounding declaration 'I do not grudge them: Lord, I do not grudge/My two strong sons that I have seen go out/To break their strength and die', which Corkery had already recycled in the words of the widow Tobin in *The Labour Leader*.[41] In this way, when hagiographic nationalists remembered the Rising they celebrated Pearse's Christological relationship with his mother, and Margaret Pearse became a key symbol for the republican movement. In 1918 Sinn Féin urged the electorate to 'vote as Mrs Pearse will vote', and after being elected herself as a Dáil deputy (TD) for Sinn Féin between 1921 and 1922, she later became a senator and a member of the Fianna Fáil executive.[42]

Margaret Pearse herself relished the role of sacrificial woman. She suggested that she had provided the inspiration for the mother who encourages a redeeming death in the increasingly popular play *The Singer*, explaining that Pádraic Pearse had 'exquisite and profound love for me', and remembering that:

> He always called me 'Little Wommie,' and 'Little Mother.' In that beautiful play, *The Singer*, when Mac Dara [*sic*] rushes into his mother's arms, it was of me, his own mother, that Pádraig was thinking. I knew that, instinctively; and Willie afterwards confirmed my belief when he told me that I was the prototype of Mac Dara's mother, Máire. His own 'Little Mother' was in my boy's brave heart when he wrote that play.[43]

Elsewhere she wrote:

> In the play of the Singer I am the supposed mother. Don't I feel proud of this, that dear Padhraic favoured me so and gave me the credit even before I deserved it, and am I, not, [*sic*] the proud mother to have given my two loving sons so willingly for the freedom of their beloved country, poor dear suffering Ireland.[44]

Margaret Pearse was the Easter Rising's most notorious incarnation of the sacrificial mother, and she owed her national prominence to the public's appetite for casting her in this role. She proudly equated her sons' love for their mother with their love for Ireland, declaring: 'Both my sons died for their country; both lived in their mother's heart; both their names will shine on the pages of their country's history'.[45]

Just as Pádraic Pearse had engaged in an act of ventriloquism in the poem 'A Mother Speaks', she in turn rejected the Anglo–Irish treaty by speaking on her son's behalf. In the Dáil she summoned his voice from beyond the grave and argued: 'As his mother I deny it [that Pádraic would have accepted the treaty], and on his account I will not accept it [. . .] my vote for accepting this is equal to his'.[46] Anyone else who invoked his name during the bitter arguments about the negotiations with Britain lacked the authority of the pre-eminent mother of

1916. In one relatively short speech Margaret Pearse managed to mention her son's name eleven times, making clear that she alone had the authority to invoke the chief insurrectionist of 1916 with full veracity:

> Pádraig Pearse would not have accepted a Treaty like this with only two-thirds of his country in it. In the name of God I will ask the men that have used Pádraig Pearse's name here again to use it in honour; to use it in truthfulness'.[47]

Michael Collins was frustrated by Margaret Pearse, and pointed out that as Pádraic Pearse was lying in his grave, nobody now had the ability to speak on his behalf:

> Deputies have spoken about whether dead men would approve of it, and they have spoken of whether children yet unborn will approve of it, but few of them have spoken as to whether the living approve of it [. . .] There is no man here who has more regard for the dead men than I have [. . .] I don't think it is fair to be quoting them against us. I think the decision ought to be a clear decision on the documents as they are before us – on the Treaty as it is before us.[48]

Shortly afterwards Collins was ambushed and murdered by Republicans who sided with Margaret Pearse.

Michael Collins had tried to prevent Margaret Pearse from assuming a central position in the Dáil, and in *The Plough and the Stars* Sean O'Casey similarly attempted to displace the stereotype of the sacrificial mother from her prominence in the Irish theatre. Instead, O'Casey's play scornfully connects the Rising to a hopelessly inadequate kind of child rearing. Fluther Good remembers that his mother instructed him to be faithful to the Shan Van Vocht when he was young. But Fluther turns out to be a drunkard and a brawler rather than an ascetic nationalist hero. When another rebel dresses in his battle uniform he looks like 'th' illegitimate son of an illegitimate child of a corporal in th' Mexican army!' (p. 182). These were hardly depictions of dignified sons following the poor old woman's exhortations to battle. In O'Casey's opinion, Easter 1916 symbolised the catastrophic failure of Irish motherhood rather than its triumph, and so at another point Mrs Gogan wheels a pram because she is going looting rather than because she is caring for an infant, and Nora, by attempting to keep Jack away from the fighting, inadvertently kills her unborn child. 'Mother' sounds particularly sinister on the lips of British Corporal Stoddart, a soldier who repeatedly uses the word when speaking to Mrs Gogan even though he is her political enemy, has invaded her home, and intends to imprison her male friends.

Some of the worst examples of mothering occur in Act II, and it is no coincidence that after watching this act the Abbey audience erupted. In this part of the play Mrs Gogan brings a baby into the pub and feeds it with whiskey. She then insults and tries to fight with Bessie, and when Mrs Gogan leaves the pub she forgets to take the nursling with her, provoking panic among the men who are left with it. The barman says, 'Take it up, man, an' run out afther her with it, before she's gone too far. You're not goin' to leave th' bloody thing here, are you?' (pp. 206–7).

It is also in Act II that an unnamed orator appears, standing offstage and speaking just four times. He addresses a meeting in the street outside the bar, and the fragments of oratory that he speaks were originally written by Pádraic Pearse. Yet despite a common assumption – that O'Casey himself shared – Pearse never intended all of these words to be delivered in speeches. The bombast of the rhetorician in *The Plough* was torn from writings that were originally composed by the rebel leader as a variety of lectures and newspaper articles, and were only anthologised after the Rising.[49]

O'Casey's speechmaker, who appears only in this act of the play, gives an address that is sardonically mirrored by the appalling mothering in the pub. Mrs Gogan drunkenly abandons an Irish child only moments before the orator claims that nationalist sentiment is succoured from one generation to another; and the barman describes the baby as a 'bloody thing' (p. 207) shortly after hearing of the need for a blood sacrifice. In *The Plough and the Stars* O'Casey dissociates Pádraic Pearse from the symbolic motherhood that his mother advocated, and instead connects the rebel leader with the intoxicated and brutish procreation of a poverty-stricken underclass that would remain unaffected by any nationalist posturing.

O'Casey's insult to Margaret Pearse was exacerbated by another character who, like the orator, appears only in Act II of *The Plough and the Stars*. Rosie, a prostitute, enters and exits the play at almost exactly the same time as the speaker, and the volatile Abbey audience was quickly driven to apoplexy by her presence. The actor who played the prostitute, Ria Mooney, had already interrupted her rehearsal schedule to ask her extremely amused priest whether she ought to play the part, and on the first Wednesday of the play's run her appearance was greeted with jeers. On Thursday the audience loudly cursed and threatened the terrified actor, before pelting her with coal and pennies.

The audience objected to more than Rosie's profession. After all, Ria Mooney had previously starred as Darling Dora in G.B. Shaw's *Fanny's First Play*, and this interpretation of Shaw's character had been received warmly by spectators at the Abbey. The theatre's denizens were also familiar with real-life courtesans. On their way to and from the auditorium many in the audience would have noticed the girls who worked in the lane behind the Abbey, who had inspired Mooney's portrayal of Rosie.[50] Indeed, the *Irish Times* initially praised O'Casey for 'giving us Dublin life as it was lived'.[51]

Yet when Rosie appeared alongside the orator, the nationalists in the audience were repelled. In 1907 the *Playboy* rioters had objected to the word 'shift' not because of its fairly innocuous meaning but because of the context in which it was used: Synge's audience ignored two mentions of the word and then exploded when it was spoken by Christy Mahon, a character who mocks both Christianity and nationalism.[52] Similarly, those who objected to *The Plough and the Stars* detested the whore because she subverted the idea of sacrifice that had developed around Pádraic Pearse and his mother. The reviewer for the *Voice of Labour* fulminated:

> She [Rosie] comes into the play at the second act, and with the close of the act she passes out of the play. She hardly justifies her introduction. She is, at best, a theatricality. The nationalism of Pearse may have fallen amongst strange companions in the days that witnessed its first manifestations, but it never lost its nobility. Mr O'Casey, whatever his purpose may be, takes away that, an unforgivable thing.[53]

Pádraic Pearse's mother and the women of the earlier plays about 1916 had encouraged their men to fight. Yet in O'Casey's play Rosie uses seduction to persuade Ireland's men away from participating in nationalist rebellion. Mimicking the quasi-religious rhetoric of Pádraic Pearse's words, she laments that the rebels are being 'holy' and acting like 'th' glorious company of th' saints, an' th' noble army of martyrs' (p. 193). Instead, she enjoins such men to fall for the more earthly delights that she has to offer.

O'Casey envisaged Rosie as a '*well-shaped girl of twenty; pretty*' (p. 192), and the first Abbey audience saw her played by the ravishing Ria Mooney. This portrayal was unlikely to make many people think about the purity and sexual abstinence evoked by Pádraic Pearse's Marian poems about his mother. Rosie is the antithesis of the old and feeble woman who persuades men to join the nationalist rebellion, something that O'Casey makes clear at the end of the act when Rosie leaves the stage with her arms around Fluther, inverting the celebrated ending of *Cathleen ni Houlihan* which saw a young male patriot led out by the old woman to forgo sexual fulfilment and fight for his country.

In fact, the prostitute could have proved even more distasteful to those who treasured the image of Pádraic Pearse's mother. O'Casey originally wrote Act II of *The Plough and the Stars* as a short one-act play, but it was rejected by the Abbey directorate.[54] When O'Casey returned it to the Abbey in its reshaped form as part of *The Plough*, the directors continued to agonise about the piece and demanded that the concluding harlot's ballad should be cut. If the song had remained uncensored, the audience would have seen Rosie describe a cartoonish version of motherhood that portrays procreation as unconsidered, and the passage from conception to birth condensed into the space of only one night. Rosie was to sing:

> We cuddled an' kissed with devotion, till th' night from th' mornin' had
> fled;
> An' there, to our joy, a bright bouncin' boy
> Was dancin' a jig in th' bed! (p. 214)

Margaret Pearse symbolised the great pain of being a mother, but Rosie's song describes a parent who knows little about her child. Rosie has felt none of the agonies of birth and feels only the thrill of sex and of watching the baby boy dancing in the morning.

Margaret's view of Pádraic

In his depiction of an orator speaking the words of Pádraic Pearse, O'Casey was adapting a stage tradition that became popular a few years before the Rising. This popularity originated with a performance of Ibsen's *The Enemy of the People* at the Moscow Arts Theatre on the day of the Kazansky Square massacre in 1905, when those in the Russian audience were thrilled to hear the stage orator before them speaking of freedom. Acting like the crowd at a political rally, the spectators rose from their seats, moved to the footlights, and shook hands with Stanislavski, who was delivering the speech. Some climbed onto the stage and joyfully embraced him.[55]

In *The Enemy of the People* a stage crowd throngs around a speaker whose lecture encompasses both the fictional assembly and the real-life audience. After 1905 this stage positioning enjoyed a vogue in British political plays such as Elizabeth Robins's *Votes for Women!* (1907) and John Galsworthy's *Strife* (1909).[56] Both of these plays were popularised by Granville Barker's direction, and O'Casey may have known about Galsworthy's tale of the battle between capital and labour after the play was performed in Dublin's Gaiety Theatre at the start of the workers' strike in 1913.[57] O'Casey may also have known that Lennox Robinson used a stage orator to criticise violent nationalism in the 1912 Abbey play, *Patriots*, in which a Fenian speaker tries to give an address, but nobody bothers to turn up and listen to him. Furthermore, O'Casey had seen the Abbey performance of Corkery's *The Labour Leader* in 1919, which includes an offstage public meeting and a specific debate about how exactly the orator and his platform should be positioned in relation to the fictional audience. As he sat transfixed by Corkery's play, O'Casey was consciously learning the art of playwriting, and evidently memorised and then recycled the moment when the speechmaking firebrand of *The Labour Leader* is told, 'You're on the wrong side of the partition: the platform is on the other side'.[58] Lennox Robinson had produced the Abbey's version of *The Labour Leader* and had written *Patriots*, and when he came to direct *The Plough and the Stars* in 1926 he loathed the offstage oratory, perhaps because his Dublin rival seemed to be impinging on Robinson's own earlier work.[59]

In *The Plough and the Stars* O'Casey's speaker addresses the auditorium from offstage, and this means that the audience members are no longer included in the crowd at the public meeting as they were in the plays of Ibsen, Robins, and Galsworthy, but instead listen along with the prostitute and drunkards of the pub. In *The Plough*, Pádraic Pearse's words are delivered by a character who is nameless and who appears only in silhouette through a window, veiled from the audience and backlit. Just like Millet's treatment of the shadowy farmer in the painting *The Angelus*, which hangs onstage at the start of *The Plough and the Stars*, O'Casey was quite literally portraying Pádraic Pearse in a bad light.

Margaret Pearse was cut to the quick by O'Casey's use of her son's image. After Pádraic Pearse was killed, his mother developed an understandable fascination with his physical representation. She had pleaded in vain with the obdurate British authorities to hand over the bodies of her offspring for burial in consecrated ground, and consequently attached great significance to their corporeality. But the Pádraic Pearse of *The Plough and the Stars* was exactly the opposite of what she wanted theatregoers to see.

After the executions Margaret Pearse had sat in the audience at the first performance of her son's play *The Singer* and was greatly moved to see what she felt was his direct autobiographical portrayal, declaring, 'I thought I would break my heart it seemed so real'.[60] She realised that the playhouse had the power to represent her son in a way that both she and he would approve, and asked a Catholic priest, Father Gaffney, to dramatise her son's short stories. Gaffney detested O'Casey's work, and the two men traded insults in the pages of the *Irish Press* in 1935, with Gaffney criticising the 'offensiveness' of *The Silver Tassie* and O'Casey pointing out 'the peculiar, sentimental, and sometimes silly idea of Christianity that many members of Catholic societies favour'.[61] Although Gaffney's finished edition of Pádraic Pearse's stories was published after Margaret Pearse's death, her daughter Margaret Mary Pearse let it be known that certain characters in the priest's dramatisation were direct representations of Pádraic Pearse. Margaret Mary Pearse claimed '"The Man from Dublin" in *The Roads* was Pearse himself' and that 'in *The Priest* he gives us a glimpse of himself as a child'.[62] The theatrical representations of Pádraic Pearse that were commissioned by his mother emphasise the dignity of his appearance, and the primacy of his family and religious life. Rather than appearing as a liminal silhouette, Gaffney's two 'Pádraics' are situated in the middle of theatrical sets dominated by prominently positioned crucifixes, and wearing costumes that 'are neat and decent. Slovenliness should be carefully eschewed'.[63]

The shadowing of Pádraic Pearse on the Abbey stage contrasted sharply to the forthcoming plays that Margaret Pearse had sanctioned and the way in which popular culture was lionising the leader of the insurrection. By October 1916 people in Dublin were noticing 'the shop windows plastered with photos of the rebels; now with the martyr's halo round their heads'.[64] Commemorative black and white postcards of the rebels were passed around Dublin, some of which, such as the one depicting Richard O'Carroll that is now permanently displayed at Kilmainham jail, were stitched with yellow thread to form a corona around the insurrectionists.[65] The *Irish Press* recognised the insurgents 'when their portraits appeared after death, as men of the same pure type, all high of purpose, too noble for anything but the fate they met'.[66] O'Casey would have noticed these sanctified images as he tramped around Dublin, and perhaps alludes to them in *Inishfallen, Fare Thee Well* when he writes 'the fires of Easter week were still a halo round De Valera's head'.[67]

Poetry about the Easter Rising also pictured the rebels surrounded by a holy light. George Russell's poem 'Salutation' imagines the patriots 'Thronged on some starry parapet' and engulfed 'in one blaze of blinding light', and many of the other poems inspired by the Rising envision the insurgents literally aflame.[68] Joseph Campbell wrote the poem 'Fires' to describe the souls of those who fought in 1916, and Dermot O'Byrne's 'Martial Law in Dublin' asks, 'have you padlocks for our inner fire?'[69] In 'The Leaders' and 'Requiem' Seumas O'Sullivan also calls the rebels 'tenders of the Phoenix Flame' and 'Spirits of wind and fire and flame'.[70]

The Pearse women supported the depiction of Pádraic Pearse as a hallowed and illuminated hero. Margaret Pearse anticipated the day when the rebels' 'bones shall be lifted as if they were the bones of saints', and in an oration on her brother, Mary Brigid Pearse testified that:

> Like that other wondrous fire which was kindled by St. Patrick on the hill of Slain [sic], and [w]hich was destined never to be extinguished, so the white flame which had been lighted from the hallowed fires of Easter week, would never again be quenched.[71]

Pádraic Pearse's other sister, Margaret Mary Pearse, concurred that her brother was concerned to make things 'as bright and as artistic as possible'.[72]

Pádraic Pearse's mother went even further by adorning the walls of St Enda's school with a multitude of pictures of him, 'as boy, as youth, in scholar's robes, and finally in the uniform in which he went forth to battle against the might of an Empire'.[73] She wanted her son to be depicted with a vivid face, and was horrified to find the Abbey's portrayal of him as a grey and gloomy figure. Just as Jung would later characterise Hitler as the shadow of Germany's collective subconscious, so O'Casey had rendered the rebel leader of 1916 as the unfortunate shadow side of Irish nationalism.[74]

Women in the house

When members of the Abbey audience demonstrated against *The Plough and the Stars* Margaret Pearse herself provided their inspiration. O'Casey's play had enjoyed a rapturous reception on its opening night, but on Thursday the real-life sacrificial mother of 1916 entered the theatre to register her disapproval. The managers of the Abbey quickly switched on the house lights when the jeering and hollering began to get out of control, and when the auditorium was illuminated the spectators peered around and realised that Pádraic Pearse was not the only member of the Pearse family to have been placed in shadow at the playhouse. Margaret Pearse, now the most famous woman of the rebellion, had also been watching the play from the darkness of the stalls. Many audience members noted her arrival at the start of the play, and when the house lights again revealed her presence during Act II the theatregoers were graphically reminded of the person O'Casey's play was designed to malign. An early critic denounced the play because O'Casey's depiction of a woman 'holding back her man' from the bloodshed of 1916 was 'quite untrue', and Hanna Sheehy Skeffington pointed out that 'The women of Easter Week, as we know them, are typified rather in the mother of Padraic Pearse, that valiant woman who gave both her sons for freedom'.[75]

Worse still for the Abbey management, Margaret Pearse was not the only sacrificial mother-figure to sit in the audience on that fateful night. This was not a spontaneous protest, but was carefully contrived to reveal exactly how the women of 1916 were being wronged. Margaret Pearse was therefore joined in the Abbey stalls by Kathleen Clarke, the wife of Tom Clarke; Fiona Plunkett, the sister of Joseph Plunkett; and Hanna Sheehy Skeffington, whose husband Francis had been celebrated by O'Casey in *The Story of the Irish Citizen Army* as the first martyr of Irish socialism. When the theatre was flooded with light these women enjoyed their prominence, and in spite of O'Casey's admiration for her late spouse, Hanna Sheehy Skeffington became the most vituperative protestor against *The Plough and the Stars*. She bellowed: 'The Free State Government is subsidising the Abbey to malign Pearse and Connolly [. . .] It is no wonder [. . .] that you do not remember the men of Easter Week, because none of you fought on either side'.[76] She felt that the play had 'held up to derision and obloquy the men and women of Easter Week', and she objurgated O'Casey in the Irish newspapers as well as humiliating the valetudinarian playwright at a public meeting in Mills Hall on the following Monday.[77]

At this meeting O'Casey was also confronted by Maud Gonne, another bereaved woman of 1916. She took particular delight in playing the part of the sacrificial woman, and although she had intensely disliked her husband when he was alive and was estranged from him for years before the Easter Rising, from 1916 until her death she consistently and ostentatiously dressed in widow's mourning weeds. She told O'Casey that he had no right to introduce Pádraic Pearse into his play, and that she could clearly see why the protest was made. In his *Autobiographies* O'Casey mentions these criticisms and describes Gonne as a shadowy creature much like the political orator in *The Plough and the Stars*. In Gonne's 'crinkled, querulous face', O'Casey writes, 'Shadows now were all its marking, shadows where the flesh had swelled or where the flesh had sagged'.[78]

The playwright Denis Johnston felt that all of these women were 'intrusive ladies', and Lady Gregory called them 'women who have made demonstrations on Poppy Day and at elections and meetings; [and] have made a habit of it, of the excitement'.[79] Indeed, although some of them were still passionately committed to female equality, these women were also determined to promote their own personal sacrificial pretensions, and they did so in another Dublin playhouse later in 1926. Ten days after the meeting about O'Casey's play at Mills Hall, the women who protested at *The Plough and the Stars* participated as delegates at the historic meeting at which Éamon de Valera broke away from Sinn Féin to form the party that would dominate Irish politics for the rest of the century. In May this new party, Fianna Fáil, would be formally launched in Dublin's La Scala Theatre, which was situated symbolically close to the GPO. *The Plough and the Stars* needed to be denounced because it represented a threat to those who sought to establish a conservative version of the Easter rebellion, and the sacrificial women associated with it, at the heart of Irish political life.

Appeasing Margaret Pearse

After the controversy about his play, O'Casey retreated to England, and the Abbey directorate rejected the next play that he submitted to them. *The Plough and the Stars* remained abhorrent to certain audiences, who complained that it vilely caricatured each hero of 1916 as 'a coward or a looter, or a drunkard or an adulterer, or a hypocrite or a degenerate'.[80] When the Abbey company toured America with O'Casey's play in the 1930s, de Valera received a raft of letters from Irish–Americans who felt that it was 'worthless trash'.[81] The Fianna Fáil government warned the Abbey's directors against producing plays that were 'likely to injure the reputation of this country', and in 1966 the theatre, dependent on state funding, complied with a government request to perform no plays by O'Casey during the celebrations marking the fiftieth anniversary of the Rising.[82] For a number of years the Abbey advised playwrights to avoid depicting any of the leaders of the rebellion for fear of causing offence to the rebels' immediate relatives.[83]

Sean O'Casey had never been entirely comfortable about the way that he denigrated Margaret Pearse in order to attack the abstract notion of the sacrificial woman. Prior to the Abbey performance, he fretted about the consequences of letting Pádraic Pearse's companions watch the play, and Gabriel Fallon, who played the part of Captain Brennan in the Abbey's original production, reported that O'Casey had a disturbing premonition:

> He appeared to be somewhat worried about 'The Voice of the Man' outside the public house in Act II. Feeling that the scene was considerably heightened in drama by the Voice – indeed, that the Voice was the dramatic backbone of the scene – I assured him that he had nothing to be worried about. But his worries were not of the dramatic kind. 'You see, Gaby,' he said, 'that speech is made up of extracts from speeches delivered by Padraic Pearse and there are people who knew Pearse who might object.' I tried to assure him that, objections or not, it would be ruinous dramatically to tamper with or remove the speech.[84]

O'Casey imagined that his play might provoke a disastrous response, and in the months before *The Plough and the Stars* was first performed, he was particularly panic-stricken about the potential effect of the speeches that he had adapted from Pádraic Pearse's writings.

Despite Fallon's admonition, O'Casey therefore tried making additions to the play that significantly revised the Pearse character. On every occasion that the orator speaks, O'Casey drafted a large number of embellishments and painstakingly glued them onto his text. The demagogue was to begin with the new line: 'Soldiers of Ireland's army of Independence, this is a proud and a splendid moment for us all! Splendid and proud, for it speaks of a power that is, and of a greater power that is to come –'. And after reciting some of Pádraic Pearse's more familiar words the speaker was to continue:

> Many are they who are eager to fight for the thing that is evil, and few there be who will fight for the thing that is good, but in every age will be

found Irishmen willing and eager to fight for the sovereign freedom of their counthry.[85]

As far as we can tell, Pádraic Pearse had never written or spoken these words. Instead, O'Casey drew on his own earlier experience of penning nationalist bombast to compose new revolutionary sentiments for the orator, indicating O'Casey's worry about insulting Margaret Pearse as well as his desire to avoid an all-out confrontation with her. By diluting Pádraic Pearse's words with fictional interpolations O'Casey hoped to make the speaker a more obviously imaginary and a less incendiary figure.

However, fearing that he was turning the play into a lesser work, O'Casey eventually reverted to his original conception of the orator. The typescript alterations did not survive into performance, and there is no trace of them in the Abbey promptbook.[86] O'Casey waited for a number of years before he tried again to make amends to Margaret Pearse, but he returned to the subject in his 1945 autobiography, *Drums under the Windows*. In this later work, O'Casey opts against recreating the portrait of a crazed leader obsessed by slaughter that dominates Act II of *The Plough and the Stars*, and instead, two decades later, O'Casey praises Pádraic Pearse as a thoughtful, literature-loving educator and idealist.

In his autobiographical works O'Casey continues to attack the sacrificial women of Ireland. He mocks Ireland as 'the Woeman of the Piercing Wail', and describes bumping into 'The Poor Old Woman' who runs around the streets of Dublin yelling maniacally for absolutely no reason.[87] He also savages Cathleen ni Houlihan as an 'ignorant' 'old hag' or 'bitch' with an 'old snarly gob'.[88] But the older O'Casey regretted his specific attack on Margaret Pearse, and went out of his way to distance her son from the satire of *The Plough and the Stars*.

Indeed, O'Casey's later descriptions of the leader of the Rising emulate the way that Margaret Pearse wanted her offspring to be remembered. The Pádraic Pearse of *Drums under the Windows* is a photographic negative of the shadowy orator of *The Plough and the Stars*. Whereas the play's orator is obscured by darkness, the insurrectionist of the autobiographical writings is insistently illuminated. O'Casey describes Pádraic Pearse as coaxing 'others to come out of the dim thicket of convention into a clearer light', and claims that the rebel leader's capture showed how 'the cordon of flame has burnt out' and 'the Easter sun has gone west'.[89] Similarly, when O'Casey came to write his later drama *The Drums of Father Ned* (1959) he depicted an Irish rebel expressing sympathy for 'Poor Paudrig Pearse!' whilst three Black and Tan soldiers have their faces darkened.[90]

At the time of Fianna Fáil's inception, O'Casey bitterly criticised the party's symbolic mother. Later in the century, after Margaret Pearse's death, he retracted much of this personal vitriol, and his autobiography includes one final emendation to the Abbey play in which Pádraic Pearse does not die but causes only the meaningless butchery of others. Margaret Pearse saw her son's martyrdom as the zenith of his glorious life, and those in O'Casey's Dublin audience were accustomed to seeing the heroic deaths of patriots at the end of popular melo-dramas. For instance, before 1916 Emmet had died at the conclusion of Boucicault's celebrated *Robert Emmet*, Henry Joy McCracken was hanged at the end of Whitbread's *The Ulster Hero*, and the fictional 1798 patriot Betsy Gray was killed at the close of Patrick Bourke's *For the Land She Loved*.[91] But *The Plough and the Stars* cocked a snook at this convention. *Drums under the Windows* therefore completes its inversion of O'Casey's earlier play by including the crucial last moment of Pádraic Pearse's life; and whereas in the Abbey Theatre the actor representing the rebel leader had ended the play with a bow to the audience, in the autobiography Pádraic Pearse ends his life with a bow to the firing squad. A repentant O'Casey commemorated how 'the stupid bullets tore a way through your quiet breast, and your fall forward to death was but a bow to your enemies. Peace be with you, and with your comrades too'.[92]

3

The Dreaming of the Bones

'But it is not like 1916'.
'It wasn't like 1916 in 1916'.
There was a long silence.[1]

ANNOUNCERESS   Oh come come come, one must have breeding.
CASEMENT   For why? are yous horses?[2]

Ploughing again

After the controversy about O'Casey's play, Ireland once more settled down into the familiar routine of commemorating the Easter Rising with yearly marches and church services. The Abbey had been soundly berated in Dublin's newspapers in 1926, and in 1928 the theatre rejected O'Casey's *The Silver Tassie* and Denis Johnston's *The Old Lady Says 'No'!* It must have appeared to some that Yeats and Lady Gregory were reluctant to court trouble again, and were refusing to stage drama that challenged the nationalism of the Free State.

However, the Abbey's dismissal of O'Casey and Johnston was primarily motivated by the directorate's dislike for expressionist writing and, in actual fact, after 1926 the theatre's enthusiasm for dealing with 1916 remained undiminished. In 1931, when Ireland celebrated the fifteenth-anniversary year of the Easter Rising, the Abbey again premiered a play about the insurgency, and this time the theatre's managers decided to perform Yeats's play *The Dreaming of the Bones* in order to challenge popular perceptions of the rebellion just as they had done five years before.

The Dreaming of the Bones has attracted far less critical attention than O'Casey's work. The dominant academic orthodoxy aggrandises Yeats's poetry whilst largely ignoring his work as a playwright, and *The Dreaming of the Bones* is often seen as little more than an engaging appurtenance to 'Easter 1916'. Those scholars who have considered Yeats's 1916 play at greater length have devoted the vast majority of their energy to exploring its aesthetic relation to Japanese Noh drama rather than its political significance.[3] Yet *The Dreaming of the Bones* echoes some of the most subversive aspects of *The Plough and the Stars*, and like O'Casey, Yeats wanted the first performance of his play to demolish the shibboleths of a sentimental and mawkish kind of nationalism.

In *The Dreaming of the Bones* Yeats invoked Pádraic Pearse's writings just as O'Casey did in *The Plough and the Stars*. When Yeats scripted the lines, 'blood has returned to fields/That have grown red from drinking blood like mine', he plagiarised exactly the same gory exhortation to battle that O'Casey doctored from Pearse's 1915 article 'Peace and the Gael': 'Heroism has come back to the earth [. . .] The old heart of the earth needed to be warmed with the red wine of the battlefields'.[4] In addition, when one of Yeats's characters announced, 'No shade however harried and consumed/Would change his own calamity for theirs' (p. 313), the original Dublin audience may well have heard an echo of Pearse's famous poem 'The Rebel' that vows, 'We will try it out with you, ye that have harried and held'.[5] After all, by 1931 Pearse's poetry and speeches had been reprinted many times and were being repeatedly quoted by Yeats himself in his public lectures.[6]

Yeats, who shared a platform with Pádraic Pearse in late 1914 at a Thomas Davis centenary meeting, resurrected the rebel leader's words in *The Dreaming of the Bones* in a more allusive way than O'Casey had done.[7] But in 1931 the omens for Yeats's invocation of Pearse were inauspicious. O'Casey's combination of the dead patriot and a prostitute had proved explosive five years before, and in *The Dreaming of the Bones* Yeats again combined Pearse's brand of revolutionary nationalism with the theme of extra-marital promiscuity. Furthermore, Yeats mirrored Maurice Dalton in describing a rebel who runs away from the combat. In Yeats's play a young Easter-week insurgent from the GPO is fleeing the British reprisals, when he meets a mysterious man and woman who tell him a ghostly but smutty tale of two accursed spirits. These spirits, because of their adultery, must wander alone for eternity, perpetually longing for the forbidden touch of one another. Just as Rosie Redmond had spoken of her erotic desires in *The Plough and the Stars*, so Yeats's rebel learns that the phantoms 'once lay warm and live the live-long night/In one another's arms' (p. 313) committing a 'passionate sin' (p. 313), and that now, after death, they long again that 'hand would slip in hand' (p. 313) and that 'Lip would be pressed on lip' (p. 314). Although this ritualised play tells its story in a more abstract way than O'Casey's earthy tale of the tenements, Yeats must have remembered that the last time Pádraic Pearse's words had been presented onstage alongside a collection of sexual innuendos was in *The Plough and the Stars*. Never one to shy away from a theatrical brouhaha, Yeats had every reason to suspect that *The Dreaming of the Bones* might again provoke disquiet amongst the Abbey's spectators, and when the play was being prepared for performance he was so excited that he mistakenly dashed back from Coole Park to Dublin for the rehearsals a week before they were actually due to begin.[8]

In the event, when Yeats leapt to the stage at the end of *The Dreaming of the Bones* he rose to thank rather than berate those in the audience, who applauded politely after finding that any discomfort with the eroticism of *The Dreaming of the Bones* was tempered by a more familiar version of nationalist historiography than was to be found in O'Casey's work. For although Yeats's rebel is initially bemused that the ghosts' adultery resulted in such a pitiless punishment, his attitude hardens when he realises that he is hearing about Diarmuid and Dervorgilla, the twelfth-century adulterers widely remembered for fighting their enemies by imploring the Anglo–Normans to intervene in Ireland. When it transpires that the rebel's companions are themselves the spirits of Diarmuid and Dervorgilla the rebel finds that he is unable to pronounce his forgiveness upon them and so condemns them to exist in an ongoing state of purgatorial longing. It hardly needs to be pointed out that in real life the island inhabited by Diarmuid and Dervorgilla in the mid-1100s had already been subjected to the massive invasions of Vikings and Hiberno–Norse, but *The Dreaming of the Bones* portrays the Anglo–Norman occupation as being a unique and disastrous event.[9] Yeats's contemporaries were accustomed to hearing that a concatenation of English wrongs had originated from this particular foreign incursion, with Seán Ua Ceallaigh, for example, writing in 1935:

> From the first coming of the Anglo–Normans to Ireland, the two edges of England's Sword of Conquest may be said to have been hall-marked, Defame and Decimate on the one hand, Divide and Dominate on the other [. . .] those twin mottoes, implemented by a ruthless Tyranny, have since been England's trump cards in the subjection of Ireland.[10]

According to this nationalist version of history, Diarmuid and Dervorgilla expedited the abhorrent Elizabethan plantations and Cromwellian land clearances, and in *The Dreaming of the Bones* Yeats brings the story up to date: the adulterers now bear the additional responsibility for the occupation of Dublin by British troops in the twentieth century. Yeats's original conception for 'Easter 1916' discerned that the rebellion showed how 'terrible beauty has been born again', and in *The Dreaming of the Bones* he explores this idea in dramatic form.[11] The violent fracas in Dublin is simply another of the recurring consequences of Diarmuid and Dervorgilla's primordial sin, a repeat of all those horrors that had already been visited on Ireland as a result of their original adultery. For Yeats's rebel the Anglo–Norman intrusions of the eleventh and twelfth centuries wrought a profound and disabling change, and he is unable to pardon Diarmuid and Dervorgilla because he has recently tried to annihilate their legacy when battling the British army in Dublin.

Yet, paradoxically, in the middle of *The Dreaming of the Bones* the rebel almost gives in to the 'terrible' temptation to forgive the ghosts. He suffers considerable torment about whether to pardon them, encouraging Yeats's audience to realise that it is not only the British troops at the GPO who belong to the disastrous legacy of Diarmuid and Dervorgilla's fornication. The occupation of Ireland by the Anglo–Normans permanently affected almost the entire Irish race, including the rebel's own lineage. As Peter Ure puts it, Yeats's ghosts 'fathered' the revolutionary. The rebel 'is one of the consequences of their transgression and cannot forgive the authors of the evil which he fights and curses'.[12] Perhaps this genealogy would have been more obvious if Yeats had retained the name of the Easter rebel that he used in the draft version of the play, that is, MacDermot.[13] Here, the patronymic prefix, 'Mac', is combined with the anglicised version of Diarmuid, 'Dermot', making the rebel, in effect, a son of Diarmuid whose identity has been transmuted by the arrival of the Anglo–Normans.[14]

The rebel's blighted inheritance is also emphasised by the qualities that he shares with the ghosts: he regrets nothing, he is willing to sacrifice himself to the dictates of his 'rascal heart' (p. 311), and in the draft manuscript he agrees that:

> we both have
> the same enemies, the dawn
> or human voices.[15]

In the final manuscript the rebel's name, 'Young Man', similarly accentuates his kinship with Dervorgilla, who is called 'Young Girl'.

This bond between the ghostly apparitions and the modern patriot is so strong that Joseph Chadwick has given a plausible Freudian reading of their relationship, arguing that Yeats's work follows the pattern of a 'primal scene' in which a child witnesses a sexual act between his parents, interprets it as an act of violence, and refuses to acknowledge that it was through this act that he himself was begotten.[16] The insurgent of *The Dreaming of the Bones* curses Diarmuid and Dervorgilla, the 'parents' who brought about the racial mixing of which his own existence is now a consequence. He is therefore placed in the fearful position of being both a descendant of the adulterers and a militant who struggles to exterminate their patrimony.

Thus, even though Yeats's play apparently deals with a more recognisable and comforting nationalist fable than *The Plough and the Stars*, his message about the sacrificial mother is akin to that portrayed in Sean O'Casey's controversial work. The plays written or commissioned by Daniel Corkery, Maurice Dalton, and Margaret Pearse had promulgated the myth that the rebels of 1916 adored their fervently nationalist mothers, who fostered hatred of the British occupation in their offspring and encouraged fighting and dying for Ireland. But like O'Casey, Yeats diligently avoided bringing his rebel into contact with the maternal influence of this type. Instead, the parental figures who have necessitated the revolutionist's combat in *The Dreaming of the Bones* are the forebears he despises and who helped to destroy Celtic Ireland in the first place. And although Yeats's audience applauded, the story may well have provoked another outcry if it were played in a form other than that of an unfamiliar spiritualist dance-drama, or if Margaret Pearse had again been sitting in the theatre.

Yeats and eugenics

The Dreaming of the Bones was first staged in 1931, but it was in fact written many years earlier, at about the same time that Yeats was composing 'Easter 1916'. The play was published in *Two Plays for Dancers* and the *Little Review* in January 1919, but took a further thirteen years to be performed.[17] The reason why Yeats chose to dust off his old play and produce it at the Abbey at the end of 1931 was partly because his work could now be performed by the Abbey School of Ballet, which was organised by the stunningly beautiful, Anglo–Irish ballet dancer, Ninette de Valois, who had been coaxed to the Abbey by an obviously smitten Yeats. But more significantly, *The Dreaming of the Bones* had a newfound thematic relevance to Yeats's wider interests in the 1930s and to the plays that he was writing and producing during this decade.

A year before the first performance of *The Dreaming of the Bones* Yeats presented *The Words upon the Window-Pane* at the Abbey Theatre, depicting a spiritualist possessed by the ghost of Jonathan Swift, and relying on the same idea of 'dreaming back' that is the keystone of *The Dreaming of the Bones*. As one of the characters in *The Words upon the Window-Pane* explains, some phantoms 'think they are still living and go over and over some painful thought [. . .] Sometimes a spirit re-lives not the pain of death but some passionate or tragic moment of life' (p. 470).

The idea that restless spirits revisit the scenes of their lives and commit their sins over and over again was a spiritualist commonplace, and it was one that Yeats returned to and developed in his play of 1938, *Purgatory*. In this late play, a nameless old man excoriates the moment he was conceived because his aristocratic mother had lain with a plebeian. He curses his origins, whilst behind him the spirits of the two lovers, his mother and father, meet once more in the lighted window to re-enact their passion, caught in the same cycle of repetition as Diarmuid and Dervorgilla's dance. At the end of *Purgatory* the old man stabs his own son to death to prevent the racial 'pollution' (p. 543) being passed on, and this violent response mirrors that of the rebel in *The Dreaming of the Bones* who hates his progenitors, savages Diarmuid and Dervorgilla's legacy at the GPO, and damns the ghosts to a continuing punishment.

In *The Words upon the Window-Pane*, *Purgatory*, and *The Dreaming of the Bones*, spirits of the dead are doomed continually to re-enact the most tempestuous moments of their lives, and in all three plays these re-enactments involve characters who curse their own lineage for introducing a new and degrading element into the world. Just as the old man anathematises his parents for mixing noble and plebeian blood in *Purgatory*, so in *The Words upon the Window-Pane* the spirit of Swift argues that he cannot have children because he must not pass his genetic tendency for attacks of dizziness into 'blood that has been healthy for generations' (p. 474), and concludes the play with the heartfelt lament, 'Perish the day on which I was born!' (p. 479).

The rebel of *The Dreaming of the Bones* also fulminates against his predecessors whose sexual act brought about a woeful debasement of the nation's bloodstock. Yeats's repeated use of the word 'blood' in this play links the rebel to Pádraic Pearse's revolutionary rhetoric, but the term was also being reiterated in contemporary eugenic discourse at the time of the play's first performance. The most noxious example of this was the passing of Germany's Eugenic Sterilisation Law in 1933, when Adolf Hitler's Reich Ministry of the Interior declared, 'We want to prevent [. . .] poisoning the entire bloodstream of the race'.[18] Yet such rhetoric had been bandied around in Ireland for some time, and as early as 1914 Yeats used the title poem of *Responsibilities* to rejoice in his own 'blood/That has not passed through any huckster's loin'.[19]

The Eugenics Education Society, founded in England in 1907, had made eugenic science a cornerstone of British medicine. Susan Cannon Harris has shown that this produced a contradictory effect in Ireland, where certain nationalists affiliated themselves with the ideas of England's public health movement by adopting the same concerns about physical health and genetic hygiene, but also identified the presence of Englishness in Ireland with racial disease and degeneration. Arthur Griffith, for instance, first accepted the imperial principle of eugenics, and then attempted to turn its idiom against the British. A British effort to enforce compulsory vaccination on Ireland in 1907 was denounced by Griffith's newspaper, *Sinn Féin*, as 'polluting the pure Irish blood', and the publication stated, 'We can never hope for a virile, healthy race, when the life stream is so early polluted with an animal excrescence'. Griffith himself wrote that the British army had the highest per capita rate of venereal disease amongst European armies, and that consequently 'the British army is the most immoral army in civilisation'.[20]

In *The Dreaming of the Bones* Yeats follows Griffith in blaming the British army for bringing degeneration to Ireland. The play's characters castigate the 'alien from overseas' (p. 312) and the 'English robbers' (p. 309) for the same kind of destruction of the ancestral houses and their ancient trees that is mourned in *Purgatory*, and the rebel is even more disturbed to see that, now, people born in Ireland can end up fighting on behalf of the British army. Yeats's play remembers a mythical, prelapsarian past before the arrival of the Anglo–Normans, in which rebellions were internal affairs amongst kinfolk, who shared the same 'blood' (p. 312) and were all Celts. Diarmuid and Dervorgilla ruined this national unity and so they are doomed to spend their afterlife in a search for the elusive forgiveness of someone 'of their race' (p. 314).

The dramatic form that Yeats selected for *The Dreaming of the Bones* also helped to convey these racial concerns. The play was based on a much older Japanese piece, *Nishikigi*, which Yeats knew through its translation by Ezra Pound and Ernest Fenollosa, and which Yeats re-wrote by changing the priest who forgives two lovers in the original play into the rebel who refuses to exonerate Diarmuid and Dervorgilla. Yeats's decision to base *The Dreaming of the Bones* on the earlier Noh piece was closely related to his belief that the Japanese theatre embodied the eugenic principles he championed. He wrote:

> The [Noh] players themselves, unlike the despised players of the popular theatre, have passed on proudly from father to son an elaborate art, and even now a player will publish his family tree to prove his skill. One player wrote in 1906 [. . .] that after thirty generations of nobles a woman of his house dreamed that a mask was carried to her from heaven, and soon after she bore a son who became a player and the father of players.[21]

Noh contained 'all that high breeding of poetical style', and Yeats celebrated the way that the cryptic literary and mythological allusions of the Japanese plays could only be understood by a few old noble families as 'part of their breeding'.[22] His play about 1916 was also concerned with the lineage of the nation, and it therefore mimicked the theatrical Noh style that he associated with high breeding.

Eugenics and the Easter Rising

Yeats's enthusiasm for eugenics was more than simply 'an old man's frenzy'.[23] In the 1970s Denis Donoghue traced Yeats's interest in eugenics back to 1900, and more recently Paul Scott Stanfield showed that the poet's renunciation of Ireland's 'new commonness' in the early 1900s indicated an initial attraction to the idea of selective reproduction.[24] As early as 1907 Yeats had defined style as 'high breeding in words and in argument' and claimed that creative writers manifested 'the freedom of the well-bred'.[25]

This is not to say that Yeats had finalised the more extreme eugenic views of his old age when he actually wrote *The Dreaming of the Bones*. In this play his views are notably less coherent and consistent than they would be in his later writings. When Yeats's rebel speaks of Donough O'Brien, for example, it is clear that internal Irish battles as well as adultery helped the Anglo–Normans to debase Ireland; and, logically, we must also presume that the ascendancy culture of the eighteenth century owed its origins – and not only its ultimate destruction, which the rebel bemoans – to the miscegenation facilitated by Diarmuid and Dervorgilla.

But by lamenting the loss of an old, Celtic Ireland in *The Dreaming of the Bones* Yeats had begun exploring those ideas about irreversible cultural decline that played such a major part in his later, more fully considered conception of eugenics. In 1931, staging this play appeared particularly apposite to the poet who had firmly come to advocate the rule of an educated and able few, as opposed to that of democratically elected representatives.[26] He had been working on his notions of the Irish eighteenth century, and his examination of Burke, Swift, and Berkeley led him to formulate a central *Weltanschauung* that was essentially a race philosophy based on eugenic goals and assumptions.

Yeats shared his views about race and governance with many others at this time. The American Madison Grant published a book that was reprinted in London several times from 1917 until the 1930s, in which he popularised the notion that a fully functional state required the management of a well-bred group. He claimed:

> True aristocracy is government by the wisest and best, always a small minority in any population. Human society is like a serpent dragging its long body on the ground, but with the head always thrust a little in advance and a little elevated above the earth [. . .] To use another simile, in an aristocratic as distinguished from a plutocratic, or democratic organisation, the intellectual and talented classes form the point of the lance, while the massive shaft represents the body of the population and adds by its bulk and weight to the penetrative impact of the tip. In a democratic system this concentrated force at the top is dispersed throughout the mass, supplying, to be sure, a certain amount of leaven, but in the long run the force and genius of the small minority is dissipated, if not wholly lost.[27]

Yeats was not clumsy enough to use such an extended phallic comparison, but in the 1930s he echoed much of Madison Grant's train of thought. Yeats wrote, 'Every day I notice some new analogy between [the] long-established life of the well-born and the artist's life', and continued, 'we [artists] carry in our head that form of society which aristocracies create now and again for some brief moment at Urbino or Versailles'.[28] Like Grant, Yeats advocated the government of an exclusive coterie, pronouncing: 'Think first how many able men with public minds this country has [. . .] and mould your system upon those men [. . .] These men, whether six or six thousand, are the core of Ireland, are Ireland itself'.[29] According to Yeats, people of genius could impart to the masses a deeper and more significant sense of nationality than that expressed by popular characteristics or opinions, even if this involved bloodshed. In 1937 he attacked the heterogeneous, degenerate nature of modern Dublin, and declared, 'wherever in Europe there are minds strong enough to lead others the same vague hatred rises; in four or five or in less generations this hatred will have issued in violence and imposed some kind of rule of kindred'.[30]

Yeats endorsed the IRB's secretive organisation of the 1916 rebellion because he found that it cohered with his ideas about how the country should be run by a 'rule of kindred', and in his poetry of the 1930s Yeats repeatedly extolled the revolutionaries in aristocratic terms. In 'The O'Rahilly' he portrays a swash-buckling rebel and the poem originally included the refrain 'Praise the Proud'.[31] Similarly, in 'The Ghost of Roger Casement' Yeats commemorates Casement's noble lineage by imagining 'many a famous man' inhabiting the rebel's family tomb.[32] 'The Statues' also celebrates the small and select group that had fought in 1916:

> When Pearse summoned Cuchulain to his side,
> What stalked through the Post Office? What intellect,
> What calculation, number, measurement, replied?[33]

Yeats wanted to remind his readers that in 1916 a band of rebels had mani-festly ignored the wishes of the majority in seizing control of Dublin, and he celebrated these insurrectionists as members of a ruling elite, with power and legitimacy residing in those 'Hearts with one purpose alone'.[34] For the rebels, their strategy, whilst not being democratic at the time, depended ultimately on the future verdict of the people. But Yeats saw this revolutionary avant-gardism in terms of a reactionary oligarchic elitism, which, rather than preparing the ground for future democracy, actually served to undermine the ballot box. The poet felt that Dublin's revolutionaries had demonstrated that a small elite ought to govern the country, and that their rebellion should be kept alive after 1916 by enabling an aristocratic leadership to rule in Ireland. In his essay 'Preliminaries' from *On the Boiler*, Yeats acclaimed the Free State's defunct senate (a governing body that mainly consisted of appointed members and which de Valera phased out in favour of a largely elected upper house) by writing:

The Ministers had not been elected [. . .] their descendants, if they grow rich enough for the travel and leisure that make a finished man, will constitute our ruling class, and date their origin from the Post Office as American families date theirs from the *Mayflower.* They have already intermarried, able stocks have begun to appear, and recent statistics have shown that men of talent everywhere are much linked through marriage and descent.[35]

The spring rebellion offered a symbolic point of origin for a new, unelected elite who could reign over the country. In Yeats's view, those who had taken up arms at Easter had facilitated a future in which those who were unelected and disdainful of democracy could grasp the baton of the nation's destiny.

Although stated most clearly in his poetry of the 1930s, Yeats had been formulating his view of the rebels as being a ruling elite ever since 1916. He labelled the rebels 'the ablest and most fine-natured of our young men' and 'fellow workers' in letters written to John Quinn and Robert Bridges after the rebellion, and in 'Easter 1916' sought to show how the rebellion served to remove the insurgents from the banality of everyday life.[36] When the affray broke out in 1916 he 'felt some discomfort at being safe in England when his friends were risking their lives in Dublin, and fretted somewhat that he had not been consulted', placing himself, a poet who already had an uneasy relationship with the stubborn will of the populace, in close affinity with the leaders of the uprising.[37]

Yeats saw nobility in the Easter rebellion, just as he discerned nobility in the Noh theatre. Consequently, in the 1916 Cuala Press edition of Pound and Fenollosa's Japanese plays, Yeats announced that the Noh theatre was 'distinguished, indirect and symbolic [. . .] an aristocratic form' and added a colophon remembering that this edition was published 'in the year of the Sinn Fein Rising'.[38] Although Yeats knew that in reality the rebellion was conducted by a solid phalanx of Dublin's middle class, he felt that the rebels had prepared the way for an elite anti-democratic regime, and so the aristocratic Japanese drama was the best form with which to describe them. As a result, *The Dreaming of the Bones* presents a thoroughly ahistorical insurgent, who is nothing like MacDonagh or Connolly or their colleagues, but is very much like the priest in *Nishikigi* and like the figure imagined in Yeats's 1914 poem 'The Fisherman', who is remote and removed from the disheartening philistinism of the Irish masses.[39]

The rebellion and democratic populism

Yet, after the fracas of 1916, the rebels were increasingly seen as leaders of popular nationalist sentiment rather than being far removed from the democratically expressed opinions of their day. After the Sinn Féin election victory in 1918 Yeats could see that the uprising's original elitism had been misremembered, and that the general populace rather than just the 'ruling class' were dating their origins from the GPO. Disappointingly, the ill-bred people of no culture were venerating pictures of the rebels, and the violence of the Rising was resulting not in a 'rule of kindred' but in a rule of the 'mob'.

Yeats had long despised the mob, a title he used to deprecate his opponents during a variety of theatrical controversies and which served as an all-encompassing term for things he found distasteful in the public sphere. He felt that members of the mob were completely devoid of genuine national sentiment, and he judged that 'the pulpit and the newspaper are but voices of the mob'.[40] After the Rising he watched the journalists and churchmen who had disparaged or condemned the Rising now embracing it enthusiastically. In 1916 the Catholic Church maintained an official silence whilst certain congregations were told that it had been 'needless, wanton, terrible', 'a senseless, meaningless debauch of blood', or that the insurgents were guilty of 'murder pure and simple'.[41] The *Irish Catholic* similarly told its readers that the Rising was 'as criminal as it was insane . . . traitorous and treasonous', whilst the *Irish Independent* and *Irish Times* applauded the executions of the leaders.[42] Yet in the months and years following the uprising, printers and preachers did much to institutionalise the Rising by organising commemorative sermons, public decades of the rosary, and the distribution of adulatory poetry and stories about the rebels. When the *Irish Press* began printing in September 1931, Margaret Pearse was invited to hit the button that started the presses rolling. This was the Ireland that Conor Cruise O'Brien thought in danger of commemorating itself to death, and much of Yeats's ambivalence towards the rebellion came from its incorporation into a form of Irish nationalism that revolved around crowds and mass politics, which he had always found nauseating.

From the late 1890s Yeats had argued with Maud Gonne about the role of the crowd, and whereas she insisted that she was 'born to be in the midst of a crowd', he vilified the tendency of individuals to abandon their own conscience by losing themselves in something large, powerful, and external.[43] Since 1902 he had used 'marching feet' as a figure for this cowardice.[44] But by the 1930s the yearly commemorations of the Rising were characterised by the marching feet of the Easter-week processions in towns across Ireland. Yeats looked on with dismay as the 1916 uprising, which once had the potential to provide a foundational moment for an able stock of Ireland's governing elite, was instead promoted around Ireland by newspaper proprietors, and metamorphosed into the corrupted property of a populist mob.

Consequently, when *The Dreaming of the Bones* was first performed in 1931 the rebel was presented in a different way from the author's original conception of the character. When Yeats began writing the play in 1916 he had wanted it performed before a small audience of about fifty invited guests in the opulent drawing-room of one of his patrician friends.[45] Rejoicing in his 'freedom from the stupidity of an ordinary audience', he would ask that only lovers of poetry be invited to this exclusive event.[46] The stage on which the actors performed would blur seamlessly into the space occupied by the spectators, undivided by a proscenium arch, by a raised lip, or by any lighting effects. The audience would be placed 'within arm's reach' of the players, and sit around three sides of the stage rather than directly in front of it.[47] Yeats wanted the performers and spectators to experience a feeling of 'intimacy' with one another, and declared:

'It is well to be close enough to an artist to feel for him a personal liking, close enough perhaps to feel that our liking is returned'.[48] The actors would enter through the same doorway as those who watched them, and, in the absence of stage lights, everyone in the room would be equally illuminated. Thus, the writer intended both troupers and viewers to play a part in the spectacle, which had the power to disarm some potential onlookers. When Yeats produced another similarly styled Noh play at his house, he invited Sean O'Casey, who later remembered disliking Yeats's careful stage-management of the assemblage, and loathing having to sit amongst a group of self-important poseurs.[49]

In Yeats's original conception of *The Dreaming of the Bones* the audience's iden-tification with the Easter rebel would have been particularly strong. Yeats was entranced by the ideas of Edward Gordon Craig, and demanded that each of the other twenty-eight characters in his four Noh plays either be fitted with a mask or have their faces made up to resemble masks.[50] Uniquely, the rebel from the GPO was to bear an undisguised countenance, and this physical similarity between player and spectator was designed to emphasise the link between the rebels who had fought at the GPO and the select members of Dublin's elegant audience. David Lloyd warns against separating Yeats's aesthetics and politics too readily from one another, and in 1916 *The Dreaming of the Bones* highlighted the affinity between the two elites who could bring about the good governance of Ireland: the 1916 rebels and Yeats's influential, poetry-loving friends.[51]

But the 1931 performance of *The Dreaming of the Bones* was a far cry from Yeats's original conception of the play. To the intimate drawing-room of his 'personal friends and a few score people of good taste', the setting of the Abbey of Corcomroe was supposed to recall the impressive ruin four miles from Lady Gregory's seaside house where Yeats, Shaw, and other members of the literati holidayed.[52] However, for those sitting in the Abbey stalls in 1931 the refer-ences to the 'Abbey graveyard' (p. 312), 'The Abbey [that] lies amid its broken tombs' (p. 311), and 'the ruined Abbey' (p. 310) had a somewhat different ring. This theatre was, after all, commonly remembered for its previous incarnation as a morgue.[53] Furthermore, in 1931 the middle-class Abbey spectators – who 'prefer light amusement or have no ear for verse' according to Yeats – paid for their tickets rather than being personally invited along by the author.[54] The audience was now entirely seated in darkness whilst the actors were brightly lit, and the imposition of the Abbey Theatre's architectural dynamics meant the players were raised up on the stage and divided from the viewers in the pit. If Yeats had wanted his audience and his rebel to enjoy a special kind of intimacy when he originally wrote the play, the writer's intentions were different in 1931, when the Abbey was packed with a crowd that he kept firmly partitioned from the noble principles of the rebellion.

The relocation of Yeats's rebel between 1916 and 1931 mirrored the reposi-tioning of the insurrectionists' images outside the theatre. In the Dublin of late 1916 pictures of the rebels and their deeds were passed from hand to hand on postcards.[55] But by the 1930s images of the insurgents were instead likely to be found on massive posters that were doubly separated from touch by being framed and hoisted up on the walls of the Irish homestead, often occupying a sanctified position alongside the Sacred Heart.[56] If nationalist hagiography had raised the rebel portraits in Irish homes, Yeats's desire to keep the revolt distinct from the middle-class mob brought about a similar repositioning at the Abbey Theatre.

The loose-lipped demagogue

One of the people who Yeats saw as being representative of the mob was Éamon de Valera, who Yeats famously labelled a 'loose-lipped demagogue'.[57] In 1926 Sean O'Casey's *The Plough and the Stars* criticised the way that those involved with founding de Valera's Fianna Fáil party were remembering the Easter Rising, and in 1931 Yeats staged *The Dreaming of the Bones* to criticise Fianna Fáil's nationalism at another critical time in the development of the Free State.

The Dreaming of the Bones opened at the Abbey during the build-up to the general election of March 1932 that brought Éamon de Valera to power for the first time. On the same day as the first performance of Yeats's play, de Valera held a rally in Waterford where he gave a speech lasting nearly two hours to a crowd estimated by the *Irish Press* to be in the region of 8,000. Ordinary people had jeered de Valera after the insurrection, but in 1931 they flocked to hear his lengthy speeches, and Yeats, the poet who disliked the mob, now saw de Valera courting the opinion of those who opposed all the values of the ruling elite.

De Valera was actually strongly inclined to view his own political principles in the same way that the rebels of 1916 had done, as being validated by an inherent rightness rather than by a contemporary democratic mandate. He had explained in the Dáil treaty debates, 'when ever I wanted to know what the Irish people wanted, I had only to examine my own heart and it told me straight off what the Irish people wanted'.[58] At times Yeats had felt some admiration for this strong-headedness, and compared de Valera to Swift, as representing the nation's 'turbulent self-assertion'.[59] But by the early 1930s Yeats could see that de Valera had unfortunately started pandering to the populism of the moment rather than being an elitist whose actions would be fully vindicated over time. The poet wrote, 'De Valera has described himself to somebody as the autocrat expressing the feeling of the masses. If we must have an autocrat let him express what Swift called "the bent & current of a people", not a momentary majority'.[60]

Although Yeats's personal feelings towards individual politicians were always likely to fluctuate, he was in general an ally of Cosgrave, Yeats's 'best supporter' over the Municipal Gallery project before the Rising.[61] In the month after *The Dreaming of the Bones* was staged Yeats wrote an article that was intended to influence the election in favour of his old ally. Published in the *Spectator*, Yeats's 'Ireland 1921–1931' suggests what he disliked about de Valera and Fianna Fáil. Yeats criticises the interlinked forces of 'sentimentality', 'insincere rhetoric', and 'mob emotion', and praises the Cosgrave government for bringing 'Freedom from obsession' and proving it was not 'afraid to govern' when it executed seventy-seven republican irregulars in 1922. Yeats wrote, 'The Government of the Free State has been proved legitimate by the only effective test; it has been permitted to take life'.[62] In an essay that eulogises 'our eighteenth century', and the Easter rebels, he lauds the Cosgrave government for enforcing a strong, anti-representational government unafraid to court unpopularity and even to kill people. The first staging of *The Dreaming of the Bones* was firmly linked to this piece in the *Spectator*, with both the Noh play and the newspaper article evoking 1916 in order to praise elite and noble visionaries and to applaud anti-democratic governance. Just like the Cosgrave administration, the rebel in *The Dreaming of the Bones* is associated with the eighteenth-century ascendancy, and he is prepared to act brutally and alone against those who threaten to despoil the nation.

The first performance of *The Dreaming of the Bones*, on 6 December 1931, took place exactly ten years after the articles of agreement for the treaty between Great Britain and Ireland were signed in London. The tenth anniversary was particularly controversial because Fianna Fáil's election campaign questioned the validity of the treaty's original endorsement, and declared it to be undemocratic. In actual fact, de Valera had shown the greatest disregard for contemporary democratic opinion in 1921 by refusing to ratify this treaty that he admitted the majority of Irish people would have accepted, asserting: 'there are rights which a minority may justly uphold, even by arms, against a majority'.[63] But by 1931 de Valera wanted to win the general election and, with characteristic pragmatism, was speaking differently. Now he wanted to gain permission from the present rather than the future, and when he spoke of the 1921 agreement he maintained, 'We are asking this election mandate from the Irish people giving us authority to get rid of that', 'We ask you to give us a mandate to do certain things'.[64]

In reality, the Easter rebels had acted without first gaining a popular mandate in the same way as the treaty signatories. Michael Collins, for example, had acted by similar principles when negotiating behind closed doors in 1921 as he had done when fighting in 1916. When the significant anniversary year of both the Anglo–Irish agreement and the Easter Rising arrived in 1931, the Abbey's version of *The Dreaming of the Bones* reminded Dubliners that the heroes of Easter week were far removed from the masses just like the treaty delegates. By contrast, other plays staged to mark the anniversaries of 1916, such as Seumas O'Kelly's *The Flame on the Hearth* or Pearse's *The Singer*, portrayed sympathetic Irish people welcoming outlawed Irish rebels into their homes.[65] But in *The Dreaming of the Bones* the rebel is a lonely and isolated figure, and in 1931 he bore little resemblance to the populist self-image fostered by de Valera as the election approached.

Noh surrender

W.J. McCormack notes that until recently many critics viewed Yeats 'as if the poet transcended the quarrels of his day or – at worst – commented upon them from an olympian detachment'; and it has been particularly acceptable to discount the political commitment of *The Dreaming of the Bones* following Helen Vendler's assertion in the 1960s that the 'genetic nucleus of *The Dreaming of the Bones* is nonpolitical'.[66] In her influential book, she observes that Yeats first invokes Diarmuid and Dervorgilla in 'The Vision of Hanrahan the Red', a story that condemns the adulterers not for having facilitated a foreign invasion but for having failed to love one another properly.[67] Vendler convincingly argues that the play was therefore originally disconnected from the Easter Rising, and she could have reinforced her thesis if she had known that Yeats had also suggested that the play's rebel might have fought at Vinegar Hill in 1798 rather than at the GPO in 1916.[68] But by privileging the gestation of the text over its realisation on the stage, Vendler acknowledges only part of the significance of *The Dreaming of the Bones*. Equally, an examination of the way that Yeats's play was first printed in 1919, at the start of the Anglo–Irish War, can reveal that the work manifests an unwavering enthusiasm for anti-British rebellion. Yeats was undoubtedly thinking of the play's Anglophobic elements when he told Lady Gregory in 1917 that *The Dreaming of the Bones* might prove 'only too powerful politically', and when he told Stephen Gwynn in 1919 that it 'may be thought dangerous by your editor because of its relation to rising of 1916'.[69] But the meaning of the Easter Rising changed and mutated between 1919 and the play's first performance in 1931, and by the 1930s Yeats was unlikely to make an unequivocal statement of support for the same rebellion that was celebrated by the Church and the popular press. *The Dreaming of the Bones* espoused a nascent eugenic ideology that corresponded with Yeats's opinions in the 1930s, and in staging these sentiments in 1931 he offered a contrast to the populism that de Valera had belatedly adopted in order to win the election. Like Sean O'Casey, Yeats was unhappy about the way that the Easter Rising had been appropriated by those associated with the Fianna Fáil party, and was using the Abbey Theatre to register his disapproval.

If *The Dreaming of the Bones* was a straightforward affirmation of support for 1916, then the presence in the audience on the first night of James MacNeill, the Governor General of Ireland, seems rather odd. MacNeill, although born in Antrim, spoke on behalf of the Crown and in theory represented the British king in Ireland. He had also advised his brother to issue the countermanding order against the Rising in 1916.[70] But when the play is considered in the context of Yeats's ideas of kindred then MacNeill's presence appears less anomalous. The governor was exactly the kind of person that Yeats felt should lead the people: an able man nominated by an executive council of the Free State, appointed by a king, and willing to hobnob with Lady Gregory over tea and cakes. Educated in Dublin and Cambridge, MacNeill was, according to Brendan Sexton, 'both an excellent athlete – a fine shot, a first-rate horseman and a very useful man in a boat – and a brilliant student'.[71] He was a healthy athlete and a learned scholar, and, to Yeats, a living embodiment of the race philosophy.

Éamon de Valera, however, despised James MacNeill, and forced the Governor General to resign after the general election. Five weeks before *The Dreaming of the Bones* was staged, de Valera addressed Fianna Fáil's annual party conference and stated that when, as he hoped, his party assumed power, 'there can be no question of our continuing to provide for any period extravagant sums which are at present paid in salary and for the upkeep of the establishment'.[72] By welcoming MacNeill into the Abbey on the eve of the general election Yeats was again emphasising the underlying political convictions of the theatre.

Peter Kuch has perceptively argued that Yeats delayed the publication of 'Easter 1916' because 'As a great poet, as one who believed in the power of poetry to make things happen, he waited until the Rebellion had acquired its own myths in order that he might counter them with the fictions of his poem'.[73] The delayed staging of *The Dreaming of the Bones* demonstrated Yeats's continued desire to counter the myths that surrounded the insurgency. On the Irish stage his portrayal of a noble Rising, fought by a combatant who frets about lineage, was designed to criticise the democratic and popular version of 1916 now endorsed by Fianna Fáil. However, as the following two chapters will show, members of de Valera's party had their own ideas about how the Easter Rising should be realised in performance, and for many years it would be their authorised version of 1916 rather than the recreations shown at the Abbey Theatre that would predominate in Ireland.

4

Fianna Fáil's Easter Rising

Ireland, Mother Ireland, with your freedom-loving sons,
Did your daughters run and hide at the sound of the guns?
Or did they have some part in the fight
And why does everybody try to keep them out of sight?[1]

And when there's a tricolour over the City Hall, Donna will still be making coffee for Joe Conran, and Josie will still be keeping house for her daddy, because it doesn't matter a damn whether the British are here or not.[2]

Off to Dublin in the Green

James Joyce knew that Dublin's theatres encouraged the people of his home city to misremember revolutionary events. When Leopold Bloom, in *Ulysses*, considers the Phoenix Park murders he thinks, 'Never know who you're talking to. Corny Kelleher he has Harvey Duff in his eye. Like that Peter or Denis or James Carey that blew the gaff on the invincibles'.[3] In mentioning Duff, Bloom is referring to a character from Boucicault's melodrama *The Shaughraun*. Bloom can easily recall Duff but is unable to remember the name of the actual historical traitor. Thus, for Bloom, the fictive realm of the theatre has come to obscure the facts of the Phoenix Park murders.

In 1935 the Fianna Fáil government was inspired by the same thought about the theatre that had struck Joyce. Dramatisations of insurrections could be extremely influential, and so the Irish leadership set about re-staging 1916 for the advantage of the Fianna Fáil party. De Valera was to appear as the central character in a giant theatrical commemoration at the GPO. And although he would declare his loyalty to the dead Easter rebels, the president would erase any of their awkward feminist commitments by ensuring that militant women were largely excluded from the event. In 1935 Fianna Fáil was under fire from the IRA, which was supported by a group of troublesome female republicans, and so it was expedient for the administration to consign the rebellious women of 1916 to the dustbin of history. In addition, Fianna Fáil had clashed with the Abbey over the theatre's portrayal of Irish women, and the government planned an enormous Easter commemoration that would promote the preferred ideal of the passive and sacrificial Irish mother. Fianna Fáil's depiction of womanhood at the 1935 memorial service dovetailed with the constitution that de Valera would publish two years later, and set an influential precedent for subsequent depictions of the Rising. Just as Harvey Duff eclipsed the historical traitor in *Ulysses*, so de Valera's government camouflaged the ambiguities of the 1916 rebellion under the homogenised and anti-feminist carapace of Fianna Fáil.

By 1935 the Easter Rising had already been memorialised at the GPO. The first, crude recreation of the revolt happened at the start of July 1917, when a fire was lit inside the disfigured building to mark the release of de Valera and Gerald Boland. This occurred whilst Ulster celebrated the first anniversary of the Somme, and the sight of flames again in the centre of Dublin sent an ominous message to unionists in the North.[4] For a number of years afterwards the GPO remained a charred skeleton, but from early in 1925 it began to rise magnificently from the rubble. When the rebuilding was completed in 1929, the Cumann na nGaedheal administration held an inauguration ceremony, and invited those who customarily attended the annual 1916 services at Arbour Hill.[5] At this ceremony a small number of uniformed troops marched to the GPO, which was reopened at noon, the time at which the rebels had occupied the building in Easter week. A tricolour was then raised and the Irish premier delivered an oration. However, instead of foregrounding the national struggle, William Cosgrave's speech focused mainly on the building's original architecture, the substances used in its reconstruction, and recent advances in communication technology. Only as Cosgrave neared his conclusion did he mention the events of 1916, before making the first telephone call from the building to the British-appointed Governor General.[6]

On the wet Easter Sunday of 1935, Fianna Fáil marshalled a far grander and more stridently nationalist commemoration at the GPO. A horde of ten thousand marched through the streets of Dublin. Bayonets flashed, rifles crashed, and the Irish Republic was declared anew. In 1916 the Easter Rising had been under-resourced and under-rehearsed, but in 1935 the participants practised their manoeuvres many times and unveiled a statue of Cuchulainn that had been purchased and installed at considerable cost. The monument's £1,000 price-tag dwarfed the subsidy on which the Abbey Theatre survived for the entire year, and a peeved Yeats witheringly observed, 'Some of the best known of the young men who got themselves in 1916 had the Irish legendary hero Cuchullain so much in their minds that the Government has celebrated the event with a bad statue'.[7]

The multitudes attending the Fianna Fáil memorial contrasted starkly with the paltry few who had entered the fray during the original revolt, and only in 1966 was anything on the same scale as the 1935 commemoration recreated at the GPO. In 1966 the ceremonies reeked of extravagance and expense because they marked a significant watershed, the fiftieth anniversary of the Rising. But 1935 was a date without any such numerological importance. Instead, the recreation had a Machiavellian motivation: to establish members of the Fianna Fáil party, and in particular its leader Éamon de Valera, as the true custodians of the 1916 legacy, and to demonstrate a moment of symbolic unity for a deeply-divided state founded by a shattering and fratricidal civil war. When Fianna Fáil stormed the GPO in 1935 the party forced into a straitjacket the disparate nationalisms that had inspired a less-regimented group to invade the building in 1916, and emphasised only the aspects of the revolt that were annexed to the stabilising forces of patriarchy and the Catholic Church.

Éamon de Valera in the midst of all

Fianna Fáil's memorial service bowdlerised the Rising to make Éamon de Valera and his beliefs emerge as the epitome of the national struggle for independence. De Valera had in fact been relatively unimportant to the insurgence in 1916, and his command at Boland's bakery was bold but confused. Unfathomably, in 1916 de Valera vacillated about whether to reinforce Mick Malone at Clanwilliam House, decided to capture a train only to abandon the plan, and ordered the incineration of Westland Row before changing his mind and ordering his arsonists to turn back and extinguish the flames. Tim Pat Coogan explains that de Valera's inexplicable behaviour was caused by a nervous breakdown during the fracas, an understandable state of a mind for a man facing imminent death and engaged in an appallingly unequal fight with extremely limited resources.[8] But in 1935 de Valera was carefully choreographed to appear a purposeful and central commander rather than a discombobulated amateur soldier stationed at one of Dublin's peripheral battlegrounds.

De Valera began the memorial celebrations when a mounted escort in full dress brought him from government buildings to the Portobello barracks, where he sat in front of thousands of troops during an open-air mass. Meanwhile a loudspeaker system had been set up at the GPO by the Department of Posts and Telegraphs. At the same time that the Portobello service reached its conclusion, the official commentator at the GPO, W.F. Cullen, began to speak to the crowds in O'Connell Street (formerly Sackville Street). He addressed them from the second floor of the post office, where he himself had commanded a contingent during the Rising. At just before eleven o'clock he told the audience below, 'Once again a party of armed men are [sic] advancing on this position', and the onlookers, hearing the approach of marching feet and bands playing nationalist tunes, craned their necks to see the soldiers arrive.[9]

A company of troops commanded by an Easter-week veteran hastened to the post office roof to fire a volley. Then Cullen announced, 'The men of 1916 are about to arrive'.[10] Suddenly 2,500 people who claimed to be associated with the Rising, wearing the same regalia that they had worn in 1916 and holding many of the rebellion's guns, strode past the throngs of Dublin. The veterans, led from Parnell Square by an armed guard, lined up outside the GPO beside the banners labelled 'Four Courts', 'Liberty Hall', or 'Boland's Mills', those legendary positions where they were supposedly stationed in combat nineteen years before.

The arrival of the veterans of 1916 culminated with the appearance of Éamon de Valera, who emerged from his car at the GPO escorted by a guard of honour, to be greeted by the assembled soldiers with salutes and a rendition of the national anthem. He joined relatives of the signatories of the proclamation, and then went into the main hall of the building. Some of the veterans went with him and the remainder took up positions in front of the GPO. De Valera gave an oration and then, nineteen years to the minute since the Volunteers crashed in through the doors, he unveiled the Cuchulainn statue to the noise of drum beats and bugle blasts.

A group of trumpeters then played a stirring fanfare from scaffolding on top of the GPO, whilst alongside them sixteen veterans fired a rifle volley. Gunfire rang out from O'Connell Street Bridge at the same time. The national anthem joined the cacophony and planes from the air corps swooped overhead. Finally, de Valera took a position on the saluting platform at the front of the building, and for the following hour a massive column of seven thousand soldiers filed past him.

Those unable to travel to the GPO could listen to a re-creation of the Rising on the Free State radio stations, which broadcast an hour-long 'Pageant in Sound' on Easter Sunday. This radio pageant was produced by Gabriel Fallon, the Abbey actor who had played Captain Brennan in the original version of O'Casey's *The Plough and the Stars*. Fallon had enthused over O'Casey's scornful depiction of Pádraic Pearse in 1926, but in 1935 assumed 'a holy mood' along with the rest of Dublin.

Playing Hamlet

Contemporary observers noted that Fianna Fáil's commemoration incorporated some distinctly theatrical elements. The *Irish Press* and the *Irish Independent* labelled the spectacle, with its Brechtian narrator and applauding crowds, as 'dramatic' and full of 'artistry'.[11] Oliver St John Gogarty also accused de Valera of 'playing Hamlet', in a particularly apt description of how the Irish leader entered the patriot tomb of the GPO to vow his devotion to the dead men.[12] In addition, the 1935 commemoration was the forerunner of the 1966 Dublin pageant, *Aiseirí*, in which 'a "Who's Who" in the Irish theatre world' joined with troops to present a version of the Rising that was again attended by de Valera.[13]

Yet the 1935 memorial service had affinities elsewhere than amongst the ranks of professional thespians. It echoed the anniversary celebrations of Russia and France, where post-revolutionary governments re-staged the symbolic battles of the past for modern political advancement. On 7 November 1920, the third anniversary of the 1917 Russian Revolution, Petrograd witnessed a performance of Nikolai Evreinov's *The Storming of the White Palace*, in which more than 8,000 participants again commandeered the rebellion's most significant building. The Russian government staged Evreinov's work to stave off a dreaded counter-revolution, realising that Bolshevik forces were bogged down by Polish troops in modern Ukraine and Belarus, and that formerly revolutionary Petrograd was gripped by deep discontent.[14] Similarly, France celebrated the first anniversary of the storming of the Bastille on 14 July 1790 by marching hundreds of thousands of people from the building in a 'Festival of the Federation'. The organisers of this spectacle situated churchmen in prominent positions at the celebration, as if to disguise the fact that the Assembly had passed the 'Civil Constitution of the Clergy' two days earlier, in a legislative move that subordinated the Church to the state and stoked counter-revolutionary agitation.[15]

Revolutionary festivals conform to the 'populist' form of theatre that Augusto Boal defines as being paradoxically aimed at the proletariat but antithetical to their real interests.[16] Boal claims that this form is patronised by the dominant classes as an efficient instrument for promulgating their ideology and controlling popular opinion. 'Populist' theatre characteristically avoids 'subject-matter of any real importance to society, any all-embracing social discussions, by restricting the story and the characters', and includes dramas such as television series and cinema films shown in venues other than the playhouse.[17] Fianna Fáil's memorial of 1935 certainly avoided engagement with the important social issues of the day, such as the hardships that Irish people faced as a result of the trade war with Britain, the educational alienation of city children by the imposition of a Gaelic curriculum, and the brutal sectarian animosity in the North of Ireland. Instead, de Valera's re-staging of the Rising attempted to distract people from their everyday concerns and to unite them in common enthusiasm for a simplified and romanticised nationalism.

According to Boal, a second tactic characteristically used by the organisers of 'populist' theatre is that:

> They give prominence to, and thus reinforce, actual or fictional characteristics or ideas which perpetuate the current situation, such as the 'docility' of slaves, women's ability to cook and keep house, the 'goodness' of the peasants, the 'aversion to violence' of factory workers, etc.[18]

Dublin's 1935 commemoration reinforced the idea that the Irishwoman belonged in the home. The organisers of the spectacle erased the proto-feminism of the 1916 Rising and allowed the sacrificial woman to enjoy a notable pre-eminence. In this way, the complicated ambiguities of the original Easter proclamation were flattened and reduced in an easily-promulgated 'populist' form of theatre favoured by Fianna Fáil.

Cherish the ladies

De Valera was one of the commanders who had refused to fight alongside women in 1916, and scoffed at the idea of sending for Cumann na mBan members who were awaiting orders at Merrion Square. Indeed, he boasted about excluding women in a speech to the Dáil in 1937:

> I said we have anxieties of a certain kind here and I do not want to add to them at the moment by getting untrained women, women who were clearly untrained for soldiering – I did not want them as soldiers in any case.[19]

He later told Hanna Sheehy Skeffington that he regretted this decision as it meant some of his men had to be assigned cooking duties.[20]

In 1935 de Valera's address in the main hall of the GPO revealed that this blinkered view of the Rising was now what the Fianna Fáil party chose to remember and celebrate. With characteristic chutzpah, the president uttered the words of the 1916 proclamation that had last been spoken before a crowd at the GPO by Pádraic Pearse himself, but in this impersonation of the rebellion's leader de Valera did not celebrate Irishwomen along with Irishmen. Although he repeated Pearse's guarantees of 'religious and civil liberty, equal rights and equal opportunities', de Valera closed his speech with a new section in Irish that gave men an inviolable position in national memory. He declared: 'If we follow on the way that has been pointed out by Padraic Pearse, we shall have the blessing and the aid of Almighty God, and He will give us victory. I now unveil this memorial to the men who gave their lives for Ireland'. He also spoke of the 'august destiny to which we, with the men of Easter Week, believe that our nation has been called'.[21] Whilst Michael Collins had been at pains to emphasise that he 'admired the men in the ranks and the womenfolk thus engaged', de Valera felt no compulsion to praise the rebels of both sexes.[22]

When de Valera pulled the veil away from the statue of Cuchulainn, the inscription upon the monument consisted of only the third paragraph of the proclamation, which expresses no assurances of civil liberty or equal opportunity, and focuses solely on the national struggle against Britain rather than on the wider social struggle.[23] Despite proclaiming 'unchangeable devotion' to the ideals of 1916, de Valera had emphasised only a certain part of the rebellion. The president was engaging in a mode of celebration that John Waters believes to have become endemic amongst subsequent Irish politicians, taking part in 'elaborate rituals of pretending' to commemorate 1916 in which the participants 'show up, lay a wreath, mouth a few platitudes and go home'. Waters claims that at such ceremonies 'there is no pressure to visit the present moment with the challenges or ideals of the past', and indeed in 1935 the Fianna Fáil administration deliberately chose to ignore the disquieting commitments to wider social change that had been made by the rebel leaders in 1916.[24] Although they would have loathed the comparison, the patrons of the Cuchulainn statue had selectively edited Pearse's words in much the same way that Sean O'Casey had done in *The Plough and the Stars*.[25]

It is difficult to gauge exactly how many of the women who had courageously organised and assisted in Easter week and its aftermath actually turned out for Fianna Fáil's commemoration. The photographs reproduced in the newspapers, if representative, indicate that there were few indeed.[26] The *Irish Press* mentions the presence of nineteen members of Cumann na mBan, although this number must be considered extremely doubtful as there is nothing to indicate that the correspondent had tallied all of the women present.[27] In any case, the positioning of the female rebels may reveal more than simply a list of their names. The *Irish Independent* reported:

> The 1916 men were in the vanguard as the march to the G.P.O. began [. . .]
> Then followed the men who garrisoned the various insurgent posts during

the Rising. Each man wore an armlet indicating his 1916 service. The Magazine Fort garrison and the G.P.O. contingent led this section, the latter under the command of Mr. Diarmuid Lynch. [. . .] The old Dublin Brigade, I.R.A., Irish Citizens' Army, Cumann na mBan, 1916-1923; Connaght Rangers' Mutineers (1920) swung along behind.[28]

Perhaps some of the organisers remembered being humiliated at the Wolfe Tone commemoration at Bodenstown in 1931, when Cumann na mBan took the opportunity to show their more-advanced republicanism by marching in front of the Fianna Fáil contingent.[29] In any case, at Easter 1935 the situation was reversed, and whilst de Valera dominated the proceedings, the two organi- sations whose women had assisted by fighting, fundraising, and rallying public support in 1916 were relegated to the rear of the procession. The women of Cumann na mBan and the Citizen Army played no part in the ceremony other than marching, and the veterans holding the old Mauser guns, the guard of honour, and the soldiers who escorted de Valera into the GPO were all exclu- sively male. The sight of the rebel Irishwoman carrying her large rifle-pistol was nowhere to be seen, prompting the *Irish Times* to recall that perhaps in 1916 the women participated as 'nurses to the wounded' who took up guns once the men who were supposed to carry the weapons had fallen.[30]

At Fianna Fáil's ceremony the rebel women of 1916 were unspeakable as well as unseen. The organisers of the commemoration were aware of the danger that 'many people, including women' might feel 'bitterness' at being excluded, but nevertheless the male voice of the official narration at the GPO repeatedly droned on about the 'party of armed men' and the 'men of 1916'.[31] Besides this, Peadar Kearney's 'The Soldier's Song' had been adopted as Ireland's national anthem, and the tune was relentlessly repeatedly during the commemoration, invoking the soldiers in question as 'Sons of the Gael! Men of the Pale!', whose 'fathers fought before us'.

Mona Ozouf writes that in France:

> The entire history of the Revolutionary festivals might be presented as an illustration of [. . .] blindness: they aimed at spontaneity, yet they were really a combination of precautionary and coercive measures. Their purpose was to bring together the entire community, but they never ceased to exclude some people and to engender pariahs.[32]

In this way the French revolutionary festival prefigured Dublin's commemora- tion of 1935. Whilst de Valera's re-enactment seemed to unite the community in a spontaneous show of support for the Easter Rising, in reality it was carefully contrived to exclude and marginalise those women who had played their part in the rebellion.

Fianna Fáil members were not alone in using masculine rhetoric to describe the Easter Rising. For example, the opposition leader William Cosgrave criticised the commemoration by speaking only of the rebellion's male participants, declaring, 'It was for a noble purpose that men fought in Easter Week'; and even the Limerick journal *Bottom Dog*, a publication dedicated to looking at life from the view of the oppressed ('be it nation, class, or sex'), had celebrated James Connolly as 'a leader of men' and as the writer of 'manly, noble' songs as early as 1918.[33] But Fianna Fáil's eradication of militant women from the memorial service was politically calculated, and was not simply motivated by good old-fashioned misogyny. In 1935 de Valera had failed to co-opt the IRA, who felt that he had reneged on his former position by working within the terms of the 1921 treaty that he had once fought tooth and nail against accepting. Rather than joining their one-time republican colleagues in Fianna Fáil, the IRA had continued to conduct assassinations. The hard-liners had killed Hugh O'Reilly in December 1933 and Richard More-O'Farrell in February 1935, and from March 1935 they began shooting in earnest against de Valera's civic guard. Fianna Fáil responded by placing more than one hundred republicans in Arbour Hill jail by April 1934, and, fearing that the IRA's recent activities would be connected to the struggles of 1916, in early 1935 de Valera's party declared it would no longer sell Easter lilies, hugely popular since the anniversary of 1932 but now symbolising 'an organization of whose methods they disapprove'.[34] This Fianna Fáil campaign was largely successful, with IRA membership plummeting from 7,358 in 1935 to 3,844 in 1936.[35]

But when the Fianna Fáil party turned on the hard-line republicans it angered a number of militant women. The Women's Prisoners' Defence League organised rallies in support of the jailed IRA members, with the aging Maud Gonne as its prominent spokesperson. Cumann na mBan, which had been one of the first organisations to denounce the treaty of 1921, also stood in affiliation with its old ally the IRA, forming its own Political Prisoners Committee. In October 1935, Cumann na mBan helped to organise a mass rally of 12,000 to condemn de Valera's actions against the IRA, at which the belligerent members of the women's organisation carried placards that announced 'Republican Prisoners Tortured by Fianna Fáil'.[36] For its part, the government repeatedly threatened the Cumann na mBan offices, whilst the fascistic Blueshirts organised with separate women's divisions, and another rival organisation, Sinn Féin, elected Margaret Buckley as its president in 1934. In this atmosphere Fianna Fáil members were unable to celebrate the influence that hard-line women had exercised on the Easter Rising, and the *Fianna Fáil Bulletin* instead commemorated 'the gentle Margaret Pearse'.[37] The official Easter commemoration of 1935 debarred 1916's militant women as part of Fianna Fáil's concerted campaign to vilify those who supported the IRA; a campaign that saw 451 prosecutions of IRA members in 1934, and by 1936 saw the IRA outlawed, with its leadership interned and sentenced to hard labour.[38]

The Fianna Fáil party deliberately ostracised members of Cumann na mBan from the 1935 commemoration, as the government tried to claim sole inheritance of the rebellion. De Valera claimed that such absentees were voluntarily exiled, but in reality his government pursued a deliberate policy of making it impossible for those who opposed his administration to attend.[39] Fianna Fáil had arranged to hold a party fundraising-day when emblems would be sold, and it was hardly coincidental that this would occur on the same day as the rebellion commemoration, blurring the boundaries between support for 1916 and support for the modern government. For members of Cumann na mBan the thought of lending their support to such a festival was unendurable. In disgust, some women joined a counter-demonstration that marched past the GPO once the official ceremony had terminated. A few days earlier, Maud Gonne told a meeting that she hoped all true republicans would not go near the GPO, as it was being surrounded 'by all the forces of the State to desecrate the memory of those who died in Easter Week'.[40]

The members of the Fianna Fáil government were only too happy for such radical groups to stay away from the Dublin celebrations, and attempted to guarantee that such political enemies would be alienated from the main ceremony. In mid-March de Valera's Minister for Defence assembled a committee of veterans to coordinate turnout at the commemoration. When angry opposition TDs discovered that the Fianna Fáil administration was making the day a celebration of the ruling party alone, whose policies and leader many of the veterans found odious, a large number of committee members resigned. Supporters of Cumann na Ban, the IRA, and the opposition party Fine Gael had now been exiled from the organisation of the event. Purged of its rogue elements, the committee decided to press home its advantage, and allowed newspaper advertisements about the ceremony to appear only in the *Irish Press*, the Fianna Fáil organ. Richard Mulcahy, a prominent 1916 veteran and Fine Gael member, clashed furiously in the Dáil with Fianna Fáil members, yelling: 'no advertisements were issued to the *Irish Independent*, *Cork Examiner* or *Irish Times* [. . .] Is it still held that the Government is not making it a Party demonstration?'[41] The Minister for Agriculture, answering on behalf of the Defence Minister, gave the weak assurance that 'It is not a political thing'.[42] But few on either side could have believed him.

The sacrificial mummy returns

Members of government had learned from the theatre that unconventional women had the power to tarnish Fianna Fáil's nationalist credentials. When the Abbey toured America in 1932 with the phrase 'By Special Arrangement with the Irish Free State Government' printed on their programmes, de Valera received many disparaging letters, including two from American congressmen, criticising his apparent support for the plays of Synge and O'Casey. The government was stung, and slapped the Abbey's wrists by reducing the subsidy for the following two years. When the theatre announced the repertoire for its next tour of 1934–5, they were told, 'the President hopes that, if the Society decides on the production of Mr O'Casey's plays during the coming tour, it will be made clear that the Government is in no sense responsible for the selection of plays'.[43] At the ceremony in 1935, in answer to those who criticised the government's ostensible endorsement of *The Plough and the Stars* and *The Playboy of the Western World*, Fianna Fáil erased women from the narrative of 1916 and made sure that Dan Breen, the famed guerrilla fighter who had accompanied Margaret Pearse in opposing O'Casey's play in 1926, was invited to stand shoulder to shoulder with de Valera at the GPO.

The Abbey continued to needle de Valera. Between 1926 and 1935 the company revived *The Plough and the Stars* sixteen times in Ireland, and the play had made more than £4,000 for the theatre by 1931 alone.[44] Inspired by the success of O'Casey's work, in the early 1930s another Abbey playwright who had seen the Rising, Paul Vincent Carroll, wrote a play called *The Conspirators*, which again criticised the motherhood associated with Margaret Pearse. In Carroll's play a young rebel dies in the Easter Rising and takes his place alongside a pantheon of Irish heroes, yet his mother refuses to celebrate his demise. She has been driven frantic by worry during the combat and is distraught at the news of the bloodshed. She would have preferred her offspring to stay safe and alive, and scorns the honour of being a sacrificial mother, asking, 'Would I not give me heart's blood to Oweneen to live with?'[45] In her view, the Shan Van Vocht is nothing but an 'oul' bitch' or an 'oul' whore', and, like Nora Clitheroe, the mother in Carroll's play laments the rebel's devotion to an abstraction rather than a real girl.[46]

The Irish government distanced itself from such controversial ideas by fêting a carefully selected group of mother-figures at the GPO in 1935. Women were generally under-represented at the Easter commemoration, but at the forefront of the event were a handful of those who symbolised sacrifice. They included Pádraic Pearse's sister and Tom Clarke's widow, both of whom flanked de Valera as he masqueraded as the rebel leader inside the GPO. The ultimate symbol of 1916's sacrificial motherhood, Pádraic Pearse's mother Margaret, had died at Easter 1932, but her legacy was alive and well in her daughters. As Elena Cabezali and others have argued, the general concept that motherhood justifies a woman's existence 'may take direct form, or be transferred to images of wife or sister', and in Ireland the mantle of the passive and suffering mother had been passed on to the sisters Margaret Mary Pearse and Mary Brigid Pearse, who remained extremely reluctant to take a combative position against any of the government's decisions, unlike the more stubborn members of Cumann na mBan.[47]

Kathleen Clarke was less easily controlled by de Valera. She felt that he and his colleagues might have long remained in prison if not 'for the work done by the women after the Rising'.[48] But at the 1935 commemoration she was positioned with care by the Fianna Fáil organisers who followed in the steps of the old Fenian movement. When the Fenians organised mass protests under the guise of funerals and mock-funerals, such as the obsequies for the Manchester Martyrs in 1867, the women related to the dead patriot usually led a train of mourners behind the hearse.[49] Although visible to all in the procession, the Fenian women were powerless embodiments of the sacrificial mother, who could do nothing but mourn and inspire other men to go out to die. By positioning Margaret Mary Pearse and Kathleen Clarke at the front of a mass commemoration, in the same place once occupied by bereaved Fenian widows, de Valera's party swindled women out of their importance to the rebellion and instead made them dependent on what was done by sons, husbands, or brothers.

When de Valera was told by the Minister for Defence that the number of relatives attending the ceremony might have to be limited because of restricted space at the GPO, the Fianna Fáil leader disagreed.[50] De Valera realised that the continuing mobilisation of the IRA made it imperative for the mothers, wives, and sisters of the rebels to be seen in attendance. His government was using these relatives to demonstrate that combat under the auspices of their party alone accorded with the old sacrificial model. As Anne Dolan has asserted, after 1923 'commemoration was war by other means', and if Fianna Fáil could establish that the true bearers of 1916's motherhood were now endorsing the leadership of de Valera, the party could legitimately suppress the aberration of the modern IRA, whose warmongering lacked the blessing of Margaret Pearse.[51]

The Irish leader's own family were used to assert that Fianna Fáil enjoyed the benediction of the Shan Van Vocht. De Valera's son, Vivion, paraded at the Portobello Barracks, and the following day the *Irish Independent* printed a large picture of the premier's progeny in military uniform.[52] Vivion had previously come to public prominence when, on the Sunday before polling day in 1923, he spoke to a huge meeting in Dublin's College Green. His father was supposed to give an address but had been arrested, so Vivion, although only thirteen years old and suffering from asthma, took his place. The boy read a script that said 'I know not what they [his pro-treaty captors] will do with him . . . but they cannot kill the spirit of freedom in Ireland'.[53] Vivion also took up his revolver and accompanied his father into government in March 1932. On each of these occasions the message was clear: if Éamon de Valera was killed then his son and the sons of others, like a many-headed Hydra, would come to take his place and perpetuate his work.

Also in attendance at the 1935 commemoration was Captain Collins Powell, a nephew of Michael Collins. As the army snaked through Dublin, the captain mounted the saluting platform and stood behind Éamon de Valera, indicating that if Michael Collins were still alive he too would be supporting Fianna Fáil. The complication of the President's fatal antagonism with Collins during the Civil War was easily and deliberately elided in enthusiasm for 1916. Moreover, the prominence of Collins Powell and Vivion de Valera endorsed the idea that it was the place of male progeny to fight for Fianna Fáil rather than for any other group. A number of other self-immolating firstborn sons were already associated with the Easter rebellion, including Michael Gillane, Pádraic Pearse, 'The Singer' MacDara, and Jesus Christ Himself. The sons of the de Valera and Collins families carried weaponry at the Easter commemoration to indicate that they too were symbolically groomed to pay a blood price, but that they were to pay it only in the cause of the Fianna Fáil government.[54] By claiming to be the champion of the willingly killed sons of 1916, Fianna Fáil affirmed that nationalist sacrifice directed by any other organisation was deeply misguided.

Bunreacht na hÉireann

The Fianna Fáil party banished militant women and cherished passive sacrificial mothers at the 1935 commemoration because it helped to combat the IRA's intransigence. But the portrayal of women at the Dublin ceremony was also connected to a wider set of social policies that the party promoted during the 1930s. Ever since the Censorship of Films Act of 1923 the Free State government had been deliberately expressing fidelity to the Pope, but in the 1930s Fianna Fáil politicians pursued the link between Dublin and Rome with renewed vigour as they tried to shake off any doubt about the party's piety that may have lingered from the republican excommunications of the Civil War. In 1931 de Valera supported the dismissal of a Mayo librarian on the grounds that she was a Protestant, and went on to suggest that only Catholics should be employed as dispensary doctors in mainly Catholic areas. Soon after entering the Dáil, Fianna Fáil urged the government to take parliamentary holidays on Catholic feast days, and in October 1932 de Valera instructed his Minister for Justice to see whether it would be possible to alter the dates of public holidays to coincide with such holy days.[55] In 1933 de Valera visited the Pope, as part of Fianna Fáil's steadfast attempt to associate itself with the Church, even though the evolution of Ireland as a theocracy specifically contradicted the words of the 1916 proclamation.

Three years before the 1935 celebrations papal prelates had visited Dublin to attend another grand public commemoration, the Eucharistic Congress. As Dermot Keogh writes, this street event celebrated 'the "resurrection": the victory of the two halves of the one struggle – Catholic emancipation and national independence'.[56] Fianna Fáil evoked this twofold resurrection with similar gusto in 1935, and members of the clergy were again invited to take a prominent role at the Easter celebration. By contrast with the excluded rebel women, eight priests stood on the platform at the forefront of the GPO ceremony. Fianna Fáil's tribute to the Rising began with two large open-air masses where the old comrades of 1916 acted as altar servers, and the ensuing ceremony in O'Connell Street also duplicated elements of Catholic ritual. The veterans moved solemnly, sang tunes emphasising communal solidarity and purpose, and faced the stern, presiding figure of de Valera who embodied the dead heroes and repeated their words. When he unveiled the Cuchulainn statue it obviously relied on the convention of the *pietà* as a representation of sacrificial suffering and death, and, just like a Church feast day, the date of the entire Rising commemoration depended on the ecclesiastical calendar rather than the actual date on which the original battle had occurred.[57]

From the summer of 1936 de Valera began drafting his *Bunreacht na hÉireann*, a new constitution of Ireland that gave a 'special position' to the values of Catholicism. But Irish bishops were hardly renowned for their emancipated views of women, and a number of republican women felt betrayed by a document that included the following articles:

Article 41.2/1: In particular, the State recognises that by her life within the home, woman gives to the State a support without which the common good cannot be achieved.

2/2: The State shall, therefore, endeavour to ensure that mothers shall not be obliged by economic necessity to engage in labour to the neglect of their duties in the home.[58]

In fairness to de Valera, these paragraphs may have been designed to protect wives from the days of the Civil War when, with their men absent, they had commonly been compelled to work; and as Justice Brian Walsh explained in 1988, these words have never been invoked in any litigation.[59] Yet the constitution legislated that, first and foremost, women's lives be circumscribed by the demands of their home and their children. Hanna Sheehy Skeffington was now one of those who complained that 'the proposed Constitution placed women in a much lower position than that accorded to them in the 1916 Proclamation'.[60] She realised that, rather than following the plan outlined by the leaders of the Easter revolt, the modern political leaders of Ireland were constructing an identity for Irish women in primarily domestic terms.

The marginalising of women at the 1935 Easter commemoration corroborated the values of *Bunreacht na hÉireann*. In the re-staging of the Easter Rising, Fianna Fáil demonstrated that women were passive, quiet, and quiescent; and achieved social significance only by rearing pugnacious, patriotic sons. During the following years, de Valera presided over a country that continued to exclude women from positions of power and responsibility. For example, although thirteen women had been elected to the Dáil between 1921 and 1935, only nine more joined the assembly from the time of the 1935 Easter commemoration until 1970.[61]

The rocky road from Dublin

After 1935 the parts of the rebellion that contradicted the official narrative, such as the role of the female participants, were ignored in both popular and academic works. Frank and Sean O'Meara's ballad 'Grace', for instance, pictures Joseph Plunkett speaking in condescending terms to his wife, Grace Gifford, before his execution: 'I know it's hard for you, my love, to ever understand,/The love I bear for these brave men, my love for this dear land'.[62] This song's lyrics imply that women completely failed to comprehend the significance of 1916 and that the insurgence had been an exclusively male affair, even though Plunkett supported women's rights and Gifford herself was an active participant in the struggle for independence.[63] Similarly, in 1949, Desmond Ryan's authoritative account of the rebellion, entitled, with no apparent sense of irony, *The Complete Story of Easter Week*, managed to summarise the involvement of women in just one lonesome paragraph.[64] For many years the most popular image of the rebellion was that of its sixteen executed male leaders, which concealed the fact that Countess Markievicz was amongst those sentenced to death in 1916. The British had originally decided to shoot her, but commuted this sentence after they grew squeamish about killing a woman. Perhaps realising that her role would soon be forgotten, Markievicz despaired: 'I wish you had the decency to shoot me. Why didn't they let me die with my friends?'[65]

Later recreations of the Easter Rising took their cue from the 1935 commemoration, and less than half a year after this ceremony the GPO was commandeered again in front of a total of about 104,000 spectators.[66] At the second GPO seizure of 1935, which occurred not at the original building but at a massive replica in the Ballsbridge arena, the modern Irish military forces again joined veterans of the Rising. Many of de Valera's ministers made a special effort to be seen in attendance, and were reassured that they were indeed the most conservative revolutionaries in history.

This performance reinforced the notion of women as domesticated and dependent on the help of men. Once again, few militant women appeared. Instead, nearly three-hundred men participated in the army infantry drill, another 'vast crowd of men' performed in a gymnastic display, and a pageant of Irish history showed the exploits of a series of exclusively male heroes, from Cuchulainn to the Fenians.[67] The correspondent for the *Irish Independent* pointed out that when the replica GPO was stormed and set alight, in a spectacular re-creation of the Easter Rising, lamentably few representatives of Cumann na mBan could be seen: 'only eleven members of the original Cumann na mBan were there, but two of them were friends of mine, though I could not distinguish them in the searchlight'.[68] The officially sanctioned view of 1916 now placed the women of the rebellion in exactly the same position that O'Casey had put Pádraic Pearse – hidden from sight in the shadows.

The final part of the Ballsbridge show was the only moment at which a woman took a central role. In 'The Rally of the Nation', Éire, personified as a woman, was defended by the male heroes of Irish nationalism from many different eras. Éire sat, perturbed but inert, as Ireland's men displayed their willingness to fight on her behalf. The Bishop of Down and Connor declared that it was 'the most magnificent thing I have ever seen'.[69]

When Ireland came to celebrate the fiftieth anniversary of the rebellion in 1966, the memorial service at the GPO replicated virtually all of the ceremonial features of the first 1935 commemoration. Once more a bevy of clergymen dominated the proceedings, the relatives of the dead were displayed as meritorious examples to Ireland, and Éamon de Valera – now little more than an aged figurehead – took the salute from 5,000 members of the military. In his address to the nation the blind president continued to speak about the rebellion with characteristically patriarchal rhetoric, saying, 'We can have our people united as a family – a nation of brothers – each working in industrial harmony, not for himself only, but for the good of all. We could then march forward confidently to that exaltation of our nation amongst the nations to which the men of 1916 pledged themselves.'[70]

Cuchulainn's buttocks

The 1935 commemoration presented an adulterated version of the historical events of 1916. The participants moved in a solemn, orderly, and dignified fashion and there was none of the havoc, destruction, or death of 1916. When the soldiers fired a volley from their rifles they did not intend to kill anyone. Everyone who marched towards the GPO knew exactly where he or she ought to be, and they were drilled and timed impeccably. There was no countermanding order. The marching of the veterans represented the inexorable and dignified march towards national liberation, and obscured the disconcerting fact that Ireland's emancipation had been achieved through a series of anarchic lurches that included a civil war during which some of those who marched in step in 1935 had tried their best to kill one another. The contradictory features of the Easter proclamation had been ironed away by a Fianna Fáil government intent on enforcing a traditional gender model, on allying itself to the Catholic Church, and on crushing the hostile Cumann na mBan.

Samuel Beckett, who as a horrified ten-year-old had watched the conflagration of Easter week from a hill in Foxrock, recognised how Fianna Fáil had helped to promulgate a greatly simplified version of the Rising. Three years after de Valera's 1935 commemoration at the GPO, Beckett published his novel *Murphy*, and at one point in the book the character of Neary enters the GPO to launch a comic onslaught upon the new statue of Cuchulainn:

> Suddenly he flung aside his hat, sprang forward, seized the dying hero by the thighs and began to dash his head against his buttocks, such as they are. The Civic Guard on duty in the building, roused from a tender reverie by the sound of blows, took in the situation at his leisure, disentangled his baton and advanced with measured tread.[71]

Neary's attack on the new monument's metallic fundament is a parody of the assault with which Cuchulainn kills Ferdia in the Ulster cycle by piercing him through the anus with a spear.[72] Beckett uses this parody to complicate the simplistic view of the Rising, questioning the sexual roles associated with the GPO by making Neary, apparently involuntarily, give Cuchulainn a mock sodomising. In the Ireland of the 1930s, which had already seen the banning of Beckett's first book, government officials aggressively promoted a conservative version of the rebellion, and hence Neary faces being clobbered by a guard after lampooning the sanctified buttocks of 1916. Later on, when Neary tells Wylie about the incident, Wylie indicates that any connection between the 1916 uprising and sexuality will obviously be repressed by the governing authorities, asserting, 'there is no rump [. . .] How could there be? What chance would a rump have in the GPO?'[73]

Fianna Fáil's views about sex and gender were in part a reaction against the previous colonial administration. The 1935 mass spectacle was designed to mark the difference between modern Ireland and the old colonial civic culture, where popular celebrations had included the rituals of the British army, Union-Jack flags, and the top-hatted presence of the Irish peerage. In the 1930s those in the South were reminded of the old British ceremonies when unionists in the North commemorated the unveiling of the Carson statue outside Stormont in 1933, and again when Ulster celebrated the silver jubilee of George V in 1935. In cleaving Irish public commemorations away from those of the coloniser, the Warriors of Destiny sought to avoid the debilitating imperial stereotype of the feminine Celt at all costs, to insist on hyper-masculine men and hyper-feminine women, and thus to hide the assertive female rebels of 1916. As Declan Kiberd has shown, de Valera's vision for Ireland was in many ways a very modern one: the Irish leader's commitments to global decolonisation and to frugal comfort have found their reflection in many subsequent cultural nationalist and environmental movements around the globe.[74] Yet the conception of women promoted by Fianna Fáil was entirely unreformed. Gayatri Spivak contends that for many former colonial subjects the triumph of anti-colonial nationalism was an imperfect liberation, and this was certainly true for Irish women during de Valera's premiership. As Spivak observes, if the male subaltern is always silenced, 'the subaltern as female is even more deeply in shadow'.[75]

Yet in their amnesia, Fianna Fáil's politicians promulgated an impoverished version of the Rising. Without remembering the socially radical parts of the rebellion, 1916 stagnated around its atavism, around Pearse's focus on dead generations and the summoning of mythological heroes to his side. Perhaps, as David Fitzpatrick has suggested, we should therefore 'celebrate the memory of Eamon de Valera not for his part in the making of the Easter Rising, but for his part in its undoing'.[76]

5

Saint Joan and Hollywood

I was a bit surprised to hear a chief inspector refer to '–ing old Roger Casement'. At home Casement was regarded as a Republican saint. Rory, my
eldest brother, was named after him.[1]

Lowest basemeant in hystry![2]

The ghost of Roger Casement

At the same time that members of Éamon de Valera's party were eradicating
early feminist sentiments from the legacy of 1916, the government was also
fighting to prevent Easter week from becoming trivialised by any association
with homosexuality. Whilst Fianna Fáil prepared for the elaborate 1935
commemoration in the centre of Dublin, hundreds of miles away in California
a movie producer had decided to film a story about the dead rebel Roger Casement, one of the most controversial figures connected with the Easter rebellion.
When de Valera learned of Hollywood's intentions he vowed to crush the
project, knowing that publicising this particular revolutionary's life could pose
a severe challenge to Fianna Fáil's control of the 1916 legacy.

Roger Casement was a Dubliner, born in Kingstown (now Dun Laoghaire) to
an Ulster Protestant family. As a young man he crossed the Irish Sea to work for
the British government, and was appointed imperial consul in Portuguese East
Africa, Angola, the Congo Free State, and Brazil. Casement revealed the atro-
cious cruelty inflicted by white officials on the natives of the Congo, and his
efforts led to a major reorganisation of Belgian rule there. He also exposed
massive human rights abuses in the Peruvian Putumayo River region, where
Amazon Indians were being mercilessly exploited and exterminated. Recognis-
ing this tireless humanitarian work, the British Empire gratefully awarded
Casement a knighthood.

Yet Roger Casement had always sympathised with Irish nationalism, and he
returned to Ireland in 1912 to help found the Irish National Volunteers. After
World War I broke out, he hoped that Germany might assist the Irish independence movement as a blow against his former paymasters. He trekked to
Germany in 1914 in an attempt to recruit Irish prisoners of war, obtain
weaponry, and borrow German army officers in support of an Easter Rising in
Ireland. Germany's suspicious authorities were unconvinced by this dubious

appeal, and sent Casement back to Ireland with nothing but a few thousand guns. Realising that any uprising would now be doomed to failure, he hurried home to dissuade Pearse from leading the rebels into suicide.

Casement returned to Ireland on 12 April aboard a German submarine, and emerged near Tralee, County Kerry, but was arrested within a matter of hours and taken to London. A few days later Easter week brought its inevitable carnage, and in the aftermath a British court convicted Casement of treason and sentenced him to death.

At the time of his trial and hanging, diaries containing titillating descriptions of homosexual practices, written by Casement, were circulated privately among British officials and became that summer's main topic of gossip, quickly spreading from Whitehall to Fleet Street. For years people have debated whether these 'black diaries' were genuine or whether they were British forgeries, circulated in order to discredit Casement and to dampen calls for clemency, particularly those appeals that might come from the influential voice of American public opinion. The British Home Secretary finally made the diaries available in July 1959, and since then it has been generally agreed that the passages in question are in Casement's handwriting, although the matter is still contested.

A grave business

Fianna Fáil consistently determined that discussion about Casement's diaries should cease. In the 1960s Taoiseach Seán Lemass repeatedly insisted upon this, and attempted quite literally to lay Casement to rest. Casement's remains were shifted from a lowly quicklime grave in England to lie with his fellow patriots in the Irish Republic in 1965. Yet this re-interment served only to illustrate how Ireland was conspiring with Britain to remove Casement from the narrative of 1916.

The reburial ceremony was relatively lavish, but was prevented from coinciding with either the centenary of Casement's birth in 1964, or the extravagant celebrations marking the fiftieth anniversary of 1916.[3] Westminster was partly responsible for this timing. During the 1964 British general election Harold Wilson's Labour party wooed the British–Irish vote by promising to return Casement's remains, but on assuming power Wilson was unable to fulfil this undertaking because Winston Churchill lay dying. Wilson knew British patriotic sensibilities would baulk at seeing Casement resurrected at this time, and especially feared antagonising staunch unionists. Consequently the British government delayed the repatriation until February 1965, when the remains were excavated within a matter of hours, and hurriedly exported to Ireland.[4]

The Irish government also had a vested interest in burying Casement quickly in that low-key year and not in 1966. Although de Valera had pushed for the return of the remains, Casement's knighthood, Protestant origins, career in the British foreign service, and association with Ulster made him an awkward figure for the Fianna Fáil party to incorporate into the story of the

Easter Rising. Furthermore, George Mosse argues that nationalisms often rely on the creation of homoerotic bonds among men, ties that have to be carefully policed, contained, and deflected onto more acceptable heterosexual objects.[5] Fianna Fáil had promoted the idea that the 1916 rebellion united men in service of the nation, which was embodied as a woman. To eulogise a reputed homosexual on the uprising's fiftieth anniversary might destroy the Irish government's carefully constructed version of the Easter Rising. The idiosyncratic path trodden by Casement hardly dovetailed with the synchronised marching of Dublin's spring commemorations. This rebel was a rare and lonely character, whose life was spent forging relationships with large groups of oppressed people, whether in the third world or in Ireland. As Yeats recognised, such aristocratic men would necessarily trouble a national state built on mass politics, because high-born leaders 'are almost always partisans, propagandists and gregarious; yet because of the *Mask* of simplification, which holds up before them the solitary life of hunters and of fishers and "the groves pale passion loves", they hate parties, crowds, propaganda'.[6]

The British authorities disliked the figure of a British civil servant whom they had honoured for his humanitarian work before hanging him as a traitor, and parts of Ireland were fearful of associating the Easter Rising with Protestantism or pederasty. But 1965 was not the first time that the two countries had unconsciously collaborated to manipulate the posthumous revival of Casement. In the 1930s British and Irish officials scuppered an American depiction of the rebel, and in this they were aided by the unlikely figure of G.B. Shaw.

Casement in America

In 1934 Julius Klein, the special assistant to the head of Universal Studios, decided to produce a film version of Roger Casement's extraordinary story. Klein was a Jewish American whose own multifarious career echoed features of Casement's life. Klein had worked as a spy during World War I in Berlin, and after the armistice he felt so nostalgic about the country that he initiated the first German-language radio broadcasts in the United States. He also maintained an interest in military affairs, and launched the South Pacific edition of the *Stars and Stripes* army newspaper. During the inter-war years Klein continued to concern himself with politics and criminality, working as a crime reporter for Chicago's *State Herald* newspaper in the 1920s and running for Congress in 1932. Later, during World War II, Klein became a hero by saving many lives during an explosion in the South Pacific, and formulated an important Allied plan called 'Combat Public Relations' which covered such topics as psychological warfare and propaganda.[7]

Between 1934 and 1939 Klein worked in Hollywood, and as soon as he arrived he felt compelled to pursue a Casement project. He had developed a lasting interest in the Irish patriot since being in Germany, and the story now seemed an ideal one for Universal to tackle. Klein saw that Casement's unique adventure contained many of the elements that would make a successful

blockbuster: spying and secrecy, heroism in the face of seemingly insur-
mountable odds, and a wartime setting replete with British and German armies.

In any case, Casement's life already obeyed a kind of preordained dramatic
schema. Irish rebellions against the British had been the staple storyline of
popular melodramas for a number of years at the Queen's Theatre in Dublin,
and accusations of sexual deviancy, usually practised by malevolent British
soldiers upon virtuous Irish maidens, were a stock feature of such plays. The
villain in Boucicault's *Robert Emmet*, for example, threatens Anne Devlin, 'I'll get
you in my clutches some day, and then I'll make it hot for you, my beauty!'[8] In
Whitbread's *The Ulster Hero* another rapscallion threatens Mary Tombe with
scandal if she does not agree to 'become my wife'.[9] Stephen Watt suggests that
such storylines enjoyed popularity in the wake of Tim Healy's 1883 allegations
of sexual deviancy in the detective division of the Royal Irish Constabulary.[10]
Furthermore, one of the best dramatists to come from Ireland, Oscar Wilde,
had already been destroyed by British accusations of homosexuality, and in a
bizarre twist of fate Casement's prosecutor served as assistant in the Ulster
Volunteers to Edward Carson, the redoubtable orator who had defended the
Marquess of Queensbury during Wilde's libel suit. Tellingly, some commentators wrote of Casement's court case as if it was the continuation of a theatrical
event. New York's *Evening Post* reported that Casement's trial and his defence
speech were Shakespearean, and Joseph Holloway said, 'Sir Roger Casement's
trial for High Treason opened in London today. I remember seeing him once
with [Pádraic] Colum in the vestibule of the Abbey'.[11]

However, Klein had good reason to be wary about his filmic endeavour.
Although Casement had never been directly represented in the cinema before,
an earlier silent film had alluded to the patriot, causing considerable discomfort
to the producers. In December 1916 the Vitagraph company released *Whom the
Gods Destroy*, in which a character called Sir Denis Esmond is arrested for
conspiring against England at the time of an Irish revolt.[12] Although the character's name and circumstances are evidently based on Casement, Esmond is a
fictional heterosexual, caught in a Girardian love triangle between Mary O'Neill
and his good friend, a British naval officer. Esmond sides with the nationalists
but repents of his treason, and is saved from execution by the King's pardon
and his British friend's intervention. However, the hue and cry that greeted the
film's release might have offered Klein a disturbing premonition. *Whom the Gods
Destroy* was considered too pro-Irish to show to audiences in Britain and was
banned outright by the Board of Film Censors, whilst Irish–American audiences
abhorred the sight of a penitent nationalist styled on Casement, and Vitagraph
was forced to issue a statement declaring that the British government had not
subsidised the film's production. The Boston Board of Censors and New York
police commissioner received bitter complaints about the film from
Irish–American groups, and there was consternation at the Luna Theatre in
Brooklyn when members of the audience started shouting at the screen and
exploding stink bombs. If Klein had known of this egregious affair then he
might have realised that he too was walking on eggshells.

Casement in the 1930s

Klein had to proceed warily because by the 1930s Casement's legacy was in flux. In the rebellion's immediate afterglow Casement had been celebrated in popular doggerel that extolled him as a saint. For example, the anonymous poem 'Waiting for the Dawn: Casement's Vigil', dated August 1916, imagines him awaiting his execution and praying:

> Oh! man of Calvary,
> With all my heart I turn to thee
> Knowing, dear Lord, in sympathy,
> You'll watch with me.[13]

The poem compares Casement's predicament with the New Testament torment in Gethsemane, and exemplifies how the poetry produced after the Rising habitually followed Pádraic Pearse's last verses by equating the rebels with Christ. Another poem, Eva Gore-Booth's 'Roger Casement', also imagines Casement 'bringing hope to the hopeless' and 'bringing light to the blind', and the anonymous author of 'A Longing: Eire to R.C.', a poem that was supposedly handed to Casement as he received his death sentence, wrote:

> To kiss your brow:
> Hard pressed (to alien eyes) with crown of thorn,
> Whose thoughts and noble courage brought
> My resurrection morn.[14]

Casement's name was also taken up by balladeers, who vowed to tell the insurrectionist's story and never allow his memory to be suppressed. The song 'Rory of the Gael', which was sung in 1916, contains the lines:

> We'll shrine your name within our hearts,
> We'll praise it in our songs,
> With all the gallant men who strove
> To right our country's wrongs.[15]

Another song heard in Dublin shortly after the execution declared:

> They tried to foul your memory
> As they burned your corpse with lime
> But God is not an Englishman
> And truth will tell in time.[16]

But in the years after 1916 the accusations of Casement's homosexuality permeated the Irish consciousness, and his tarnished image sat uncomfortably with Catholic iconography.[17] Irish songsters ceased promising to commemorate the rebel's life in perpetuity, whilst in England liberal interest quickly vanished as the country set about attempting to build a land fit for heroes after the war.

However, in the 1930s, as the question of Ireland's allegiance became a hot topic once again in the face of the worsening political situation in Europe, a number of biographies of Casement were published, and the response to these books revealed that Casement's legacy had grown more complicated since the days in which he was compared to Christ. When Roger Parmiter published his biography about Casement in 1936, British contributors to the *Times Literary Supplement* protested that the story 'had been sufficiently told already by others' and that 'no more Lives of Casement should be written'.[18] The following year, W.J. Maloney's book, *The Forged Casement Diaries*, proved even more troublesome when serialised in the *Irish Press*. Maloney accused the British government of slandering Casement for propaganda purposes, and G.B. Shaw, who had already read and been unimpressed by the manuscript of Maloney's book in 1934, declared it a 'superfluous addition to the bad blood still existing between England and Ireland'.[19] Shaw wrote a response in the *Irish Press*, insisting that the diaries were simply Casement's records from South America that the British had misinterpreted in good faith. The following day the novelist Francis Stuart angrily countered Shaw's article, accusing Shaw of being nothing but a 'busybody'.[20] Meanwhile, W.B. Yeats had read Maloney's serialisation and was so incensed by Britain's perfidy that he wrote a short poem about Casement for performance on the Abbey stage and on the radio. But one of the people lambasted in Yeats's piece, the English poet Alfred Noyes, immediately apologised for having publicised the anti-Casement argument in 1916, and published a lengthy retraction in the *Irish Press* honouring Casement.[21] Accordingly, Yeats decided to revise the poem, and it reappeared in the *Irish Press* with the offending verse modified.[22] Soon dissatisfied with this alteration, he reshaped the poem again for its publication in *New Poems* the following year.[23]

The Maloney serialisation showed how complicated and self-referential any argument about Roger Casement's representation had become by the 1930s. For the Irish government, the safest course of action was stoically to turn a deaf ear to the controversial aspects of this irksome figure. A few days after the *Irish Press* published Shaw's letter, de Valera was asked if he would take up the matter of the diaries with the British government. 'No Sir,' he replied, 'Roger Casement's reputation is safe in the affections of the Irish people.'[24]

The Irish for no

Shortly before the altercation over the serialisation of Maloney's book, Julius Klein began to work on his film scenario about Casement. The *Irish Press* announced the commencement of Klein's project in July 1934, and Casement's cousin, Gertrude Parry, read the newspaper with alarm. Although she was Casement's sole heir with control over the reproduction of his copyright documents, she would exert no influence over a creative interpretation of Casement's life. Parry wrote, 'This fills me with dismay, as one has no idea what sort of horror may issue from Hollywood. I don't trust American film magnates'.[25] She also declared that a sensational Hollywood film would be 'simply revolting' because:

> Roger is a national Hero, + his life Belonged to Ireland + he sealed his faith
> with his death, + he should be treated so as to be an example for the youth
> of his Country.

> One does not want a garbled account of his life + actions to go forth to the
> world – + Even from the commercial side of the venture, the producers
> would make a much better picture if it were true + showed Roger in the
> light of an Irish patriot.[26]

Parry informed de Valera of her fears. She hoped that his government might
be able to use its weight in pro-Irish America to compel Klein to produce a
panegyric to Casement. The president felt that his influence over Hollywood
was tenuous, but nevertheless contacted the Irish Free State's consular offices in
Chicago and San Francisco in order to pressurise Universal. He was particularly
anxious that, if the Americans did insist upon making a Casement film, any
indication of sexuality should be suppressed. The Irish consular officials were
instructed 'to ensure [the] film will be dignified and in all respects worthy of its
subject', and that:

> Every effort should be made to prevent introduction [of] any unfitting inci-
> dents such as [a] love story which would be much resented in U.S. of
> America. Your representations [to the] corporation should be of course
> completely unofficial and as unobtrusive as possible.[27]

Julius Klein had in fact already visited the Chicago consulate and had been
warned to continue with caution. After de Valera sent them a cable, the consular
officials contacted a sympathetic production manager at Universal Studios who
vowed to conform to their wishes. The demurring of the Irish government
worried Julius Klein. He did not want to alienate his potential Irish–American
audience and bring the stink-bombers back into the cinema. In September
1934 he contacted de Valera directly to say:

> While the screen scenario naturally must be written with fiction to be an
> attraction for the movie audience, I will do all I can to do justice, not only
> to a great character, but also to history. As soon as the final script is finished,
> I will present same to the various governments for their consideration.[28]

De Valera, however, was unimpressed. When he reconsidered the significance of the Casement project his initial objections hardened. Fianna Fáil had
been in power for less than three years and had set about steering Irish nationalism on a conservative course that took no account of the radicalism of those
early feminists or alleged homosexuals who had invigorated the movement in
its revolutionary days. Although de Valera did mention Casement in his
speeches, the president avoided any discussion of the diaries and ensured that
Casement signalled approval for the Fianna Fáil government. That government
struggled to escape the colonial paradigm of the feminised Celt, by tacitly
asserting, as David Norris quips, 'that to be Irish is to be white, heterosexual
and Roman Catholic'.[29] To remind people of the opinions held by the dead

generation of 1916 – of Casement, Connolly, Francis Sheehy Skeffington, or Countess Markievicz – could provoke deeply subversive questions about de Valera's 'ownership' of the 1916 legacy and his creation of a state that was a celebration of all that was rural, Catholic, and petit bourgeois.

Permitting Klein to make his film would allow him to gain control of a popular portrayal of the 1916 rebellion, and thus to exercise considerable power over the Irish self-image. As Graeme Turner writes, 'If we understand our world (or our nation) through its representations, foreign control of the major media of representation does threaten the coherence of the individual's understanding of that world (or nation)'.[30] De Valera's worry about American domination of film productions about Ireland was much debated in 1934. In this year Fianna Fáil commissioned the Gaelic film *Oidhche Sheanchais* ('An Evening of Storytelling') in order to wrest control of the national narrative away from Hollywood, and the weekly 'Film Notes' of the *Irish Times* repeatedly fretted that 'As a rule, the only thing one can find to say about Irish films is that there aren't any'.[31] In addition, anxiety about films dealing with Michael Collins (*Beloved Enemy*, 1936), the Easter Rising (*The Plough and the Stars*, 1936) and *Parnell* (1938), revealed that it was not only a depiction of a homosexual relationship that worried the conservatives in Ireland, but that they feared historical figures might be trivialised by any connection with Hollywood's heterosexual 'romantic love interest' and by the subjugation of the political to a starry-eyed, intimate private sphere. Thus, Klein remained unable to mollify the Irish government, even though he carefully inserted a fictional fiancée into his script, with his version of Casement declaring, 'I would like to marry you right now, Mary [. . .] I crave a home and children'.[32]

Julius Klein received a letter from de Valera that denounced the prospective film:

> The President is of [the] opinion that no Writer outside Ireland, however competent, who had not the closest contact with events in this country during the years preceding and following the Rising of 1916 could hope to do justice to the character and achievements of this great man [Casement]. The President takes the view that a further period of time must elapse before the full extent of Casement's sacrifice can be understood and appreciated outside Ireland. He hopes that no attempt will be made to commercialize this great sacrifice either in a popular life or through a film in which fiction will play any part.[33]

Having initially concurred with Parry's sentiments, that a film on Casement could be made as long as it was treated with considerable dignity, de Valera became more intransigent as the Easter commemoration of 1935 approached, and he ordained that Klein's film should not be made. De Valera wanted to be associated with a version of Casement who was remembered as an avowedly Irish, Catholic hero; as the president indicated when he named his son after Casement by having the baby baptised with the Gaelic form 'Ruarí'.[34] But Hollywood's control of the agenda meant that de Valera was uncertain about what would be unleashed in Ireland's picture houses, and so he determined that Klein should abandon writing about Casement altogether.

The old lady says 'no!'

Meanwhile Klein was facing further objections. As well as contacting de Valera, Klein sensibly checked whether his film would cause the British to take umbrage. One of Universal Studios' largest markets was England and the British colonies, and Klein was reluctant to produce a film that would mortify this audience and harm the distribution of future Universal productions. When he informally sounded out the secretary of the British Board of Film Censors he discovered that he was likely to encounter difficulties, and so decided to make a more formal approach by sending the committee a copy of the film's synopsis.

The board read Klein's proposal at the end of October 1934, and responded with apoplexy. The British chief censor between 1930 and 1946 was Colonel J.C. Hanna, who had been stationed in Ireland from 1918 to 1922. He was disinclined to license narratives about controversial Irish topics, such as the 1939 Civil War film *Irish Story* that he prohibited Warner Brothers from distributing. Hanna saw Casement as an insignificant 'traitor' who had been justly punished, and knew it would be highly inappropriate, when the British government was in the course of spending £1.2 billion on weaponry between 1933 and 1938, to allow the British taxpayer to watch a war film in which their own soldiers were depicted as malevolent, and the upper echelons of the imperial civil service were mired in deviousness and scandal.[35] Klein's film looked likely to encouraged a British audience to identify with a revolutionary Irish nationalist, something that Colonel Hanna was unable to stomach, and he threatened Klein: 'my Board considers a film based on the life of this individual extremely undesirable. It would be quite impossible for us to issue our certificate for any such film'.[36] Worse still for Universal, in 1935 Lord William Tyrrell was appointed president of the censorship board, and was determined not to allow a film on Casement to be shown because the two men had been loyal friends at the foreign office.

Klein was thunderstruck, and passed the news of Hanna's decision to the British and Irish press. In response, one group of Fianna Fáil members, ignorant of de Valera's involvement in helping to quash the film, wrote to their leader to 'protest against the showing of all films from British studious [*sic*] in the Irish Free State and we call on all nationals to boycott same as a protest on account of the boycott on the Casement Film by the British authorities'.[37]

G.B. Shaw

When opposing Universal's Casement film, de Valera also found an unexpected ally in a dramatist who, a few months later, would be speaking out in public against the censorship of films, particularly those with a troublesome sexual content. In 1935 G.B. Shaw declared that:

The Archbishop [of Canterbury] speaks of undesirable films. There are no undesirable films. No film studio in the world would spend fifty thousand pounds in making a film unless it was a very desirable film indeed [...] The censorship method, which is that of handing the job over to some frail and erring mortal man, and making him omnipotent on the assumption that his official status will make him infallible and omniscient, is so silly [...] Others are obsessed with sex appeal. Now, sex appeal is a perfectly legitimate element in all the fine arts that deal directly with humanity.[38]

Shaw delivered this radio talk because he was confronting the same prudishness encountered by Julius Klein. Shaw had written a screenplay of *Saint Joan* in 1934, but it was soon obvious that antagonism from the Catholic Church, whose support Twentieth Century Fox regarded as vital, would prevent the film's production.

Shortly before Shaw's radio outburst, he had received a letter from Klein asking for support in the matter of the Casement project. Klein reasonably expected that Shaw would help tackle the obduracy of de Valera and the British censor. The playwright had written more than fifty articles against censorship, had signalled his resolute opposition to the Lord Chamberlain's office, and had claimed that censorship was discredited by the pernicious trash it allowed and by the good work it suppressed.[39]

But Klein knew nothing of Shaw's close friendship with Gertrude Parry, who objected to the film about her cousin. Shaw decided to support Parry against Hollywood's film-makers, whom he was already accustomed to offending. In 1933 he had visited MGM studios in California where he refused to sign an autograph for the leading actor John Barrymore, and reduced the star Ann Harding to tears by responding to the news that she had acted in *Captain Brassbound's Conversion* with the terse observation, 'I'm sure it must have been a piratical performance'.[40]

Shaw felt no compulsion to be any more tactful with Julius Klein, but told him:

> I cannot encourage you in the matter of the film. America may be pro-Irish and to that extent pro-Casement; but America is not pro-German; and Casement's German adventure will not be popular.
>
> In England the film will probably be forbidden.
>
> Film Corporations are often very foolish, especially when politics (which they don't understand) are in question; but I doubt if any well advised firm will back Casement as a winner.
>
> Casement's relatives view the threat of a film with consternation.[41]

However, Shaw also sent a more supportive message. Klein told Shaw that as well as producing a film he intended to write a book about Casement, to 'do justice to this great martyr'.[42] In response Klein received a long statement from Shaw outlining what Casement had tried to achieve, and explaining Shaw's own involvement with the affair.[43] Unlike de Valera, Shaw wanted to succour Klein's interest in Casement; it was the cinematic representation that the playwright opposed.

Shaw and the courtroom

Scholars have tended to overlook Casement's influence on Shaw, and yet, like Julius Klein, Shaw personally knew the difficulty of trying to depict Casement. Shaw was, in fact, the first person to produce a dramatic text on Casement, which he wrote before the notorious hanging, and Shaw was also the first to see his script fail to reach performance.

Prior to the summer of 1916, Shaw's work had been greatly admired by Roger Casement. The unconventional civil servant owned a copy of *John Bull's Other Island*, which he annotated heavily, and recommended that Shaw's newspaper article about the Easter Rising 'ought to go to all European countries, and would have good effect'.[44] Consequently, after his arrest Casement thought that Shaw might be able to intercede on behalf of Max Daulhendy, a German detained in Java. But Casement's friends believed that Shaw might be able to help Casement himself, and in June and July 1916 the rebel's American lawyer, Michael Doyle, and Gertrude Parry (then Gertrude Bannister) were both eager to contact Shaw.

After the Easter Rising Shaw received several written appeals from those connected to the insurgents, urging him to use his intellectual gifts and political leverage to help his jailed countrymen.[45] He and his wife were almost persuaded when visited at Adelphi Terrace by Gertrude Bannister. He subsequently organised meetings with a group of friends to decide how best to help, but Casement's pro-Germanism repelled most of the group, which then disbanded after hearing rumours of the 'black diaries'. In the summer of 1916 Shaw was visited by Alice Green, who called to solicit money, as she required funds for Casement's defence lawyer, but Shaw felt that this was pointless, as the facts of the affair were incontestable. Instead he decided to write a speech for Casement to deliver in the dock, arguing for the status of a prisoner of war who could not be found guilty of treason by a British court. In language reminiscent of Pearse's Easter-week rhetoric, Shaw insisted that Casement's defence would be a 'daring frontal attack on the position of the Crown'.[46]

Beatrice Webb wrote disapprovingly of Shaw's plan:

> Casement was to defend his own case; he was to make a great oration of defiance which would 'bring down the house'. To this Mrs Green retorted tearfully that the man was desperately ill; that he was quite incapable of handling a court full of lawyers; that the most he could do was the final speech after the verdict. 'Then we had better get our suit of mourning,' Shaw remarked with an almost gay laugh. 'I will write him a speech which will thunder down the ages.' 'But his friends want to get him reprieved,' indignantly replied the distracted woman friend.
>
> The meeting turned out to be a useless and painful proceeding. The Shaws were determined not to pay up – not 'to waste our money on lawyers'. G.B.S. went off to write the speech which was 'to thunder down the ages'. Alice Green retired in dismay, and I felt a fool for having intervened to bring Irish together in a common cause [. . .] The Shaws don't care enough about it to spend money; and Shaw wants to compel Casement and

Casement's friends to 'produce' the defence as a national dramatic event. 'I know how to do it,' was G.B.S.'s one contribution to the tragedy-laden dispute between the weeping woman friend and the intellectual sprite at play with the life and death of a poor human. And yet the man is both kindly and tolerant, but his conceit is monstrous.[47]

However, Casement himself appreciated this gesture. 'I shall be so grateful if you will convey to Bernard Shaw my warmest thanks', he told his solicitor Gavan Duffy after he received Shaw's script.[48] But although grateful, the rebel opted against incorporating the speech into his defence. Perhaps, like Pearse, Casement realised the necessity of his own death. The handwritten notes that he made to his copy of Shaw's script include the words 'The only good Irishman as I have said before is a dead Irishman – by the English Canonization of Irish rebels.'[49] Ominously, Casement also underscored Shaw's words 'I ask for no mercy, no pardon, no pity.'[50]

After the trial Casement did express his regret at jettisoning 'the only defence possible, viz. my own plan and that of G.B.S.', and also cited a portion of Shaw's script when rising to address the court after the draconian sentence had been pronounced.[51] But by this time of course neither Shaw nor anyone else could save Casement, as the rebel's fate had already been sealed.

Shaw felt quite sure that if his work had been performed then Casement would have been saved. Turning away from scriptwriting, Shaw desperately changed strategy and wrote a flurry of articles and a petition in a last ditch attempt to save Casement.[52] But the government, armed with the 'black diaries', was unflinching. Shaw might as well have saved his ink.

Saint Joan

Shaw's response to Julius Klein was paradoxical, advising the American to dwell on Casement but to avoid the patriot's direct dramatic portrayal. In this recommendation, Shaw was encouraging Klein to follow the example of *Saint Joan*, which the playwright was striving to cinematise at the same time as he was corresponding with Klein about the Casement film. It is generally accepted that after 1916 Casement had no more than a very minor impact upon Shaw's writing, warranting only the occasional mention in letters and newspaper articles; and scholars usually assume that Shaw wrote no other dramatic work about Casement after the execution. Yet, although the playwright never again attempted to compose a dramatic script that would directly represent Casement, the hanged rebel did influence *Saint Joan* in a profound if allusive way.

When Shaw sat down to write *Saint Joan* in 1923 he had been considering his subject-matter for ten years.[53] After visiting Orléans in 1913 he mulled over the saint's life, and continued to ruminate about it throughout the years of conflict in mainland Europe and in Ireland, including during his personal involvement with Casement. Consequently, when *Saint Joan* was first staged, shortly after the cessation of the Irish Civil War in December 1923, Shaw's depiction of Joan leading the French army to rout the English evoked the recent battles between Britain and Ireland. In addition, Shaw envisaged the play taking place in an Irish setting. He attempted to establish an Irish film industry in order to produce *Saint Joan*, wanting to promote Ireland's actors and 'scenic beauties' around the world.[54]

Shaw wrote most of *Saint Joan* in the summer of 1923 whilst in Glengariff, County Cork and Parknasilla, County Kerry, and tested out his trial scene by reading it to two Irish Catholic priests.[55] Declan Kiberd observes:

> Writing in the heart of republican Kerry, the backdrop of so many recent battles, Shaw must have sensed many local resonances in the theme of a nation fighting free of the shackles of foreign ownership. Like many of the Irish rebels, Joan was not a landless peasant but the offspring of strong farmer stock.[56]

This is entirely correct, but it is also worth noting that Kerry was the county in which Casement had been apprehended after having attempted to land in a German submarine, and that writing and reciting Joan's trial scene here must have had a curious resonance with the trial scene that Shaw had penned earlier for the region's most famous prisoner.

When writing *Saint Joan*, Shaw had explicitly equated the Catholic saint with the Irish patriot. In the play's preface Shaw names Casement twice, discerning that both Joan and Casement were tried by politically partisan assessors and that, despite the different implications of their trials, they both suffered the same kind of persecution.[57]

In the play itself Casement is a hidden referent, treated by Shaw in much the same way as he is treated by James Joyce. In *Finnegans Wake*, where rumours of sexual crime and deviancy follow HCE, Casement's name appears in a variety of cryptic rearrangements, and in *Ulysses* Casement is named in the 'Cyclops' chapter, where Bloom is troubled by divided national loyalties and by aggressive Irish nationalists.[58] As Robert Spoo shows in his erudite examination of 'Nestor', the action of *Ulysses* is ostensibly concerned with 16 June 1904, but Joyce brings this day into contact with subsequent historical events.[59] Hence, the 'Cyclops' chapter invokes Casement's eventual fate by referring to his 1904 Congo adventure before mentioning the courtroom, homosexuality, and the gallows.

Saint Joan is also constructed in this double time frame, which was recognised by reviewers of the original performances. A.B. Walkley wrote in *The Times*, 'It is a nuisance that he [Shaw] is so obsessed with the present period as to drag it into every period, however remote, that he dramatizes'; and the *Christian Science Monitor* scorned the play's 'local gags'.[60] Shaw's preface speaks of the necessity of constructing *Saint Joan* with two time periods in mind, 'having thus to make a twentieth-century audience conscious of an epoch fundamentally different from its own' (p. 73), and the playwright wrote that his characters have an anachronistic awareness of the peculiarities of the Middle Ages because 'the play would be unintelligible if I had not endowed them with enough of this consciousness to enable them to explain their attitude to the twentieth century' (p. 74). The play's proto-Brechtian epilogue, which aroused hostility from contemporary critics, explicitly encourages the audience to recognise this chronological duality. Yet, although Stanley Weintraub notes that Joan mirrors T.E. Lawrence, and William Irwin Thompson indicates that Shaw's heroine emulates Pádraic Pearse, critics have been slow to scrutinise Roger Casement's influence upon *Saint Joan*.[61]

Sir Joan and Saint Roger

In *Saint Joan* the siege of Orléans recalls Dublin's Easter Rising, another spring-time revolt that enabled a country to break free of its overweening English neighbour. Joan's battle begins on 29 April, the date on which the Irish rebels surrendered in 1916, and prior to the fight she seeks armed support and persuades soldiers to join her campaign, echoing Casement's thirteen-month mission to raise an Irish brigade in Germany. By contrast with Casement, Joan does enjoy significant military success, yet her initial appeal for one horse and three soldiers seems as unlikely to shift the occupying power as his ragged group of prisoners of war.[62] Like the leaders of the Rising, she is described as someone who 'will go ahead when she has only ten men to do the work of a hundred' (p. 150).

Joan's aim, like Casement's, is 'to make the English leave' (p. 92), and her military tactics mirror his. Just as he wanted the Germans to sail to Ireland, so her troops 'must come by water, and take the English in the rear' (p. 121). She echoes the requests made by Casement to the Germans, demanding, 'make rafts and put big guns on them; and let your men cross to us' (pp. 121–2). Moreover, the details of Roger Casement's life before and after his attempt to requisition weaponry also parallel Shaw's depiction of Joan. Casement was raised as a Protestant but was secretly baptised a Catholic, and Shaw's heroine is similarly affined to both religions, professing devotion to Catholicism but asserting the primacy of individual conscience and dying as one of the first Protestant martyrs. After his capture, Casement declared in his speech from the dock, 'I am proud to be a rebel, and shall cling to my "rebellion" with the last drop of my blood', whilst in Shaw's play Joan is labelled with the same rhetoric, as 'a rebel' whose 'rebellions are only excuses for her great rebellion against England' (p. 140).[63] Although she is burned at the stake rather than hanged like Casement, the gallows are mentioned several times: the archbishop predicts that Gilles de Rais will be lynched, the chaplain vows to hang himself, and Joan declares that anyone who tells too much truth will dangle from a rope.

Shaw's historically-allusive approach to the 1916 rebellion was echoed by his friend Lady Gregory. The year after the premiere of *Saint Joan*, Gregory wrote *The Story Brought by Brigit*, which supposedly takes place in Jerusalem at the time of Christ's crucifixion, but in which the Roman occupation parallels the modern British incursion into Ireland. One Roman soldier observes:

A little Rising now and then is no harm at all. It gives us an excuse to get rid
of disturbers and to bring more of our armies in. A Rising too is very apt to
lead to splits, and splits are a great help when you want to keep a country
down.[64]

However, Shaw sustains the analogy between Easter 1916 and the struggles of
a previous era more consistently than Gregory. Indeed, in Shaw's trial scenes the
narratives of Joan and Casement almost merge, as if the unperformed script he
wrote for Casement in 1916 became the template for his play in 1923.

Shaw wanted both Joan and Casement to rely on the same basic legal argument, to claim that the courts had no jurisdiction to condemn them, and
therefore that the judges lacked the authority to pronounce death sentences.
Joan maintains that that the higher court of God, revealed internally to her by
celestial voices, must be obeyed ahead of the earthly apparatus of Pope and
bishops. By comparison, Shaw's Casement was to claim that Ireland had bifur-
cated from England and that therefore he was a prisoner of war, 'an Irishman,
captured in a fair attempt to achieve the independence of my country'.[65]

In Shaw's two speeches from the dock, the defendants remain unapologetic,
with Joan claiming that whatever 'God made me do I will never go back on' (p.
173), and Casement explaining that he 'had no apology whatever to make [. . .]
it was his plain duty to his country'.[66] Both accept the prosecution case, but
they deny that they have done anything criminal or to be regretted. Indeed, at
times Casement and Joan were proudly supposed to reaffirm the details with
which their detractors charged them.

In Shaw's writing, Joan and Casement's language is suffused with Christian
rhetoric, and both defence speeches conclude with the recognition that the
death of martyrs serves a lofty purpose. Both defendants face execution boldly
because it will release them from a people amongst whom they do not belong
into a realm of patriotic or heavenly glory. The fact that in real life Joan and
Casement were then escorted to their deaths reinforced the grim affinities
between the two nationalists.

Moreover, Joan and Casement both challenged conventional ideas about
sexual and gender identity. Like James Connolly, Casement was enthusiastic
about the involvement of women in the conflict of 1916, declaring: 'There will
also be work for women to do, and there are signs that the women of Ireland,
true to their record, are especially enthusiastic for the success of the Irish Volunteers.'[67] More notoriously, when Casement sought a reprieve from his death
sentence the British government circulated the 'black diaries' to expose his
homosexuality. Echoing Casement, Joan proves eager to help in the cause of
militant nationalism, and at her trial her cross-dressing and masculine behaviour are pivotal indictments, as her prosecutor declares:

I must emphasize the gravity of two very horrible and blasphemous crimes
which she does not deny. First, she has intercourse with evil spirits, and is
therefore a sorceress. Second, she wears men's clothes, which is indecent,
unnatural, and abominable. (p. 176)

Her transgressive behaviour is considered outrageous even amongst the French court where the Dauphin's paternity is questioned, where Dunois is known as 'Bastard', and where Le Hire's manners are 'camp' (p. 99).

Since Joan refuses to 'stay at home' to do 'woman's work' (p. 173) she troubles both the English and the French for whom she fights. Like the apparently homosexual and rebellious Casement who vexed the Irish and British authorities, Joan refuses to accept rigid and impassable definitions of gender and sexuality. Roberta Maxwell, who played the part of Joan at the Seattle Repertory Theatre in 1979, commented that even wearing a feminine costume 'didn't stop me from playing the nonfeminine aspects of her character, at the risk of people saying, "My goodness, that girl is a bit boyish, isn't she?".'[68] Although *Saint Joan* broaches the gender issues of the Easter rebellion in a less direct way than O'Casey and Yeats, Shaw's dramatisation also disdains the passive and powerless image of the conventional nationalist woman.

As we have seen, post-revolutionary Irish nationalism often has difficulty in incorporating figures who unsettle traditional gender roles, and Shaw's play shows the political difficulties of dealing with sexual dissidence. The epilogue to *Saint Joan* is set twenty-one years after Joan's death, when she is being canonised by the Catholic Church, and it is at this point that the play judiciously comments on the posthumous political treatment of nationalists who challenge sexual and gender roles. At the end of the play Joan is commemorated, but the reality of her life remains unexamined. When her spirit hears news of the canonisation she asks whether, as saints have the ability to work miracles, she ought to rise from the dead. The Vatican official and others who celebrate her memory greet this question with alarm, and each steals away from her side. One character declares that she is 'better dead', whilst another pleads, 'do not come back: you must not come back' (p. 207). King Charles declares that if it were possible to 'bring her back to life, they would burn her again within six months, for all their present adoration of her' (p. 193).

This moment reflects the way that Casement troubled politicians like de Valera. For much of the twentieth century Irish leaders mouthed empty words of praise for Casement whilst dreading any re-emergence of the reality of his life and beliefs, and such politicians therefore resembled those who praise Joan after her death in Shaw's play. Conor Cruise O'Brien, for example, when working for the Department of Foreign Affairs, noted that the Irish government's policy was always to take 'no official action' in the matter of Casement's diaries.[69] Quite consistently, when confronted with hints of the Rising's homosexuality and proto-feminism, de Valera reacted in the same way as the characters who flee from Joan in Shaw's drama. That plea, 'do not come back', expresses the fears of Fianna Fáil in the twentieth century as much as those of the French who lived five hundred years before. Shaw could not have been surprised by de Valera's reaction to Universal's film about Roger Casement, as it was precisely what *Saint Joan* had predicted.

A painful Casement

By the start of 1935 Universal Studios realised that the objections of the British censor and the Irish government would make a film about Roger Casement financially unworkable. Hollywood's executives decided to forsake the delayed project completely, and Julius Klein never completed his script. He wrote to de Valera in March 1935 to confirm that the film was being abandoned 'due to the many complications that have arisen'.[70] Klein continued his Casement study and research, hoping to publish a book instead, but the outbreak of World War II and his entry into active service frustrated these plans.

Since 1935 there has been a prolonged cinematic silence about Casement. A large number of films about him have been mooted, but each has fallen by the wayside. In 1954 Robert Monteith set to work on a Hollywood script based on his book *Casement's Last Adventure*, and it was even rumoured that the tall Galway actor Sean McGlory had been cast as Casement, but the production lapsed into abeyance.[71] In the 1980s David Collins declared his intention of creating a Casement screenplay, and in the early 1990s Isaac Julian penned a Casement script.[72] But both ventures again proved abortive. Thaddeus O'Sullivan worked on a failed cinema project that received a great deal of development money between about 1993 and 1997, and today Dublin is rumoured to contain a number of un-produced Casement scripts.[73] Yet the only time that Casement's story has reached the screen has been in passing allusions: *The Lost World*, based on Conan Doyle's novel, includes an Amazon explorer called Lord John Roxton, and David Lean's *Ryan's Daughter* features an attempted landing of guns by Irish revolutionaries during World War I.[74] In the cinema, Casement remains the rebel who dares not speak his name.

In 'Autumn Journal' Louis MacNeice wrote of his fear of Casement's appearance:

> And I remember, when I was little, the fear
> Bandied among the servants
> That Casement would land at the pier
> With a sword and a horde of rebels.[75]

As MacNeice indicates, unease about Casement extends beyond the cinema. Lucy McDiarmid has shown how the patriot has become 'over-remembered' in ballads, newspapers, anecdotes, and other flotsam, yet his posthumous appearances have regularly provoked furious controversies, which are reflected in historical studies about him.[76] Angus Mitchell and Roger Sawyer, for instance, signed a contract in 1993 to edit Casement's diaries of 1910, but subsequently found that they disagreed about the material so fundamentally that they were unable to work together. Instead each man published his own edition of the diaries.[77]

Although a *rapprochement* has taken place between popular culture and Roger Casement in the 1990s, the patriot's literary and dramatic representation has often presented a conundrum. On Saint Patrick's Day in 1992 Paul

Muldoon published the poem 'A Clear Signal' in the *New York Times*. This poem urges Gerry Adams to make a commitment to peace in the North of Ireland, and it also assaults Irish–American homophobia. In 1992 the Ancient Order of Hibernians had refused to let the Irish Lesbian and Gay Organisation march in the New York Saint Patrick's Day parade, and some marchers planned to brandish anti-gay and anti-lesbian banners, prompting Muldoon to ask:

> would they have stopped Casement when he tried to land
> a boatload of guns on Banna Strand?
>
> The ghost of Roger Casement would now call 'enough'
> to the claymore and Kalashnikov.[78]

But since 1992 Muldoon has perhaps grown dissatisfied with the politically-candid nature of this poem, and it has not been anthologized or reprinted in Ireland or Britain.

Medbh McGuckian is another Northern Irish poet who has encountered problems when using Casement's image in her work. He is the mysterious 'R' of her poem 'The Moses Room' and the subject of many of her unpublished poems.[79] Yet when she wanted to use some of his words as an epigraph to her collection, *On Ballycastle Beach*, an editor at Oxford University Press forbade her from doing so. Apparently a member of the Casement family worked at the press and was unhappy with the idea.[80] Instead, McGuckian used the quotation as an epigraph to the Gallery Press edition of her selected poems.[81]

From time to time, Casement has also continued to be embroiled in dramatic controversy. In 1972 the Abbey Theatre refused to produce Richard Stockton's Casement play under the author's preferred title, *The Royal Rape of Ruari Macasmunde*, but changed its name to *The Prisoner of the Crown*.[82] Nearly thirty years later, a Martin McDonagh play that involved Casement in a small but important way, *The Lieutenant of Inishmore*, nearly failed to reach the stage altogether. McDonagh's play pokes fun at nationalist paramilitary groups, and includes a character called 'Sir Roger' who is a cat. Like his predecessor, this 'Sir Roger' is disguised and then executed: the cat is painted with shoe polish and shot by an obnoxious ruffian called Padraig. At the end of the play Padraig is himself killed by the cat's vengeful owner whilst asking, 'Sir Roger who? Sir Roger Casement? [. . .] What has that oul poof to do with dead cats, Mairead?'[83] Martin McDonagh has parodied the Easter rebels elsewhere, most notably in his brutal rewriting of Pearse's Christological children's stories in 'The Little Jesus' of *The Pillowman*, and the playwright's decision to include Casement's name in the deliberately shocking play *The Lieutenant of Inishmore* indicated that the dead gunrunner had maintained a lingering air of contro-versy.[84] Although *The Lieutenant of Inishmore* eventually enjoyed a lucrative run with the Royal Shakespeare Company, it took five years to reach the stage. Several theatre companies (including the British National Theatre), rejected the play, with Trevor Nunn, the artistic director of the National, apparently declining *The Lieutenant of Inishmore* because he feared it would endanger the peace process in the North of Ireland.[85]

Thus, Julius Klein's project was neither the first nor the last abortive attempt to speak about Casement, and Hollywood has yet to find an adequate way of telling his story. Casement's identity, like that of Shaw's Saint Joan, is unstable and indeterminate, and therefore proves difficult to incorporate into conventional masculine narratives about the 1916 insurrection. Ever since Fianna Fáil led the campaign against Klein's movie, the revolutionary has caused problems for film-makers, despite the fact that screenwriters have frequently been seduced by the remarkable story of his life. The ghost of Roger Casement might be beating at the cinema door, but since 1935 that door has been firmly locked and bolted.

6

Later Representations

It's the same old theme since nineteen-sixteen.
In your head, in your head, they're still fighting,
With their tanks and their bombs,
And their bombs and their guns.
In your head, in your head, they are dying.[1]

'I told you the truth,' I say yet again, 'Memory's truth, because memory has its own special kind. It selects, eliminates, alters, exaggerates, minimizes, glorifies, and vilifies also; but in the end it creates its own reality, its heterogeneous but usually coherent version of events; and no sane human being ever trusts someone else's version more than his own.[2]

Roger Casement and *Insurrection*

As the twentieth century wore on, Irish theatres were continually haunted by the disputes about the Rising that had been conducted between 1916 and 1935. In spite of the various social and cultural upheavals that affected Ireland after the mid-1930s, the unresolved tensions that existed between the varying nationalisms of 1916 continued to encourage and to goad subsequent writers into action. Although prevailing attitudes to the insurrection vacillated in the ensuing years, playwrights and producers of differing political standpoints consistently repeated the arguments that had already been conducted by dramatists in that formative period after the revolution, as though these debates and contradictions were a nightmare from which the Irish theatre was powerless to awake.

In the years following independence the new leaders of Ireland had, more often than not, proved extremely conservative when dealing with social legislation. In 1923, following aggressive lobbying from the Catholic Truth Society and from newspapers such as the *Irish Ecclesiastical Record* and the *Catholic Mind*, film censorship was introduced; divorce was prohibited in 1925; and in 1935 public dance-hall events were restricted and contraceptives were banned from sale. By 1930 the Municipal Gallery had hidden all of its nudes away from the impressionable eyes of the general public, and the work of notorious 'pornographers' such as Joyce and Beckett was falling victim to the notorious Irish Censorship Board.[3] Fittingly enough, in 1935 de Valera's government had also eviscerated the Easter Rising of its links with a kind of early feminism and struggled to prevent the rebellion from becoming connected with homosexuality. At the start of their lengthy tenure in office, Fianna Fáil's politicians were instead anxious to promote and institutionalise a Catholic vision of the nation's founding revolution, to cohere with the reactionary ethos of the newly independent state. And this conservatism proved remarkably durable, with Fianna Fáil's version of 1916 comfortably predominating in Ireland for at least another thirty years. For much of this time a number of dramatists eagerly assisted the government by writing plays that aligned the insurrection with the social attitudes of de Valera and his ministers. In the preceding years Yeats had positioned his rebel onstage with two infamous adulterers and O'Casey had placed his nationalist orator next to a whore, but by contrast, many of the lesser playwrights who followed in the wake of Yeats and O'Casey affirmed a more prudish set of values. Moreover, in an act of Oedipal slaying, these subsequent writers often described the Rising by directly inverting certain features of *The Dreaming of the Bones* and, even more frequently, *The Plough and the Stars*.

Amongst those who emended the earlier dramatic works were Roger McHugh and Alfred Noyes. In 1957 McHugh, a forty-nine-year-old lecturer at the English department of University College Dublin, and Noyes, a seventy-seven-year-old British poet, were each already known for having become embroiled in newspaper controversies involving the Rising. Noyes, of course, still regretted his accusations about Casement for which Yeats had upbraided him in 1937, whilst McHugh had gained a degree of notoriety for disrupting a production of *The Plough and the Stars* in 1947 in order to protest at the Abbey's mid-century lack of artistic vision.[4] By 1957 McHugh and Noyes had decided to write a play that would retell the story of Roger Casement, who had drawn Noyes into the headlines twenty years earlier.[5] In doing so they would also revamp the second act of Sean O'Casey's *The Plough and the Stars*, which had raised McHugh's profile in Dublin only ten years before.

McHugh's and Noyes's play, *Roger Casement*, features a scene in which two drinkers listen to an offstage orator from a hotel bar. The unseen speaker tells a raucous crowd that his cause is divinely guided and he urges blood sacrifice with the same fervour as the agitator of O'Casey's play. Yet McHugh and Noyes decided to invert their audience's expectations, and so in *Roger Casement* the rhetorician is no Irish nationalist but the unionist leader, Edward Carson. McHugh and Noyes then further moderated Act II of *The Plough and the Stars* by rebutting O'Casey's provocative combination of Pádraic Pearse and a prostitute. In fact, in *Roger Casement* the rebel displays a strong aversion to manifest displays of sexuality. This Roger Casement is presented as heterosexual in inclination, but has no girlfriend because his roving consular life prevents him from forming any romantic attachments. As a gentleman, he abhors the thought of having to 'drag any woman through the jungles [...] or condemn her to stay at home playing bridge', and so in this version of Casement's life his reputed homosexuality is nothing more than a nasty slander cooked up by a hyperactive British imagination in a wily plot to calumniate the chivalrous nationalist.[6]

Liam O'Flaherty, who joined with Fianna Fáil's noisy founders to denounce the Abbey's production in 1926, also targeted the second act of *The Plough and the Stars* in his own writing about Easter week. In his 1950 novel *Insurrection* O'Flaherty depicts the main character, Bartly Madden, eavesdropping on Pádraic Pearse's words and then being inspired to fight in the GPO. O'Flaherty draws a deliberate comparison between this scene and O'Casey's less flattering portrayal by describing those listening to Pearse as being 'like an audience at a theatre'.[7] But in O'Flaherty's version of events Pearse stands in a central position, addresses an enormous crowd who listen in hushed reverence, and speaks words that make Dublin serene and heroic instead of reducing the city to the shambles depicted in *The Plough and the Stars*. When Madden hears Pearse's declaration he falls into a meditation about wildlife and longs 'for the beauty that the poet proclaimed'.[8]

O'Flaherty also adapted the kind of female character that O'Casey had presented on the Abbey stage. *The Plough and the Stars* had shown women who want to protect their men and cannot bear to see their family slaughtered for any noble cause whatsoever. O'Flaherty realised that some mothers would naturally want to prevent their men from being placed in danger, and presents the character of Mary Colgan, whose son is fighting with the Citizen Army even though she has begged him, on her knees, to stay out of the conflict. However, O'Flaherty also attempted to reconcile this woman with the maternal image of Margaret Pearse. After Mary Colgan's son proves determined to fight, Mary boasts of having pride in her offspring's actions, before cajoling someone else's son into fighting and dying in the rebellion. In Ireland in the middle of the twentieth century women lost the right to sit on juries unless they applied specifically to do so, and married female civil servants were forced into compulsory retirement. At this time O'Flaherty's novel revealed the paradoxical link between Fianna Fáil's and Sean O'Casey's depictions of women, neither of which helped real-life women gain autonomy. Ironically, in depoliticising the mother role the Fianna Fáil party had followed O'Casey's consensual maternal figure, pitting the unifying emotional space of the home against a violent, strife-torn public sphere.

Sean O'Casey had also linked the rebels with the licentious desires of the alehouse, but in O'Flaherty's work the rebellion is far more ascetic. In making his way to the GPO, Madden chooses to abandon the sex life that he had already planned, and although he is *en route* to his fiancée Barbara at the time of the Rising, he gladly (perhaps too gladly?) forsakes his impending wedding for the militarism of the Volunteers. Elsewhere, by the middle decades of the century the insurgents of 1916 were repeatedly being presented as latently heterosexual men who nevertheless unhesitatingly abandoned the physical delights of the mattress for the more lofty, spiritual call of the Shan Van Vocht. Pádraic Pearse's hagiographers invented a tale of a lost fiancée, and Michael Collins's biographer emphasised that although the hero wanted a romance with a 'demure young lady', Collins remained chaste and unsullied by any fully realised love affair.[9] In a similar vein, both *Roger Casement* and *Insurrection* invoke O'Casey's play only to repudiate it, presenting the rebels as distanced from the forthright eroticism of *The Plough and the Stars*.

Easter Christening and Lost Light

However, it was not only Sean O'Casey's work that was reappraised by a newly-prudish generation of writers. In 1940 Donagh MacDonagh, the son of Thomas MacDonagh, scripted the radio play *Easter Christening*, which modified Yeats's *The Dreaming of the Bones*. MacDonagh's play features a 'Seeker' who wishes to establish whether the rebellion has been a success, and although initially uncertain, he is finally reassured of its triumph by meeting with the spirits of the dead rebels. The main character's quest thus revolves around Yeats's familiar idea that the deceased constantly re-enact the most significant moments of their lives, and that:

> Perhaps
> Some spirit that once lived within these walls
> [. . .]
> Possessed all Dublin for a week,
> And cannot leave the earth it has enriched.[10]

Like *The Dreaming of the Bones*, Donagh MacDonagh's play about Easter week uses music, a chorus, and nameless characters; and it also situates ghostly apparitions in a dreamlike scenario. MacDonagh pointedly mentions Yeats's determinative influence by summoning words from 'Easter 1916', 'I have seen not vivid light shine on those faces' (fol. 9), and by appropriating a line from *The Dreaming of the Bones*: Yeats's 'never, never/Shall Diarmuid and Dervorgilla be forgiven' becomes MacDonagh's 'Never, never more can they be parted' (fol. 17).[11]

But MacDonagh allied this Yeatsian dramatic form to the social attitudes promoted by the Fianna Fáil government. In *Easter Christening* the 1916 Rising is the rebellion of 'a thousand men' (fol. 18), and the play's only significant woman is the figure of Mother Ireland, who glorifies her dead sons. By contrast with this abstract mother, real women are responsible for distracting the men from republican purposes. The play describes the stagnation of one former rebel, who now languishes in bed with his spouse:

> Sometimes he wonders,
> Lying quiet and wakeful in early morning
> Beside his sleeping wife, if he or some mad twin
> Sang that brave song of Spring. (fol. 5)

By contrast with the sacrificial mother, real women can only corrupt the rebellion, as one of the veterans confirms when he says, 'Marriage sealed me from daring' (fol. 6). Such enervated rebels are contrasted with those who had the good fortune to die in 1916. The dead men do not sleep with female lovers but 'lie in brotherhood' (fol. 17), an infinitely preferable state where they exist perpetually 'in the spring of youth' (fol. 10). In *Easter Christening* women are absent from the rebellion, and when they do appear they hinder the male rebels from achieving laudable nationalist goals.

Three years after Donagh MacDonagh wrote *Easter Christening* the Abbey Theatre staged another play that recalled *The Dreaming of the Bones* but which aligned itself with the view of women outlined in de Valera's constitution. Robert Farren's *Lost Light* tells of an Anglophile Irishman named Dermot, who has one son fighting in Flanders whilst the other, Niall, falls in the GPO. Farren's Dermot, like the characters in Yeats's play, obsesses about breeding, and accuses his wife of bearing 'contagion!' when he discovers that her ancestors were Fenian rebels.[12] He repeatedly asserts that she has passed her malign inheritance on to their progeny, blaming Niall's revolt on 'the same fanatical spark, [that] spring[s] from your blood'.[13]

Yet, whilst affirming the importance of genetic inheritance, Farren's play is far removed from Yeats's view of motherhood. As we have seen, Yeats's *The Dreaming of the Bones* presents the adulterous lover Dervorgilla, who is a cause of disgust to the rebel she has engendered, and who is light years away from the maternal image of Margaret Pearse. But in *Lost Light* Farren redeems the sacrificial woman. Dermot and his wife discover that Niall has married in secret shortly before the rebellion, and that Niall's new spouse sent him out to die straightaway. Niall's mother is initially irresolute about her son's demise, yet by the end of *Lost Light* she too relishes the fact that he has been slain for Ireland. In this way, under its new managing director Ernest Blythe, who had been a member of the IRB at the time of the Rising, the Abbey revived the devouring woman and offered a *mea culpa* to conservative nationalists.[14] Furthermore, in the Abbey's premier of Farren's play the original Rosie Redmond, Ria Mooney, was cast in the role of Niall's nationalist mother. Whereas Mooney had appeared as O'Casey's lascivious hussy in fourteen revivals of *The Plough and the Stars* at the Abbey before the 1940s, in Farren's play she conjured up a completely different image, portraying that dignified woman who revels in her son's immolation on behalf of Ireland.[15]

The gallant allies

In the middle of the twentieth century a variety of Irish playwrights promoted a version of the Easter Rising in which the rebels were celibate heterosexual men who obeyed the insistent call to fight that was demanded by Ireland's passive women. But by contrast, when foreign writers dealt with the Rising they were unhindered by such restrictive mores. It was as though, unwelcome in Ireland, the subversive inheritance of O'Casey and Yeats had temporarily fled abroad.

Mein Leben Für Irland ('My Life for Ireland') was an anti-British propaganda film made in 1941 by those 'gallant allies in Europe', the German film industry.[16] The movie refigures the contemporary conflict between the Axis powers and Britain in terms of the 1916 struggle between Pearse's soldiers and the Crown forces. Although supposedly set in 1921, this production presents an anachronistic Easter Rising that features a World War II tank, rebels who lob grenades, and the final comeuppance of a distinctly familiar-looking, cigar-smoking British commander.

At the start of *Mein Leben Für Irland*, in a flashback sequence, a group of violent British soldiers evict a Dublin family from a misty cottage. Several Irish rebels attack these British forces, but are overwhelmed and captured. The girl-friend of one of the Irishmen visits her jailed lover, and reaches through the prison bars to tell him that she is pregnant. They subsequently marry in the prison chapel, whilst bearskin-hatted British prison guards look on. The rebel then passes his spouse a locket, and as a drumbeat sounds he is led to the gallows.

This prison wedding is a garbled version of the real-life story of the 1916 rebel Joseph Plunkett and his wife Grace Gifford. Plunkett was betrothed to Gifford in December 1915 and they were due to be married on Easter Sunday 1916. However, on the morning of the wedding he was so busy with the military council that the pair agreed to postpone their nuptials, deciding that if he were imprisoned she would wed him in detention. Plunkett duly fought and was captured. On 3 May Gifford was allowed into Kilmainham prison chapel where her fiancé was under guard, and where a priest was waiting. The lovers pronounced their marriage vows by candlelight before being parted for the final time. They were denied any privacy in the jail cell, and Plunkett was shot the following day.[17]

In Ireland, nationalists celebrated Plunkett as a heterosexual who remained celibate, forsaking Grace Gifford's arms for the embrace of the Shan Van Vocht. Straight after the rebellion the poet Wilfred Maynell emphasised Plunkett's association with the Virgin Mary, and later Grace Gifford wrote poetry comparing her husband to Christ.[18] The chorus of the ballad 'Grace' similarly depicts Plunkett declaring his chastity: 'there won't be time to share our love, for we must say goodbye'.[19] Yet in real life there is considerable evidence that Gifford was pregnant at the time of her marriage, and that she suffered a miscarriage shortly after the Rising.[20] By contrast with the Irish mythologising, German film-makers were at liberty to reinterpret the story without being encumbered by any sanctimonious views of the rebels, and so *Mein Leben Für Irland* described a more realistic version of the relationship, with the nationalist's girlfriend already being pregnant before her wedding day.

Irish sexual pieties also carried little weight with Frenchmen. When Raymond Queneau wrote his novel *On est toujours trop bon avec les femmes* in 1947 he told of a band of rebels, named after the characters from *Ulysses*, who take over the GPO whilst one of the female clerks, Gertie Girdle, is indecorously trapped inside the lavatory. Although initially a virgin who is rancorous towards the rebels she soon changes her mind and decides to seduce her captors:

> Prends-moi, murmura-t-elle.
> Elle ajouta:
> Longtemps.[21]

By the end of the novel Gertie has been remarkably successful, making sexual contact, in one way or another, with six of the seven rebels. Realising that the nobility of their effort will be remembered incorrectly by posterity because of their prurience, the final two rebels decide to violate Gertie in such a way that she will never be able to tell anybody about her Easter-week liaisons, and she protests:

> Mais, je vous assure, avec une femme, ce n'est pas la manière. Mais vous êtes un ignorant. Vous vous croyez entre gentlemen. Mais je vous dis que ce n'est pas comme ça.[22]

There was little chance that the censorship board would have allowed Irish readers to lay eyes on this sort of account. Queneau's Joycean portrayal of Easter week shows the insurgents being distracted by a beguiling siren; includes a candid presentation of female erotic desire; and suggests that the 'heroic', 'valiant', and 'pure' way in which the rebels wanted to be remembered was secured only through a brutal act of anal rape.

A green, white, and golden jubilee

Back in mid-century Ireland, where a theatre director who instructed his actors merely to mime the dropping of an imaginary condom could find himself imprisoned and his theatre ruined, the Irish government staged another elaborate celebration of the Easter insurrection to mark the fiftieth anniversary of the conflict.[23] The official commemorations at the GPO were ostentatious and modelled on those seen in O'Connell Street more than thirty years before. Almost all of the ceremonial features of the 1935 memorial service were repeated, from the marching troops and rifle salutes, to the trumpet fanfares and swooping planes. The militant women, of course, found themselves unremembered once again. The following day the *Irish Times* reported that the ceremony included 'line after line of striding men' sporting banners with mottoes such as 'Stand together, Brothers', whilst the front page of the *Irish Independent* bore the legend 'NATION HONOURS MEN OF 1916'.[24] The *Irish Times* repeated de Valera's claim that '"A Nation of Brothers" was [the] ultimate goal of the seven signatories', and the most eccentric veneration of the masculinity of Easter week happened in Kilkenny, where a ceremony saw sixteen male athletes lay a wreath before running a race around the town.[25]

In 1966 Dublin's theatres were at the centre of the anniversary celebrations just as they had been at the heart of the Rising fifty years before. But unlike in 1916, women were entirely ousted from the performance space. The Adelphi cinema hosted a tribute concert by the Clancy brothers, Jack Cruise performed his patriotic if somewhat bizarre review *Easter Parade* at the Olympia Theatre, and at Gemini's Theatre Eugene McCabe produced a one-act show about the Rising which starred only two men.[26]

The Abbey players, having agreed to boycott work by O'Casey, spent their Easter week performing Robert Farren's *Lost Light*, Pádraic Pearse's *The Singer*, and the 1907 play which helped inspire Yeats's play about the Rising, Lady Gregory's *Dervorgilla*.[27] But Pearse's play contained a controversial erotic subtext and some Fianna Fáil members still harboured lingering suspicions about the

Abbey, so the party's newspaper complained that the company could have given an even more explicit portrayal of the sacrificial woman and a more Christ-like depiction of the revolutionary. The *Irish Press* critic grumbled that although an attempt had been made to capture the spirit of 1916, the actor playing the part of MacDara in Pearse's play:

> . . . did not convey the appeal of the revolutionary, the attractiveness of the visionary, or the fatalism of a martyr, and his last lines, evoking his messianic role, were too subdued [. . .] Yeats' [*sic*] 'Cathleen Ni Houlihan' would have been a greater expression of the forces of the time and the motivations of the period.[28]

To satisfy such appetites, RTÉ broadcast Yeats's *Cathleen ni Houlihan* alongside its own version of Pearse's *The Singer* on Easter Sunday, to accompany the rambling, Catholic ceremonies televised from St Patrick's Cathedral and Parnell Square. Although the Department of the Taoiseach had originally wanted a more ecumenical service at the Garden of Remembrance, the cabinet finally caved in to the Archbishop of Dublin's refusal to share a blessing with any non-Catholic clergymen, and his desire to maintain his Church's exclusive association with the Rising.[29]

On Easter Tuesday, de Valera attended the first performance of a pageant at Croke Park that retold the story of Ireland's independence struggle through a series of male-only tableaux and culminated with a depiction of the Rising. Just like Daniel Corkery's earlier play the event was named *Aiseirí* ('Resurrection'), and the pageant once more excluded the rebellion's militant females. The absence of women was unwittingly emphasised by the *Irish Press*, whose correspondent eulogised the event by exclaiming that to 'select members of the cast for special mention would be to pick a hero from Irish history and say – "he was our greatest man"'.[30] The pageant may have shown greater theatrical sophistication than its counterparts in 1935, but the gender message remained relatively unreformed. Irish revolutionary history largely continued to marginalise women in 1966, and the official Fianna Fáil interpretation of the uprising still remained in the ascendant.

Revising the Rising

Yet the celebrations of 1966 proved to be the swansong for this version of the Easter Rising. As the crowds cheered in O'Connell Street, a group of revisionist historians, who felt little need to genuflect to nationalist tenets, were asking awkward questions about the rebellion. Those associated with *The Bell* magazine, founded in 1940, and the *Irish Historical Studies* journal, first published in 1938, emphasised the need for professional, international standards of historical scholarship, and attempted to wrench Irish history away from its obsession with a narrative of progressive national revolution towards an analysis of the country's underlying social, economic, and cultural experience.[31] The revisionists broadly believed that veritable 'history', which was acquired through scientific methods, should be separated from 'myth', which was gleaned from popular, often oral traditions. The leading revisionist F.S.L. Lyons was particularly venomous about the stultifying myths that surrounded Pearse and the 1916 rebels, declaring that all the people of Ireland were 'in a sense children of the revolution [. . .] and for the past sixty years scholars and statesmen alike seem to have been mesmerized by the Easter Rising of 1916'.[32]

Towards the end of the 1960s the revisionist reassessment of 1916 elbowed its way into popular and academic work. In 1966 Father Francis Shaw, a professor of early and medieval history, wrote an article 'The Canon of Irish History – A Challenge' in which he observed that Pearse's equation of Calvary with the GPO was blasphemous, and argued that placing the 1916 rebels on a pedestal belittled the efforts of those constitutional nationalists who had also worked to liberate Ireland.[33] This article was suppressed by journal editors in that fiftieth-anniversary year of the Rising, but proved influential when published posthumously in 1972. Writers such as Conor Cruise O'Brien, Roy Foster, and Fintan O'Toole aligned themselves with Father Shaw's views, and in 'Some Truths and Jokes about the Easter Rising' David Krause praised such 'noble Irishmen' whose reassessments of 1916 'nauseate the die-hard nationalists'.[34] When the North headed towards violent conflict in 1969 moderate nationalists generally avoided speaking of the revolutionary violence of 1916. Only the IRA and Sinn Féin continued evoking the Easter rebellion, and some scholars who were repulsed by the return to bloodshed struck at the paramilitaries by deriding the mythology that appeared to underpin the modern atrocities.

When the revisionists examined the rebellion of 1916 they often asked questions about sexuality that had been shunned by earlier historians. In 1942 one of the original contributors to *The Bell*, Patrick Kavanagh, wrote his poem 'The Great Hunger', which asserts that a mother's encouragement of her son to devote himself to the feminised land was likely to create an emotionally dysfunctional and disaffected manhood, masturbating into the dead ashes of the fireplace.[35] This poem typifies the attitude that revisionist historians brought to bear on the dominant view of the Easter Rising, with its sacrificial mothers and asexual, saint-like rebels. In 1977 Ruth Dudley Edwards published her book *Patrick Pearse*, which displaced the conventional Christ-like champion with a diminished dullard whose maladroit career was motivated by neurosis, Anglophobia, and sexual frustration. Before this, in 1967, William Irwin Thompson published *The Imagination of an Insurrection*, a psychological study of the rebel leaders in which he proclaimed the heroes ascetic and inhibited, and noted that the Rising was an outlet for the disappointments and idiosyncrasies of their personal lives. He observed that Pearse manifested 'the religious fanatic's fear of sin: a fear that causes the devout to castrate himself, lest he fall into carnal sin'.[36]

In her 1965 novel about the rebellion, *The Red and the Green*, Iris Murdoch also presents an Easter revolutionist, Pat Dumay, who has a debilitating fear of having sex with women. When one of Murdoch's characters asks whether Dumay 'might conceivably be interested in boys', the reader is none-too-subtly steered towards viewing the rebel as a closet homosexual.[37] In the same year, when Casement was reburied, wags in Dublin told a spate of jokes about the distance that de Valera had kept between himself and the coffin, and at the seemingly conservative *Aiseirí* pageant in 1966 some attentive listeners may have been intrigued to hear that the omniscient 'Voice of History' was played by Michael Mac Liammoir, the director of the Gate and one half of Ireland's 'only visibly gay couple'.[38]

Brendan Behan and Denis Johnston

Despite the general prudery of the new Irish plays written after 1935, *The Plough and the Stars* had remained consistently popular, and was revived by the Abbey for more than one hundred performances in each decade from the 1930s to the 1970s.[39] Alan Brien feared that O'Casey was in danger of being 'relegated to the attic as an antique' at the start of the 1960s, but this prediction never came true, as the revisionist reassessment of the Easter insurgents and renewed speculation about the rebels' sex lives made O'Casey's play appear freshly pertinent.[40] Shortly after the rebuilt Abbey Theatre opened its doors in 1966, the company performed *The Plough and the Stars* for seven weeks. In 1976 the Abbey staged a lavish golden-jubilee production of the play, and perhaps mischievously, the theatre managers appointed Tomás MacAnna to direct this performance even though he had previously organised the hagiographic fiftieth-anniversary pageant for the Rising, *Aiseirí*. MacAnna perceived the contemporary relevance of *The Plough and the Stars* to the situation in the North, and gave Ulster accents to the Dublin Protestant characters, which quickly became the theatrical norm.[41] There followed major revivals by the British National Theatre in 1977 and by the Abbey in 1984. In 1991, when the seventy-fifth anniversary of the Rising was sheepishly celebrated with a low-budget ceremony at the GPO, there were, by contrast, two expensive revivals of *The Plough and the Stars*, one at the Abbey in Dublin and another at London's Young Vic. These two versions were directed by *Wunderkinder* of the theatre, Garry Hynes in Ireland and Sam Mendes in England, and both productions had an impressive air of glamour: Judi Dench played Bessie Burgess in London, and in Dublin a prestigious gathering of Irish celebrities, including Mary Robinson, attended the first night.[42]

While producers and directors re-staged *The Plough and the Stars*, Irish playwrights wrote new works that re-interpreted O'Casey's ideas. In 1958 Brendan Behan and Denis Johnston were amongst the earliest writers of a revisionist bent to produce plays that, as Johnston put it, followed *The Plough and the Stars* like the 'smell following the motor car'.[43]

In a newspaper article of 1955 Behan wrote:

> In my childhood I could remember the whole [of Easter] week a damn sight better than I can now, for I have learned enough arithmetic to know that I could not possibly have taken part in the Rising, which happened seven years before I was born.[44]

Behan may have missed seeing the Rising itself, but when young he had seen patriotic revues at the Queen's Theatre, where his uncle Patrick Bourke had been the manager. Such shows had stirringly evoked Pearse's oratory and the image of the GPO just as the Fianna Fáil commemoration of 1935 had done. But Behan was keen to show that such notions of 1916 were elaborately constructed fictions, which were now hopelessly outdated. The newspaper article joke of asking 'where were you in 1916?' to someone who could not possibly have been involved in the rebellion is repeated several times Behan's other writings, echoing the disillusionment and cynicism of O'Casey.

In particular, in the 1958 Irish-language play *An Giall* Behan sought to echo Sean O'Casey's criticism of Pádraic Pearse. The play is again set in the Dublin tenements, but this time it is long after the Rising, in a 1950s room where the IRA hold and inadvertently kill a British soldier. Rather than including Pearse himself in the play, Behan makes a seventy-year-old character called Monsúr stand for the Pearsean ideals of sacrifice and martyrdom, showing how the republicans of Behan's day were trapped in a time-warp and still obsessed by the outmoded struggles of more than thirty years before. Monsúr repeatedly revels in the idea of death for Ireland, and when he hears that a young man is to be hanged in Belfast he repeats the sentiments of Pearse's famous oratory at O'Donovan Rossa's grave, declaring that such sacrifice is a reason for pride and joy. But just as Pearse's ideas are rubbished in *The Plough and the Stars*, so Monsúr is mocked and declared stupid by the other characters in *An Giall*. The audience is drawn to concur that Monsúr's views are indeed risible, as Monsúr repeatedly – and ridiculously – appears playing the bagpipes and failing to notice that his IRA barracks is in fact a brothel.

Monsúr consistently praises both the male and female soldiers of the country, and is evidently one of the republicans who sympathised with the sexual equality championed by Connolly and MacDonagh in 1916. However, Behan shows that this is not necessarily an admirable thing, as the conflict of 1916 is largely an irrelevance to the women of 1958. At one point, we learn Monsúr has been singing 'Soldiers of Cumann na mBan' and praising the help that women are giving to the cause of independence because he mistakenly believes that two of the women in the house, who are in fact rushing to collect coal, are hurrying to help in the fight against the British.[45] For Behan, as for Sean O'Casey, the women of Ireland can ill afford to worry about revolutionary nationalism because they have more pressing and more practical concerns. In Behan's Ireland it matters little whether women were or were not in the Easter Rising, because the rebellion itself has become fictive and distanced from people's everyday lives. Later in 1958, when Behan and Joan Littlewood translated and altered the play to suit the English stage, the portrayal of the Irish struggle for independence was even less sparing, with the introduction of an ironically framed version of the song 'Who fears to speak of Easter Week?' and the morphing of Monsúr into Monsewer.[46]

Denis Johnston's work, *The Scythe and the Sunset*, recalls Act II of O'Casey's play more directly than *An Giall* by using the setting of Dublin in April 1916.

Johnston places an ill-assorted group of characters in a dingy café opposite the GPO during the insurrection, where they listen to a nameless orator reading the proclamation. Rosie the prostitute had distracted from those in a holy mood in *The Plough*, but it is the male doctor, MacCarthy, who provides a sexual distraction from the oratory of *The Scythe*. He boasts of his extra-marital affairs, propositions both of the play's female characters, and articulates his lascivious desires at the climactic moment when the unseen speaker declares Ireland a republic.

In effect, *The Scythe and the Sunset* is a version of O'Casey's 1916 play with the male and female characters reversed. *The Plough and the Stars* features gung-ho men who are fired with enthusiasm for revolutionary nationalism whilst the play's women generally remain humane and sentimental. But in *The Scythe and the Sunset* Johnston's men are the ones who agonise about the consequences of political violence, and are so reticent about firing their guns that, despite making bellicose threats, they repeatedly 'freeze [. . .] into inaction'.[47] The Volunteer O'Callaghan is reduced to paralysis when he discovers a British intelligence agent escaping from the café:

> O'CALLAGHAN　　I'll shoot you [. . .] I warn you. You'll be plugged. I mean it [. . .]
> PALLISER　　　　Why didn't you shoot? No ammunition, I suppose.
> O'CALLAGHAN　　None of . . . your damn . . . business. (p. 131)

In fact, every single man in the play avoids firing a gun. But Johnston's women, on the other hand, grow more aggressive. Roisin slaps the face of a rebel, and at the end of the play she marches out to join Michael Collins in fighting a guerrilla war against the British. The other female character, Emer, encourages the man she loves to fight and die, but she is hardly a passive woman. She is the only character to pull a trigger on the stage, and instead of firing just one bullet she launches an entire machine-gun volley at the British negotiating officer from a position marked as a Red Cross post. Johnston admired *The Plough and the Stars*, but sought to rewrite O'Casey's women in a more combative vein. He wrote that the 'women of Ireland, ever since the Maud Gonne era, have been the most vocal part of its militancy [. . .] when it comes to the point – both my women are killers' (p. 86).

RTÉ and *The Patrick Pearse Motel*

Hugh Leonard, who decided to become a playwright after watching *The Plough and the Stars*, followed Behan and Johnston in writing works that were largely influenced by Sean O'Casey.[48] In Easter week 1966, RTÉ broadcast *Insurrection*, an eight-part mini-series scripted by Leonard, which gives a gripping factual account of the Rising in the format of a documentary news programme.[49] It features 'live' footage of the rebellion, analysis of the fighting 'as it happens', and interviews with the protagonists and observers of the conflict.

The series was well received, but Leonard and his historical advisor, the revisionist scholar Kevin Nowlan, were alarmed that their programme inspired children to play 'Rebels and Brits' where once they had played 'Cowboys and Indians'. After all, RTÉ scheduled *Insurrection* alongside a number of commemoration services, and the series concludes with the ominous question, 'The insurrection is over. Or is it?' Consequently, when the North of Ireland erupted into conflict at the end of the decade, Leonard, like Yeats before him, feared that his drama might have encouraged certain men to fight and die. The executives of RTÉ were similarly apprehensive, and never rebroadcast the series on television.

Yet this fear was somewhat overstated. Leonard was, after all, strongly influenced by *The Plough and the Stars*, and some of his television characters are lifted directly from O'Casey. In *Insurrection* the golfer from Howth mirrors O'Casey's lady from Rathmines, and the combative women who loot Noblett's toffee shop resemble Mrs Gogan. At another point a version of O'Casey's Corporal Stoddart appears in the guise of Leonard's nameless Tommy who laughs at the rebel digging a trench, and shouts, 'Go to it, Paddy, that's the stuff!' Elsewhere, *Insurrection* depicts a comic drunk who, like Fluther, espouses his befuddled support for the insurgents, and the series also shows a woman of the slums who resembles Bessie Burgess in singing 'God Save the King' and mocking the rebel 'bastards'. As a result of O'Casey's influence, *Insurrection* gives a far more nuanced and a far less adulatory portrayal of the uprising than the official celebrations of that anniversary year. Just as O'Casey had shown that there was little to choose between either group of combatants, Leonard humanises a number of British characters and reveals the villainous murderer of Francis Sheehy Skeffington, Captain Bowen Colthurst, to be an Irishman. Although Pearse emerges as a hero when he decides to call for a ceasefire and save civilian lives, his role in directing the fighting is mocked. Connolly is irked by the new president's obsession with rhetoric, and declares, 'If that man [Pearse] decided to move his weight from his left foot to his right, he'd put it in dispatches.' By consistently giving a greater emphasis to the Citizen Army rather than the Volunteers, examining the Rising's effects on the urban poor, and emphasising the terrible carnage wrought by both sides in the conflict, Leonard continued to follow in O'Casey's footsteps. Even if those in the North of Ireland could receive the RTÉ signal in 1966, it is far from clear that this series would have given a ringing endorsement of modern armed republicanism.[50]

However, Hugh Leonard felt that he had offered a sop to violent nationalism, and tried to make amends by writing a bedroom farce based on *The Plough and the Stars*. Set in 1966, and staged at the Olympia Theatre in 1971, *The Patrick Pearse Motel* reacts against the part that Leonard believed he had played in the triumphalist fiftieth-anniversary celebrations, and mocks the reverence of the official ceremonies.[51] *The Patrick Pearse Motel* attacks Pádraic Pearse as being 'full of ou' codology', and repeats Sean O'Casey's sacrilegious connection of Pearse with fornication.[52] In Leonard's play, multiple adulteries are attempted in a motel bearing the rebel leader's name, where, with the rebellion's flag stoutly flying over its roof, the 'Patrick Pearse' provides an opportunity for 'Lust under the Plough and the Stars'.[53]

In *Insurrection* Hugh Leonard had signalled his intention of challenging conventional views about the role of the women. Although official celebrations since 1935 had largely ignored the female rebels, Leonard depicts a number of women throughout the series, and he devotes particular attention to the bravery of Connolly's secretary, to Constance Markievicz, and to Elizabeth O'Farrell, who helped negotiate the ceasefire. In *Insurrection* Connolly urges, 'let us not forget the splendid women who everywhere stood by us', and Pearse insists that the women 'have inspired the Volunteers by their courage to resist to the end. And by their own bravery they have won a sure place in the records of the fight for freedom.'

The Patrick Pearse Motel similarly scorns the ideal of motherhood associated with 1916, but does so in a far more cynical manner. In Leonard's stage play the business company that owns the Pearse motel is called 'Mother Ireland Motels Limited', and so whilst the poor old woman is unlikely to lure young men into fighting for their nation, she is extremely likely to coax randy adulterers into their bedchambers. Leonard also lampoons the celebrated stage version of the nationalist woman by presenting the figure of 'Hoolihan', a senile and feeble drunkard who goes out alone at the end of the play to die in the cold.

Leonard's television drama had been influenced by a number of O'Casey's other themes and characters, but his stage play revives the kind of female sexuality embodied by Rosie Redmond. The main female character of *The Patrick Pearse Motel*, Grainne, leaves her children languishing permanently offstage while she schemes to seduce an old acquaintance. She is married to the man who part-owns the 'Patrick Pearse', and assiduously plots to commit adultery in the motel whilst her husband is away. For Grainne, it is a patriotic duty to fornicate, and she justifies her sexual desires in terms of equality and national liberation: 'I love Ireland. I believe that whatever English women have, we owe it to our pride as a nation to let Irish women have some of it, too.'[54] *The Patrick Pearse Motel* thus offers a comic reappraisal of the patriotic Irish motherhood that Fianna Fáil promoted in their recreations of the uprising; and shows a woman who, like Rosie Redmond, is perfectly happy to express her need for sex.

The non-stop O'Casey show

By the later decades of the twentieth century O'Casey had come to dominate the dramatic memory of 1916 to such an extent that writers began to represent him directly in performance. In the Liberty Hall in 1975 Margaretta D'Arcy and John Arden staged an enormous twenty-six-hour cycle play, *The Non-Stop Connolly Show*, in an effort to do what O'Casey most certainly did not want to do: make a hero of James Connolly and contradict those who argued that the Easter Rising was unnecessary.[55] D'Arcy and Arden further differentiated their work from O'Casey's play by giving a complete portrait of the struggles of the era rather than limiting their scope to Ireland in 1916, and by using an assortment of dramatic techniques taken from Hindu mystery plays, Brechtian theory, and agit-prop productions. Yet even here D'Arcy and Arden paid tribute to *The*

Plough and the Stars and repeatedly invoked parts of O'Casey's drama. In 1975 the Liberty Hall audience saw Pearse delivering the familiar oratory that O'Casey had used in his play, and also watched this rhetoric again being undercut as Connolly criticised 'too much poetry'.[56] Just as if they had been seeing *The Plough and the Stars*, the audience members watched as *The Non-Stop Connolly Show* repeatedly returned to the tenements of Dublin, abjured the sacrificial woman, and made numerous jokes about sex, 'How's it off for cunt, Paddy, in the city of Cork? [. . .] for a stone of potatoes they'd sell ye the hole in the arse of a pig and pretend it's their ain sister'.[57] A few years earlier Behan had referred to O'Casey by name in *An Giall*, but Arden and D'Arcy went one step further, bringing a depiction of O'Casey himself onto the stage, where they showed him spouting the socialist sentiments of The Covey and carrying a flag depicting the plough and the stars.[58]

Far away from the left-wing ideology of D'Arcy and Arden's show was the ABC television series, *Young Indiana Jones*, which George Lucas created in the early 1990s as an offshoot from his internationally profitable film franchise. And yet here again O'Casey became surprisingly prominent. In 1992 ABC broadcast an episode in which Indy, on his way to fight for the Allies in World War I, arrives in Dublin on the eve of the Rising.[59] In Lucas's version of Easter week the ideas of *The Plough and the Stars* are again central; with Indy befriending Sean O'Casey, who refuses to help the rebels and finds his early writing rejected by Yeats. Pearse is once more seen delivering his rhetoric to cynics ('They'll not be wanting stamps' observes one onlooker) and the traditional sacrificial woman is rejected when O'Casey vows to write plays that are nothing like 'bloody *Cathleen ni Houlihan* [. . .] I want to write plays that stink of life, real life'. The Poor Old Woman is even more clearly discarded in the second half of the episode, when Indy moves from supporting the rebels in Dublin to sympathising with female emancipation in London; where Pearse's wartime struggle, his uniform, and his crumpled proclamation are mirrored by a group of English suffragettes; as if the nationalist and women's causes were two sides of the one coin.

After its American television premier, *Young Indiana Jones* was subsequently sold to broadcasting companies around the globe, whilst *The Non-Stop Connolly Show* has hardly ever been performed, and was even jokily referred to in 1975 as 'the cheapest doss in Dublin'.[60] But by the final decades of the twentieth century O'Casey's views about 1916 had grown dominant enough to appear in both productions, and it was now the turn of those with more conservative opinions than him to feel under threat. In 1980 the Abbey Theatre refused to stage Criostoir O'Flynn's *A Man Called Pearse*, a theatrical pageant that emphasises the stable and orthodox family life enjoyed in the Pearse household. The Abbey directors had paid an advance on royalties, and an outraged O'Flynn seethed at their change of heart as a signal of 'official political disapproval of the totality of Pearse as a theatrical topic'.[61] But the theatre's directors were unmoved by his protests: Ireland was turning its back on the economic and social policies of de Valera, and the Irish stage no longer felt the need to associate the Easter Rising with heterosexuality, family life, and Catholicism.

Out of the Closet

Instead, a familiar homosexual character began to enjoy the limelight. In 1935 de Valera had tried to suppress the aspects of Casement that he found distasteful, but by the 1970s writers began to celebrate Casement's homosexuality. At the Abbey Theatre in 1972 Richard Stockton's *The Prisoner of the Crown* showed Casement's prosecutor declaring:

> What has happened, I say, to *pervert* that man's character from his earlier high promise, I cannot tell you. What it was that *seduced* his private energies, causing them to *degenerate* from lofty principle to *vulgar practice*, I may not say. It is like some *grotesquely inverted fairy-tale* the way this prisoner's affections have *descended* to the *basest*. (Stockton's emphasis)[62]

Despite re-inscribing the rumour in this way, Stockton's play concluded that Casement was probably not gay, but during the following year the BBC broadcast a radio play by David Rudkin, *Cries from Casement as his Bones are Brought to Dublin*, in which the hero admits explicitly to an assortment of homosexual acts. Rudkin's play celebrates Casement's brilliance and bravery but also gives graphic descriptions of his gay desires: 'Indian lad, black thighs astride, his proud yard up – black as the Earl of Hell's waistcoat, hard as iron, thick as a wrist: oh, shovel thon intill me deep, deep.'[63]

The 1980s saw the publication of Frank McGuinness's *Innocence*, and the Abbey Theatre's productions of Brian Friel's *The Gentle Island* and Thomas Kilroy's *The Death and Resurrection of Mr Roche*, which still showed homoeroticism inevitably leading to death, disfigurement, and disempowerment.[64] But by the 1990s Irish stage companies like 'Muted Cupid', 'Room B', and 'Out-to Play' targeted gay and lesbian audiences. The Republic liberalised its laws on sexuality, and in 1993 abolished anti-homosexual legislation in a move initiated by David Norris's earlier victory in the European Court of Human Rights. In the 1990s, in the more sexually open Ireland that came in the wake of Sinéad O'Connor's controversial protest against sexual abuse and Annie Murphy's revelation that she had borne the child of Bishop Eamonn Casey, popular culture became comfortable and familiar with the long-suppressed image of the gay Irish male. Television viewers in Britain and Ireland were bombarded with the flamboyant Irish camp of figures like comedian Graham Norton, children's presenter Brian Dowling, or pop star Stephen Gately. In 2002 Siobhán Kilfeather observed that since the early 1990s 'an in-your-face gay aesthetic has emerged' that sets a high value on 'controversial ways of living, ways of writing and modes of dispute'.[65]

At the start of the new millennium, the homosexual Roger Casement achieved iconic status, and Irish writers were eager to raise the issue of homosexual patriotism. In 2001 Jamie O'Neill published his novel *At Swim Two Boys*, a gay love story about Easter 1916 in which 'rising' is often an obscene pun, and which depicts one character naïvely insisting that 'Sir Roger' must be referred to by the name of 'Casement', because the revolutionary 'has never liked to be Sir

Rogered'.[66] The ironic effect of this comment relies on a clash between the speaker's innocence and the knowingness of a reader in the early twenty-first century, when Casement's homosexuality was so widely accepted that it provided a variety of organisations with a valuable marketing tool. In early 2002 Picador books promoted Colm Tóibín's new book, *Love in A Dark Time: Gay Lives from Wilde to Almodóvar*, by allowing the *Irish Times* to print an extract about Casement under the enticing headline, 'Sex, Lies and the Black Diaries'.[67] Several months later, London's National Portrait Gallery hung Casement's long secreted picture alongside Churchill, Lloyd George, and King George V, and publicised the rebel's prominent new position in the press.[68] In 1999 and 2000 even Tony Blair and Bertie Ahern were publicly seen to exchange letters about Casement.[69]

Suddenly the homosexual patriot was a saleable 'brand', and organisations were falling over themselves to share in his success. In spring 2002 the BBC launched their digital television channel, BBC 4, and one of their opening programmes was about Casement.[70] His gaunt, bearded image stared out from the new channel's glossy advertising literature and was also repeatedly broadcast on BBC 4 as part of a visual montage between scheduled programmes. Within hours of the BBC programme RTÉ rushed to televise half of a two-part documentary, *The Ghost of Roger Casement*, at a popular evening viewing time.[71] Britain and Ireland's national television channels had ploughed money into a handwriting analysis carried out by a London expert, and both documentaries breathlessly revealed the results: that Casement was indeed the author of overtly homosexual reminiscences. The two broadcasters were simultaneously associating themselves with the image of the 1916 rebel whose gay identity was newly re-established, and his use as a promotional tool was particularly valued by the BBC management, who wanted the public to subscribe to a new and unfamiliar channel.

The homosexuality of Dublin's rebellion was also shown on the big screen. Six decades after de Valera had attempted to suppress Casement's appearance on film, the producers of a lavish and expensive Hollywood movie hinted at the gay identity of the 1916 rebels, although Casement himself remained perennially concealed. Neil Jordan's 1997 film *Michael Collins* presents its audience with a Girardian triangle, as Michael Collins and Harry Boland compete over Kitty Kiernan. Collins and Boland share an attachment that is just as strong as that linking either of them to Kiernan, and this is made obvious when the two men are parted by the malicious intervention of de Valera, who is stung by Collins's affection for Boland:

DE VALERA   What's so special about Harry?
COLLINS   I know my men, and I can't do it without him.
DE VALERA   Do what?
COLLINS   I can't run a war without Harry Boland.
DE VALERA   You could run it without me.[72]

Jordan's adulatory biopic demonstrated that by the 1990s hints about the homosexuality of patriots could do little to diminish the rebellion's heroism, and the film is far from anti-nationalist. *Michael Collins* consistently sides with the Irish revolutionaries, portrays every single British character as baleful, and won high praise from the Sinn Féin organ *An Phoblacht* ('The Republic') upon its release.[73]

Irish women's writing and traditions

Homosexuals were not the only marginalised group to reap the benefits of increasingly liberal attitudes in Ireland. Towards the end of the twentieth century there was a change in views of women's sexuality, reproduction, and place within the family. From 1979 contraception became more accessible, divorce was legalised, and the Irish populace received the right to information about abortion. When Ireland had celebrated the fiftieth anniversary of the Rising only five per cent of married women were in the workforce, but at the end of the century the figure had risen to forty per cent.[74]

By the 1980s and 1990s the arguments between revisionists and their opponents had been contested many times, with scholars often entrenched in intractable oppositions and alliances. As Irish academics struggled to escape the confines of these tired historiographical debates they began to re-evaluate and recover women's words and experience.[75] In particular, Margaret MacCurtain of University College Dublin worked to recover women's role in Irish history, and, with Mary Cullen, established the Irish Association for Research in Women's History. Ailbhe Smyth and Eilis Ní Dhuibhne compiled anthologies of Irish women's poetry during the 1980s and 1990s, and most famously, when Seamus Deane collated the *Field Day Anthology* of 1991 he faced an outcry from feminists who discovered that the publication ignored their concerns.[76] During the following eleven years *Field Day* made its recompense by coordinating the printing of a further two enormous volumes entirely dedicated to 'Irish Women's Writing and Traditions'.[77]

The changed atmosphere of Irish studies in the 1980s and 1990s fostered a rediscovery of women's experience of the Rising. In 1983 Margaret Ward published a study emphasising the place of women in the Irish revolution, *Unmanageable Revolutionaries: Women and Irish Nationalism*, and Ruth Taillon followed in 1996 with *When History was Made: The Women of 1916*. Taillon used a picture of Molly Childers and Mary Spring-Rice importing armaments in 1914 as the frontispiece to her study, and the image of the gun-toting female rebel preponderated on Irish bookshelves during the 1990s. The portrait of Constance Markievicz cradling her Mauser rifle appeared on the front covers of Marjorie Howes's *Yeats's Nations*, W.J. McCormack's *Ferocious Humanism*, and the paperback reprint of Anne Marreco's *The Rebel Countess*.[78] By the end of the century, Sinn Féin, the organisation that consistently adopted the rhetoric of 1916 during the Troubles, had introduced positive discrimination to ensure that women served on its executive.

Creative accounts of 1916 also contradicted the amnesia of Fianna Fáil's earlier commemorations. Roddy Doyle's bestselling 1999 novel, *A Star Called*

Henry, portrays the women of 1916 intrepidly cycling around Dublin to fetch communiqués, firing guns 'as well as any man', and being exasperated by the asinine derision they suffer at the hands of sexist male commanders.[79] One woman complains, 'They [the men] never wanted us there in the first place. All we were good for was cooking stew and sewing haversacks. I'm a better shot than the lot of them.'[80]

Meanwhile, Irish dramatists were eager to reinstate women at the heart of 1916. Ronan Bennett depicts the Easter uprising in the first episode of a four-part television drama shown on RTÉ and the BBC in 2001, *Rebel Heart*.[81] Although Bennett's male lead, Ernie Coyne, later becomes one of Ireland's most dependable guerrilla fighters, he is initially uncertain and befuddled. By contrast, the main female character, Ita Feeney, is a Belfast republican who is knowing, courageous, and militarily important from the outset. She and her friend Ursula are first seen, like Markievicz, fighting on St Stephen's Green during the insurrection. Ita is a capable markswoman, and is able to demolish British machine-gun positions with a single shot. She is also demonstrably braver than the men with whom she fights. She asks to conduct missions that her commander describes as 'suicide', and clambers onto the exposed roofs of Dublin where she is seriously wounded. She also possesses greater military nous than her male colleagues when she declares, 'I told you, Hugh, this was a terrible mistake. Why try to take the Green when we couldn't take the buildings 'round it?' In this televised version of the Easter Rising, Bennett encourages his viewers to consider that a rebellion commanded by women may well have been organised with more commonsense.

At the end of the twentieth century, organisations such as Eleanor Methven's 'Charabanc' theatre company signalled that women had found their own voice on the Irish stage, and dramatists simultaneously depicted the rebellious women of 1916 rather than just the quiescent mothers idolised in 1935.[82] Tom Murphy's play *The Patriot Game* premiered at the Peacock Theatre in 1991, as an antidote to Charles Haughey's parsimonious Easter ceremony, but Murphy did not revert to the way that the nation builders of 1935 had envisaged women. *The Patriot Game* echoes Robert O'Donoghue's lost play, *The Witness*, which was staged for a delighted audience in Cork's Father Mathew Hall in 1966.[83] O'Donoghue's work apparently revolved around a man who is initially scathing about the rebellion, but who renounces his hostility after watching the nobility with which it is conducted, and the play eventually concluded with a Yeatsian role call of the rebel names. Murphy's piece unconsciously repeats O'Donoghue's story, but with one crucial difference: this time the central witness is a woman. Furthermore, in *The Patriot Game* it is a female rebel who bears the most hatred for her enemies, screeching, 'Rotten English! – Sassanach! – Dirty rotten English Protestants!', and Murphy's original production followed the gender-bending example of plays such as Caryl Churchill's *Cloud Nine* by giving the roles of Plunkett, MacDermott, Ceannt, and MacDonagh to female actors.[84] When Murphy's play transferred to the Tramway Theatre in Glasgow a woman also took the part of Tom Clarke.

Like so many other dramatists, Murphy took his cue from Sean O'Casey but avoided any slavish adherence to the political message of *The Plough and the Stars*. Whereas in O'Casey's play Pádraic Pearse the orator was a peripheral figure, in *The Patriot Game* he delivers his speeches from the middle of the stage. If O'Casey had allowed Pearse to speak only from the gory ending of the panegyric to O'Donovan Rossa, then, by contrast, Murphy was intent on presenting a version of Pearse who speaks extensively from this graveside oration. Murphy felt that *The Plough and the Stars* gave undue attention to Pearse's bloodlust, and wanted to show that this formed only a part of a more reasoned political philosophy.

Yet, although Murphy distanced his play from O'Casey's denigration of the rebels, *The Patriot Game* does follow *The Plough and the Stars* in abjuring syco-phantic praise for Pádraic Pearse's mother. Murphy's play directs Margaret Pearse to deliver Pádraic Pearse's poem 'The Mother' according to the actor's own interpretation of whether to celebrate or disavow Pádraic Pearse's views, showing that the Irish mother does not necessarily and unreservedly push her sons to die for Ireland.

In his 1985 play *Observe the Sons of Ulster Marching Towards the Somme*, Frank McGuinness went even further than Murphy in dismantling the idea of Margaret Pearse as a passive and suffering mother. McGuinness's character McIl-waine, an Ulster Protestant at the Somme, asks:

> Did you hear about this boy Pearse? The boy who took over a post office because he was short of a few stamps [. . .] He took over this big post office in Dublin, kicks all the wee girls serving behind the big counter out on to the streets. When the place is empty, him and his merry men all carrying wooden rifles land outside on the street. Your man reads the proclamation of an Irish republic. The Irish couldn't spell republic, let alone proclaim it. Then he's caught, him and all hands in gaol. He starts to cry, saying he has a widowed mother and he had led the only other brother astray. Anyway, he didn't plan to take over this post office. He walked in to post a letter and got carried away and thought it was Christmas. Nobody believes him. They're leading him out to be shot. He's supposed to see the widowed ma in the crowd. He looks at her and says, pray for me, mother. The ma looks back at him, looks at the Tommy, he's guarding Pearse, the old one grabs the Tommy's rifle. She shoots Pearse herself. She turns to the Tommy and she says, 'That'll learn him, the cheeky pup. Going about robbing post offices. Honest to God, I'm affronted.[85]

In *Observe the Sons of Ulster*, Frank McGuinness, like so many playwrights before him, had written a dramatic account of the Easter rebellion that recalled the earlier work of the Abbey Theatre. Nearly sixty years after O'Casey had caused the audience to riot, Margaret Pearse's motherhood was still being re-examined and re-mythologised by a mesmerised Irish stage. And when the Abbey celebrated its centenary with a troubled season of plays in 2004, the Easter women and words of *The Plough and the Stars* reappeared in Colm Tóibín's *Beauty in a Broken Place*, which tells the story of the disturbances of

1926 and shows how O'Casey's portrayal of the sacrificial woman and the prostitute affected the Abbey audiences. Tóibín's play focuses on the key role played by Dublin's women in producing, acting, and objecting to *The Plough and the Stars*, with Hanna Sheehy Skeffington and Lady Gregory emerging as the heroes of the hour, united by the grief of having recently lost either a husband or a son. On hearing about the theatre riot, Tóibín's Lady Gregory declares:

> We are arguing against grief, against the lines that run between hurt and pride. These women want their men back. Those who have given up wanting them by day want them more fiercely when night falls. They wake in the night, going over and over how the news came and how it might have been otherwise; they long for more innocent times, and they cannot admit they have such longings, for the child back in their arms, or the young man's first embrace or his return to them. They must be proud instead of hurt.[86]

In this play, Tóibín restores the humanity of the women who protested against *The Plough and the Stars*, reminding his 2004 audience that at the heart of the notorious riot was a group of families who were struggling to cope with the pain of bereavement and loss.

From spring insurrections to Ann Summers

The dramatisations of the Easter rebellion that were staged in the first twenty years after 1916 have echoed throughout the subsequent annals of Irish literary history. Both the Abbey Theatre in its heyday and de Valera's early administration have had a lasting effect upon how the Irish stage remembers the uprising; and later actors, writers, and producers have engaged with the ideas and dramatic forms explored by W.B. Yeats, Fianna Fáil, and, overwhelmingly, Sean O'Casey, even when wishing to refute the political messages that these performances had conveyed. Indeed, the skirmishes between the early dramatisers still exert an almost inescapable force upon modern playwrights, particularly when combined with Ireland's recent tastes and mores. Tom MacIntyre recounts that when he began writing a play about Michael Collins in the mid-1990s, people instantly, and correctly, anticipated that his work would revolve around the rebel's sex life.[87] It would, in fact, be refreshing to see a dramatic production that focused instead on some of the other unexplored aspects of the rebellion – such as the humanitarian work of Casement, the terminal illness of Plunkett, or the educational ideas of Pearse – and yet since 1935 dramaturges dealing with the Easter Rising have often preferred to focus their attention instead upon debates about sex, gender, and reproduction. The other histories of 1916 remain largely untold, as each subsequent generation uses the ideas of the 1920s and 1930s in order to inspire new versions of the insurrection that suit their current ideological needs. It may be that the appearance of homosexuals and women in recent depictions of the rebellion shows only that one form of political correctness has superseded another, telling us more about our contemporary preoccupations and attitudes rather than bringing us any closer to the 'truth' about the Rising.

The confrontations between Yeats's theatre and de Valera's government can even be discerned in the cultural geography of modern-day Dublin. The stern portico of the GPO still looms large over O'Connell Street, but in recent years it has been surrounded by an assortment of constructions with more bawdy purposes and nicknames. At the end of September 1999, the management of the British-based Ann Summers chain of sex shops decided to open a branch of their store opposite the GPO and sell crotchless knickers and sex toys a few metres from where Pearse had proclaimed the Irish Republic. Nearby, a bronze statue of Anna Livia was unveiled to mark Dublin's millennium in 1988, and became commonly known as the 'Floozy in the Jacuzzi' and the 'Whore in the Shower'. More recently, to commemorate the millennium, Bertie Ahern's administration erected an enormous spire in O'Connell Street, in the place where the statue of Nelson had stood until the IRA blew it up in 1966. When the new monument was unveiled in the spring of 2003 it did not take Dubliners long to christen it with an unofficial name. Outside the pock-marked facia of the GPO it is now possible for tourists to locate the 'Stiffy by the Liffey'. But some people have objected to these lewd developments. The Dublin corporation first attempted to close the Ann Summers shop and then tried to disguise it from view by planting a row of trees; the floozy was hauled away in 2001; and the National Graves Association appealed that the spire should be christened with a name to 'honour Padraic Pearse'.[88] Every year, to this day, Easter weekend is marked by a succession of well-attended, solemn processions and speeches outside the GPO, where Sinn Féin celebrates the revolutionaries in the same way that the young Fianna Fáil party did. Many years after they began, the ideas of Éamon de Valera's party are still locked in conflict with those of Yeats's Abbey Theatre, and fittingly clash with one another not only in Ireland's playhouses, but also on the tarmac and the paving stones of Dublin.

Notes

Introduction

1   W.B. Yeats, 'Cathleen Ní Houlihan', *The Collected Works of W.B. Yeats: Volume II: The Plays*, ed. by David R. Clark and Rosalind E. Clark, part of 14 vol. collected works (Houndmills: Palgrave, 2001), II, 83–93 (p. 93).

2   Alan Simpson, 'O'Casey and the East Wall Area in Dublin', *Irish University Review*, 10:1 (1980), 41–51 (p. 49).

3   Ó Crualaoich, 'Responding to the Rising', in *Revising the Rising*, ed. by Máirín Ní Dhonnchadha and Theo Dorgan (Derry: Field Day, 1991), pp. 50–70 (p. 50).

4   Benjamin, 'Unpacking My Library: A Talk about Book Collecting', in *Illuminations*, ed. by Hannah Arendt, trans. by Harry Zorn (London: Pimlico, 1999), pp. 61–9 (p. 63).

5   Ní Dhonnchadha and Dorgan, p. ix.

6   Bobby Ballagh, '1916 – Goodbye to All That?', *Irish Reporter*, 2 (1991), 6–8 (p. 7).

7   Declan Gorman, 'Prejudice on Parade', *Irish Reporter*, 2 (1991), 9–11 (p. 9).

8   Waters, 'Giving the Memory of 1916 more than a Ritual Nod', *Irish Times*, 17 May 1994, p. 12.

9   Barnes, 'Vision and Revision', in *The Page and the Stage: The Plough and the Stars*, ed. by Martin Drury (Dublin: Abbey Theatre, 2003), pp. 47–9 (p. 49).

10   O'Brien, *Ancestral Voices: Religion and Nationalism in Ireland* (Chicago: University of Chicago Press, 1995), p. 116, p. 171.

11   Ní Dhonnchadha and Dorgan, p. ix.

12   Martin, 'Eoin MacNeill on the 1916 Rising', *Irish Historical Studies*, 12:47 (1961), 226–71. Wall, 'The Background to the Rising, from 1914 until the Issue of the Countermanding Order on Easter Saturday, 1916/The Plan and the Countermand: the Country and Dublin', in *The Making of 1916: Studies in the History of the Rising*, ed. by Kevin B. Nowlan (Dublin: Stationery Office, 1969), pp. 157–251.

13   Conor Cruise O'Brien, 'The Embers of Easter 1916–1966', in *1916: The Easter Rising*, ed. by O. Dudley Edwards and Fergus Pyle (Dublin: MacGibbon and Kee, 1968), pp. 223–40.

14   Bew, 'The Easter Rising: Lost Leader and Lost Opportunities', *The Irish Review*, 11 (1991/2), 9–13 (p. 13).

15   Esslin, *An Anatomy of Drama* (London: Temple Smith, 1978), p. 101.

16   Williams, *The Long Revolution* (London: Chatto and Windus, 1961), p. 246.

17   See for example Seamus Deane, *Strange Country* (Oxford: Clarendon Press, 1997); and David Lloyd, *Ireland After History* (Cork: Cork University Press, 1999).

18   G.B. Shaw, *The Matter With Ireland*, ed. by Dan H. Laurence and David H. Greene, 2nd edn (Florida: University Press of Florida, 2001), p. 125.

19   Gregory, *Seventy Years: Being the Autobiography of Lady Gregory* (Gerrards Cross: Colin Smythe, 1974), p. 547.

20   *Poems of the Irish Revolutionary Brotherhood*, ed. by Padraic Colum and Edward J. O'Brien, rev. edn (Boston: Small, Maynard & Co., 1916), p. xxxv.

21   Desmond Rushe, 'The Abbey Presents Works on the Rising', *Irish Independent*, 12 April 1966, p. 4.

22   Johnston, *The Dramatic Works of Denis Johnston*, 2 vols (Gerrards Cross: Colin Smythe, 1977), I, 85–6.

23   *The Modern Irish Drama: A Documentary History*, ed. by Robert Hogan, James Kilroy, Richard Burnham, and Daniel P. Poteet, 6 vols (Dublin: Dolmen, 1975–1984 and Gerrards Cross: Colin Smythe, 1992). Welch, *The Abbey Theatre, 1899–1999: Form and Pressure* (Oxford: Oxford University Press, 1999). Herr, *For the Land They Loved: Irish Political Melodramas, 1890–1925* (Syracuse: Syracuse University Press, 1991). Watt, *Joyce, O'Casey, and the Irish Popular Theater* (Syracuse: Syracuse University Press, 1991).

24   Kiberd, *Inventing Ireland: The Literature of the Modern Nation* (London: Vintage, 1996).

25   McCormack, *Fool of the Family: A Life of J.M. Synge* (London: Weidenfeld and Nicolson, 2000). Foster, *W.B. Yeats: A Life: I, The Apprentice Mage* (Oxford: Oxford University Press, 1997). Foster, *W.B. Yeats: A Life: II, The Arch-Poet* (Oxford: Oxford University Press, 2003).

26   Murray, *Twentieth-Century Irish Drama: Mirror up to Nation* (Manchester: Manchester University Press, 1997). Grene, *The Politics of Irish Drama: Plays in Context from Boucicault to Friel* (Cambridge: Cambridge University Press, 1999). Pilkington, *Theatre and the State in Twentieth-Century Ireland: Cultivating the People* (London: Routledge, 2001). Morash, *A History of the Irish Theatre 1601–2000* (Cambridge: Cambridge University Press, 2002). Levitas, *The Theatre of Nation: Irish Drama and Cultural Nationalism 1890–1916* (Oxford: Clarendon Press, 2002).

27   D. George Boyce, '1916, Interpreting the Rising', in *The Making of Modern Irish History: Revisionism and the Revisionist Controversy*, ed. by D. George Boyce and Alan O'Day (London: Routledge, 1996), pp. 163–87 (p. 172).

28   Ward, *Unmanageable Revolutionaries: Women and Irish Nationalism* (London: Pluto, 1995). Taillon, *When History was Made: The Women of 1916* (Belfast: Beyond the Pale, 1996).

29   Dudgeon emphasises the genuine nature of Roger Casement's homosexuality in *Roger Casement: the Black Diaries: With a Study of His Background, Sexuality and Irish Political Life* (Belfast: Belfast Press, 2002); whilst Susan Cannon Harris discusses the same-sex erotic desires that motivated Pádraic Pearse's nationalism in *Gender and Modern Irish Drama* (Bloomington: Indiana University Press, 2002), pp. 123–66.

30   Nandy, *The Intimate Enemy: Loss and Recovery of Self Under Colonialism* (Delhi: Oxford University Press, 1988), pp. 1–18.

31   Arnold is quoted by Elizabeth Butler Cullingford, *Ireland's Others: Gender and Ethnicity in Irish Literature and Popular Culture* (Cork: Cork University Press, 2001), p. 15. Thatcher is quoted by David Beresford, *Ten Men Dead: The Story of the 1981 Hunger Strike* (London: Grafton, 1987), p. 236, p. 275.

32   See Marjorie Howes, *Yeats's Nations: Gender, Class and Irishness* (Cambridge: Cambridge University Press, 1996), p. 16.

33   Particularly influential feminist scholarship came with the founding of the *Irish Journal of Feminist Studies* in 1996, and *The Field Day Anthology of Irish Writing: Irish Women's Writing and Traditions*, ed. by Angela Bourke, Siobhán Kilfeather, Maria Luddy, Margaret Mac Curtain, Gerardine Meaney, Máirín Ní Dhonnchadha, Mary O'Dowd, and Clair Wills, 2 vols (Cork: Cork University Press, 2002).

34   Susan Cannon Harris, 'Performance, Sexual Difference, and National Identity in the Irish Plays of Frank McGuinness', *Genders*, 28 (1998): <http://www.genders.org/g28/g28_watchyourself.html> [accessed 12 December 2002]. *Sex, Nation and Dissent in Irish Writing*, ed. by Walshe (Cork: Cork University Press, 1997), pp. 1–15 and pp. 150–69.

35   For some unsubstantiated gossip about Pearse see W.J. McCormack, *Roger Casement in Death: Or Haunting the Free State* (Dublin: University College Dublin Press, 2002), p. 8; for gossip about Casement see Chapter 5 of this book; for gossip about de Valera see Tim Pat Coogan, *De Valera: Long Fellow, Long Shadow* (London: Hutchinson, 1993), p. 150; and for gossip about Collins see Susan Cannon Harris, 'Performance, Sexual Difference,

and National Identity' (para. 1 of 53) or Diarmaid Ferriter, *The Transformation of Ireland 1900–2000* (London: Profile, 2004), p. 224.

36 McDiarmid, 'The Posthumous Life of Roger Casement', in *Gender and Sexuality in Modern Ireland*, ed. by Anthony Bradley and Maryann Gialanella Valiulis (Amherst: University of Massachusetts Press, 1997), pp. 127–58 (p. 129). Gibbons, 'The Camel in the Koran: Rumour in Irish Politics', *Irish Reporter*, 5 (1992), 12–15 (p. 14).

37 Coogan, 'The Exile', in *The World of Sean O'Casey*, ed. by Sean McCann (London: Four Square, 1966), pp. 106–28 (p. 115). Said, *Yeats and Decolonization* (Derry: Field Day, 1988).

38 Kiberd, *Inventing Ireland*, p. 224.

39 This early work is reproduced by Roger McHugh, '"Always Complainin'": The Politics of Young Sean', *Irish University Review*, 10:1 (1980), 91–7 (p. 92).

40 O'Casey, *The Complete Plays of Sean O'Casey*, 5 vols (London: Macmillan, 1984), I, 255.

41 In his original Field Day pamphlet Said claimed Yeats's work remained an 'achievement in decolonisation', but in the revised essay that appears in *Culture and Imperialism* he asserts only that Yeats's poetry and plays were an 'achievement in cultural decolonisation'. Said, *Yeats and Decolonization*, p. 24, and *Culture and Imperialism* (London: Chatto and Windus, 1993), p. 288.

42 Corkery, *Synge and Anglo-Irish Literature* (Cork: Mercier, 1966), p. 13.

43 Pilkington, pp. 1–5.

44 Yeats, *The Letters of W.B. Yeats*, ed. by Allan Wade (London: Hart–Davis, 1954), p. 295.

45 Thompson, *The Imagination of an Insurrection: Dublin, Easter 1916: A Study of an Ideological Movement*, 2nd edn (West Stockbridge: Lindisfarne Press, 1982), p. 171.

46 The letter is rendered in its corrected form in Yeats, *The Collected Letters of W.B. Yeats: Volume Two, 1896–1900*, ed. by Warwick Gould, John Kelly, and Deirdre Toomey (Oxford: Clarendon Press, 1997), p. 176.

47 In 1916 the Dublin rebellion failed to inspire the countrywide revolt that its leaders hoped for, and little rebel activity occurred outside the capital.

48 Trotter, *Ireland's National Theaters* (Syracuse: Syracuse University Press, 2001), p. 2.

49 Kowsan, *Littérature et spectacle*, rev. edn (Paris: Mouton, 1975).

50 Schechner, 'Approaches to Theory/Criticism', *The Drama Review*, 10:4 (1966), 20–53 (p. 27). Pfister, *The Theory and Analysis of Drama*, trans. by John Halliday (Cambridge: Cambridge University Press, 1988), p. 11.

51 For an eloquent discussion of various theoretical approaches to performance see Marvin Carlson, *Performance: A Critical Introduction* (London: Routledge, 1996).

52 Norris, 'Homosexual People and the Christian Churches in Ireland: A Minority and its Oppressors', *Crane Bag*, 5:1 (1981), 31–7 (p. 31).

53 Trimble, *The Easter Rebellion of 1916* (Lurgan: Ulster Society, 1992), pp. 33–4.

54 P.H. Pearse, *The Story of a Success: Being a Record of St. Enda's College, September, 1908, to Easter, 1916*, ed. by Desmond Ryan (Dublin: Maunsel, 1917). Ruth Dudley Edwards, *Patrick Pearse: The Triumph of Failure* (London: Gollancz, 1977).

55 For instance, the editors of the original 1991 volumes of *The Field Day Anthology of Irish Writing* glossed Pearse and Casement almost exclusively in terms of nationalist activities, mentioning homosexuality only as a British slander against Casement. But the following two volumes, published under different editors in 2002, repeatedly mention Pearse and Casement primarily in terms of homosexual habits and desires. Compare, for example, the descriptions found in *The Field Day Anthology*, ed. by Seamus Deane, Andrew Carpenter, and Jonathan Williams, 3 vols (London: Faber, 1991), II, 295–6, 369, and 824, with *The Field Day Anthology: Irish Women's Writing and Traditions*, IV, 759, 891, and 1041.

1. The Rebellion of 1916

1 Taken from the unpublished journal of Charles Robert Ashbee, November 1916. King's College Cambridge, Ashbee Journals, fols 1042.140, 1045.141. Ashbee was an English

architect and socialist who regularly met in Dublin with George Russell and James Stephens in the months after the Rising.

2   Yeats, 'Easter 1916', *Collected Works of W.B. Yeats: Volume 1: The Poems*, ed. by Richard J. Finneran, part of 14 vol. collected works, rev. edn (Houndmills: Macmillan, 1991), I, 181.

3   Diana Norman, *Terrible Beauty: A Life of Constance Markievicz 1868–1927* (London: Hodder and Stoughton, 1987), p. 15.

4   Morash, p. 152.

5   Michael Foy and Brian Barton, *The Easter Rising* (Phoenix Mill: Sutton, 1999), p. 145.

6   Margaret Mary Pearse, 'Patrick and Willie Pearse', *Capuchin Annual* (1943), 86–8 (p. 87).

7   The boys performed Standish O'Grady's *The Coming of Fionn* and Douglas Hyde's *An Naomh ar Iarraidh* ('The Lost Saint').

8   Quoted by Dudley Edwards, p. 123.

9   I am grateful to Declan Kiberd for this information about his great-uncle.

10 This letter came from Mabel FitzGerald, the mother of future Taoiseach Garret FitzGerald. BL, G.B. Shaw Papers, Letter of 23 May 1916 to Shaw from Mabel FitzGerald, Add.50,517, fols 396–9 (fol. 398).

11 NLI, Ernán de Blaghd Papers, Letter of 22 August 1916 from Helena Molony, MS 20,702.

12 Yeats, 'Three Songs to the One Burden', *Collected Works*, rev. edn, I, 330.

13 Bourke, 'For the Land She Loved', in Herr, pp. 311–59 (p. 339).

14 This story was originally recorded by MacBride's confessor on 5 May 1916, six months after Bourke's play. *Last Words*, ed. by Piaras F. Mac Lochlainn (Dublin: Stationery Office, 1990), p. 103.

15 Gregory, *Seventy Years*, p. 549.

16 Sheehy Skeffington, '"Under Which Flag?": James Connolly's Patriotic Play', *The Workers' Republic*, 6 April 1916, p. 6.

17 De Rosa, *Rebels: The Irish Rising of 1916* (New York: Fawcett Columbine, 1990), p. 278.

18 Yeats, 'Man and the Echo', *Collected Works*, rev. edn, I, 345.

19 *Roscommon Herald* quoted by J.J. Lee, *Ireland 1912–1985: Politics and Society* (Cambridge: Cambridge University Press, 1989), p. 35. J.P. Gaynor, 'A.O.H. and Rebellion: A Reply to Critics of Our Organisation', *Hibernian Journal*, 6:3 (1916), 271.

20 See Coogan, *Michael Collins: A Biography* (London: Hutchinson, 1990), p. 54.

21 Misha Glenny, *The Balkans 1804–1999: Nationalism, War and the Great Powers* (London: Granta, 2000), pp. 105–6.

22 Anthony Arblaster, *Viva la Libertà!: Politics in Opera* (London: Verso, 1992), p. 78, p. 49.

23 Yeats, *Uncollected Prose*, ed. by John P. Frayne and Colton Johnson, 2 vols (New York: Macmillan, 1975), II, 141.

24 Levitas, pp. 223–4. The theatre staged plays that emphasise realism and pragmatism over ideological zeal, such as Eimar O'Duffy's *Phoenix on the Roof* and *The Walls of Athens*, but also produced Pearse's play, *The Master*, which describes the triumph of an isolated visionary.

25 Ward, *Unmanageable Revolutionaries*, pp. 106–7.

26 Reprinted by Lee, p. 33–4.

27 Southwoman, 'To the Young Women of Ireland', *Irish Freedom/Saoirse na hÉireann*, November 1913, p. 2.

28 Kathleen Clarke, *Revolutionary Woman: My Fight for Ireland's Freedom*, ed. by Helen Litton (Dublin: O'Brien, 1991), pp. 212–13.

29 The entire proclamation is reprinted by Mac Lochlainn, pp. 1–2.

30 Cullingford, '"Thinking of Her . . . as . . . Ireland": Yeats, Pearse and Heaney', *Textual Practice*, 4:1 (1990) 1–21 (p. 1).

31 Ward, *Unmanageable Revolutionaries*, p. 91.

32 For more details of Inghinidhe na hÉireann's activities see Trotter, pp. 73–100.

33 For a number of years Connolly's play was considered lost, even by the editors of *The Oxford Companion to Irish Literature*. But *Under Which Flag?* can be found in manuscript

at the NLI amongst the morass of papers belonging to Connolly's literary executor, the labour leader William O'Brien, who refrained from fighting in 1916 but would have served on the provisional government if the rebellion had been successful. *The Oxford Companion to Irish Literature*, ed. by Robert Welch (Oxford: Oxford University Press, 1996), p. 113. NLI, William O'Brien Papers, *Under Which Flag?*, MS 13,945. Further references to this manuscript will be given after quotations in the text.

34 Stephens, *The Insurrection in Dublin* (Dublin: Maunsel, 1916), p. 82. De Rosa, p. 150.
35 Connolly, *James Connolly: Selected Writings*, ed. by Peter Beresford Ellis (London: Pluto Press, 1997), p. 191.
36 Quoted by Ward, 'Gender: Gendering the Irish Revolution', in *The Irish Revolution 1913–1923* , ed. by Joost Augusteijn (Houndmills: Palgrave, 2002), pp. 168–85 (p. 168).
37 Cullingford, 'Thinking of Her', p. 2.
38 Sheehy Skeffington, p. 6.
39 See Levitas, p. 216.
40 Thomas MacDonagh, *When the Dawn is Come: A Tragedy in Three Acts* (Dublin: Maunsel, 1908), p. 47.
41 Thomas MacDonagh, *When the Dawn is Come*, pp. 14–15.
42 Johann A. Norstedt, *Thomas MacDonagh: A Critical Biography* (Charlottesville: University of Virginia Press, 1980), p. 52.
43 Thomas MacDonagh, *Pagans: A Modern Play in Two Conversations* (Dublin: Talbot, 1920), p. 36.
44 Thomas MacDonagh, *Pagans*, p. 40.
45 Shelia Walsh, 'A Mother's Letter', *Irish Press*, 27 April 1966, p. 12.
46 Padraic Pearse, *Collected Works of Padraic H. Pearse: Plays, Stories, Poems* (Dublin: Maunsel, 1917), p. 44. Further references to this edition will be given after quotations in the text.
47 Girard, *Deceit, Desire and the Novel: Self and Other in Literary Structure*, trans. by Yvonne Freccero (London: John Hopkins University Press, 1976).
48 Padraic Pearse, *Collected Works: Plays, Stories, Poems*, appendix p. iv.
49 The *Irish Times* is quoted by Conor Kostick and Lorcan Collins in *The Easter Rising: A Guide to Dublin in 1916* (Dublin: O'Brien, 2000), p. 63. The symbolism of the GPO is further described by F.X. Martin, '1916; Myth, Fact, and Mystery', *Studia Hibernica*, 7 (1967), 7–126 (pp. 10–11).
50 Taillon, pp. xxi–xxvii.
51 Maire Nic Shiubhlaigh and Edward Kenny, *The Splendid Years: Recollections of Maire Nic Shiubhlaigh as Told to Edward Kenny* (Dublin: Duffy, 1955), p. 185.
52 Clarke, p. 170.
53 Ward, 'Gendering the Irish Revolution', p. 179.
54 Ward, 'Gendering the Irish Revolution', pp. 176–7.
55 Ward, 'Gendering the Irish Revolution', p. 177.
56 Davies, 'Guerrilla Theatre', *Tulane Drama Review*, 10:4 (1966), 130–6. Schechner, 'Guerrilla Theatre: May 1970', *Tulane Drama Review*, 14:3 (1970), 163–8 (p. 163).
57 Marvin Carlson, p. 165.
58 'Guerrilla Girls Bare All', <http://www.guerrillagirls.com/interview/index.shtml> [accessed 22 January 2005] (section 5 of 44). The website also details the recent activities of the Guerrilla Girls.
59 Frances Babbage, *Augusto Boal* (London: Routledge, 2004), pp. 17–18.

2. *The Plough and the Stars*

1 Pádraic Pearse, 'To My Mother', in Mac Lochlainn, p. 21.
2 Margaret Pearse wrote this to the head of the San Francisco Gaelic League in 1919. Her letter was reprinted by the *Irish Press* on the fiftieth anniversary of the Rising. See Walsh, p. 12.

3 'Abbey Theatre Scene', *Irish Times*, 12 February 1926, p. 7. Variants of this speech also appeared in the *Irish Independent*, *Evening Mail* and *Manchester Guardian*, but the *Irish Times* version is probably the most accurate: Yeats personally dashed a copy to this newspaper, which in 1916 had called for the execution of the Easter rebels.

4 Foster, *Yeats: A Life*, II, 306.

5 Johnston, *Orders and Desecrations: The Life of the Playwright Denis Johnston*, ed. by Rory Johnston (Dublin: Lilliput, 1992), p. 187.

6 For an account of the failed kidnapping see Ria Mooney, 'Playing Rosie Redmond', *Journal of Irish Literature*, 6:2 (1977), 21–7 (pp. 25–6).

7 The following week Granville Barker's new play *Doctor Knock* took only £156, although the run was a day shorter because of Ash Wednesday. When *The Plough and the Stars* was revived by the company in May it again took over £421. In fact, it took until December for an Abbey play to take more money, and that was O'Casey's *Juno and the Paycock*. Abbey Theatre Archives, Abbey Theatre Papers, vol. 17, P8134.

8 Gregory, *Lady Gregory's Journals*, ed. by Daniel J. Murphy, 2 vols (New York: Oxford University Press, 1987), II, 64.

9 Robert G. Lowery, 'Prelude to Year One: Sean O'Casey Before 1916', *Sean O'Casey Review*, 2:2 (1976), 92–103 (p. 96).

10 *Songs of the Wren* (Dublin: O'Connor, 1918).

11 Sean O Cathasaigh, *The Story of Thomas Ashe* (Dublin: O'Connor, 1918), pp. 3–4, and P. O Cathasaigh, *The Story of the Irish Citizen Army* (Dublin: Maunsel, 1919).

12 Greaves, *Sean O'Casey, Politics and Art* (London: Lawrence and Wishart, 1979), pp. 82–93. Jack Mitchell, 'Desmond Greaves *contra* Sean O'Casey', *O'Casey Annual*, 1 (1982), 195–211. McDonald, *Tragedy and Irish Literature: Synge, O'Casey, Beckett* (Basingstoke: Palgrave, 2002), p. 111.

13 O'Casey, *The Letters of Sean O'Casey*, ed. by David Krause, 4 vols (London: Macmillan, 1975, 1980 and Washington: Catholic University of America Press, 1989, 1992), I, 64.

14 See Garry O'Connor, *Sean O'Casey: A Life* (London: Hodder and Stoughton, 1988), p. 315.

15 Lenin, 'The Irish Rebellion of 1916', in *1916: The Easter Rising*, ed. by O. Dudley Edwards and Fergus Pyle (London: MacGibbon and Kee, 1968), pp. 191–5 (p. 193).

16 'Public Meetings in Dublin: Mansion House Meetings Postponed', *Irish Times*, 23 April 1917, p. 4.

17 John O'Connor, *The Story of the 1916 Proclamation* (Dublin: Abbey, [1986?]), p. 22.

18 See *The 1916 Song Book*, 9d edn (Dublin: Irish Book Bureau, [1938?]), p. 7; and Patrick Buckland, *'Ireland in Schools': Irish History in Song 2: Some Notes* (Liverpool: Ireland in Schools, 2002), p. 6.

19 The Bishop's words are quoted by Coogan, *De Valera*, p. 89.

20 'Bishop O'Dwyer and Maxwell', in *The 1916 Song Book*, p. 19.

21 Ferriter, *The Transformation of Ireland*, p. 182.

22 O'Casey, *Autobiographies* (London: Macmillan, 1981), I, 506–20.

23 Dalton's play was premiered in Cork's Father Matthew Hall in May 1918. Dalton, *Sable and Gold* (Dublin: Maunsel, 1922). Further references to this edition will be given after quotations in the text. Corkery, 'Resurrection', *Theatre Arts Monthly*, 8:4 (1924), 259–72.

24 Another play about the Rising was staged in 1922 to commemorate the sixth anniversary of the revolt but unfortunately has now been lost. Like *Resurrection* and *Sable and Gold*, Brian O'Kennedy's *The Awakening* apparently concerned 'the effect of the Rising on a Dublin family. Early in the play most of the characters are "engrossed" in Imperialism; but as the action develops, the characters, one by one, are redeemed by the spirit of nationality'. This was the description of the action contained in a 1922 commemoration pamphlet quoted by John Coddington Countryman, 'Life Imitates Art: The Drama of the 1916 Easter Uprising in Ireland' (unpublished doctoral thesis, Bowling Green State University, 1977), p. 116.

25 Corkery, 'Resurrection', p. 259, p. 265.

26   Corkery, 'Resurrection', p. 266, p. 265.
27   Corkery, 'Resurrection', p. 271.
28   Corkery, *The Labour Leader* (Dublin: Talbot, 1920), pp. 68–9.
29   Corkery, *The Labour Leader*, p. 113.
30   Garry O'Connor, pp. 131–2.
31   The Dubliners, *More Dubliners Songs* (London: Wise, 1979), pp. 44–5.
32   O'Casey, *Letters*, I, 169.
33   O'Casey, *The Complete Plays of Sean O'Casey*, 5 vols (London: Macmillan, 1984), I, 27.
      Further references to this edition will be given after quotations in the text.
34   Deane, 'Irish Politics and O'Casey's Theatre', *Threshold*, 24 (1973), 5–16.
35   Dalton, p. 42.
36   Printed in Mac Lochlainn, p. 21.
37   Printed in Mac Lochlainn, p. 22.
38   P.H. Pearse, *The Mother and Other Tales*, trans. by T.A. Fitzgerald (Dundalk: Dundalgan,
      1916). Pádraic Colum and Edward J. O'Brien, p. 40.
39   Padraic Pearse, *Collected Works: Plays, Stories, Poems*, p. xvii.
40   Ni Chathain, 'The Old Woman of the House', *Irish Freedom/Saoirse na hÉireann*, Decem-
      ber 1926, p. 7.
41   Padraic Pearse, *Collected Works: Plays, Stories, Poems*, p. 333. Corkery, *The Labour Leader*,
      p. 68.
42   Ward, 'Gendering the Irish Revolution', p. 179.
43   Pádraic Pearse, *The Home-Life of Pádraig Pearse: As Told By Himself, His Family and Friends*,
      ed. by Mary Brigid Pearse (Dublin: Browne and Nolan, 1935), p. 47.
44   Walsh, p. 12.
45   Pádraic Pearse, *The Home-Life*, p. 49.
46   Deputies of Dáil Éireann, *Tuairisg Oifigiúil: Díosbóireacht ar an gConnradh Idir Éire Agus
      Sasana*, ed. by Dáil Éireann staff (Dublin: Talbot, 1922), pp. 221–2.
47   Deputies of Dáil Éireann, *Díosbóireacht ar an gConnradh*, p. 223.
48   Deputies of Dáil Éireann, *Díosbóireacht ar an gConnradh*, p. 36.
49   O'Casey draws on three sources for his depiction of Pearse, but only one, the O'Donovan
      Rossa oration, was actually delivered verbally. The other two were newspaper articles:
      P.H. Pearse, 'The Coming Revolution', *An Claidheamh Soluis*, 8 November 1913, p. 6; and
      the anonymous 'Peace and the Gael', *The Spark*, December 1915, pp. 1–2. O'Casey read
      all three pieces in Padraic Pearse, *Collected Works of Padraic H. Pearse: Political Writings
      and Speeches* (Dublin: Maunsel, 1922), pp. 133–8, pp. 89–100, pp. 213–18.
59   Mooney, p. 22.
51   This *Irish Times* article is reprinted in *A Whirlwind in Dublin: The Plough and the Stars Riots*,
      ed. by Robert G. Lowery (Westport: Greenwood Press, 1984), p. 23. In addition,
      Holloway mentions how, as the audience was dispersing from the first night of the show,
      'In Abbey Street a policeman was stalking after four "Rosie Redmonds" who flew before
      him'. Yet Holloway himself would later hold that the play was abominable because
      'There were none [no prostitutes] in Dublin till the Tommies brought them over'.
      Holloway, *Joseph Holloway's Abbey Theatre: A Selection from his Unpublished Journal, Impres-
      sions of a Dublin Playgoer*, ed. by Robert Hogan and Michael J. O'Neill (London: Southern
      Illinois University Press, 1967), p. 252. Gregory, *Journals*, II, 65.
52   Stephen Tifft, 'The Parricidal Phantasm: Irish Nationalism and the *Playboy* Riots', in
      Nationalisms and Sexualities, ed. by Andrew Parker, Mary Russo, Doris Sommer, and
      Patricia Yaeger (New York: Routledge, 1992), p. 316; and Nicholas Grene, *The Politics of
      Irish Drama*, p. 80.
53   Reprinted by Lowery, *A Whirlwind in Dublin*, p. 52.
54   Unfortunately the one-act piece is no longer extant, but we know it probably formed the
      basis of *The Plough*'s Act II because in 1957 O'Casey wrote, 'it was, practically, word for
      word, the present 2nd act of The Plough'. *The Letters of Sean O'Casey*, III, 428. In his
      autobiographical writings he also mentions that the original work was 'full of wild

discussions and rows in a public-house [. . .] and later was used to form the second act of another play'. O'Casey, *Autobiographies*, II, 103.

55 Konstantin Stanislavski, *My Life in Art*, trans. by J.J. Robbins (London: Methuen, 1948), p. 379.

56 Robins, 'Votes for Women!', in *The New Woman and Other Emancipated Woman Plays*, ed. by Jean Chothia (Oxford: Oxford University Press, 1998), pp. 135–210. Galsworthy, *Strife*, ed. by Non Worral (London: Methuen, 1984).

57 Levitas, p. 203.

58 Corkery, *The Labour Leader*, p. 100, p. 112.

59 For Robinson's dislike of the offstage orator see Hogan et al., VI, 294.

60 See Walsh, p. 12.

61 Gaffney, 'Readers' Views: "The Silver Tassie"', *Irish Press*, 12 September 1935, p. 6; O'Casey, 'Mr. O'Casey and the Abbey Theatre: "Defensive Words" on *The Silver Tassie*', 11 September 1935, p. 8.

62 See Padraic Pearse and M.H. Gaffney, *Stories of Padraic H. Pearse: Dramatised by M.H. Gaffney, O.P.* (Dublin: Talbot, 1935), pp. 7–8.

63 Padraic Pearse and M.H. Gaffney, p. 228.

64 Mordaunt Croft, 'Ireland – the Weak Spot in the Empire', *The Times*, 16 October 1916, p. 9.

65 Richard O'Carroll was arrested after an engagement near Jacob's biscuit factory and killed by the same insane British Captain who shot Francis Sheehy Skeffington.

66 Roddy the Rover (the penname of Aodh de Blácam), 'Poems of Easter Week', *Irish Press*, 22 April 1935, p. 6.

67 O'Casey, *Autobiographies*, II, 4. This halo has proved persistent, with pictures of Bobby Sands often featuring a white aureole around his head. See for instance the picture hung by Sinn Féin in *Endgame in Ireland*. Prod. Norma Percy and Brian Lapping. BBC 2. 15 July 2001.

68 *Nineteen-Sixteen: An Anthology*, ed. by Edna C. Fitzhenry (Dublin: Browne and Nolan, 1935), pp. 59–60.

69 Fitzhenry, p. 90, p. 44.

70 Fitzhenry, p. 88, p. 91.

71 Margaret Pearse's words are quoted in Deputies of Dáil Éireann, *Díosbóireacht ar an gConnradh*, p. 223. The manuscript of Mary Brigid Pearse's speech is found at the Pearse Museum, Rathfarnham, MB108.

72 Margaret Mary Pearse, 'Patrick and Willie Pearse', p. 87.

73 'Mrs. Margaret Pearse Dies at St Enda's', *Irish Press*, 23 April 1932, p. 1.

74 Jung, *The Collected Works of C.G. Jung: Civilization in Transition*, trans. by R.F.C. Hull, 2nd edn (London: Routledge, 1970), p. 223.

75 P.S. O'Hegarty, 'A Dramatist of New-born Ireland', in *Sean O'Casey: Modern Judgements*, ed. by Ronald Ayling (London: Macmillan, 1969), pp. 60–7 (p. 64). Sheehy Skeffington's words are included in O'Casey, *Letters*, I, 173.

76 Quoted in Hogan et al., VI, 300–1.

77 O'Casey, *Letters*, I, 168.

78 O'Casey, *Autobiographies*, II, 152.

79 Johnston, *Orders and Desecrations*, p. 188. Gregory, *Journals*, II, 62.

80 Father Gillis, *Irish Rosary* (September 1935), 651.

81 This condemnation is found in NAI, Department of the Taoiseach, Abbey Theatre Objectionable Productions, Letter of 24 September 1934 to de Valera from John Devine, S8208.

82 NAI, Department of the Taoiseach, Abbey Theatre Objectionable Productions, Draft document of April 1933 to Abbey from government, S8208. The injunction on O'Casey in 1966 is discussed by David Krause, 'Some Truths and Jokes about the Easter Rising', *Sean O'Casey Review*, 3:1 (1976), 3–23 (p. 3).

83 In 1943 when Robert Farren was writing his play *Lost Light* the Abbey directorate

cautioned him against depicting the any of the leaders of the Rising in case he riled the relatives of the dead. See Countryman, p. 321.

84 Fallon, 'The House on the North Circular Road: Fragments from a Biography', *Modern Drama*, 4:3 (1961), 223–33 (p. 232).

85 NLI, *The Plough and the Stars* Typescript with MS Annotations, MS 29,407, fol.II–2, 3. O'Casey made similar alterations to every speech given by the orator. For instance, on either side of the 'Comrade soldiers' speech he appended the following words: 'The earth is speaking with a new and terrible voice, stirring the hearts of the people with the quickening pulse of patriotism. and [sic] we have heard that voice and we are ready to answer [. . .] We have sworn to make that sacrifice, even unto the shedding of our own blood that our country may be redeemed from the toil and shame of slavery'. NLI, *The Plough and the Stars* Typescript with MS Annotations, MS 29,407, fol.II–5. Reproduced with kind permission of the Estate of Sean O'Casey.

86 Abbey Theatre Archives, *The Plough and the Stars* Promptbook, 1926/A/6. Nicholas Grene has written an excellent article on O'Casey's other alterations to *The Plough and the Stars* in 'The Class of the Clitheroes: O'Casey's Revisions to *The Plough and the Stars* Promptbook', *Bullán: An Irish Studies Journal*, 4:2 (1999/2000), 57–66.

87 O'Casey, *Autobiographies*, I, 506, 509.

88 O'Casey, *Autobiographies*, II, 125, 150.

89 O'Casey, *Autobiographies*, I, 617, 662.

90 O'Casey, *The Complete Plays of Sean O'Casey*, V, 138, 135.

91 Boucicault, 'Robert Emmet', in *Forbidden Fruit and Other Plays*, ed. by Allardyce Nicoll and F. Theodore Cloak (Bloomington: Indiana Press, 1963), pp. 263–313. BL, The Lord Chamberlain's Collection, *The Ulster Hero*, 1905/19N. Bourke, 'For the Land She Loved', in Herr, pp. 311–59.

92 O'Casey, *Autobiographies*, I, 624.

3. *The Dreaming of the Bones*

1 Bernard MacLaverty, *Cal* (London: Vintage, 1998), p. 66.

2 David Rudkin, *Cries From Casement As His Bones Are Brought To Dublin* (London: BBC, 1974), p. 44.

3 The link between *The Dreaming of the Bones* and Japanese Noh was first explored by David R. Clark, 'Nishikigi and Yeats's *The Dreaming of the Bones*', *Modern Drama*, 7:2 (1964), 111–25; Shotaro Oshima, *W.B. Yeats and Japan* (Tokyo: Hokuseido, 1965); and Hiro Ishibashi, *Yeats and the Noh: Types of Japanese Beauty and their Reflection in Yeats's Plays*, ed. by Anthony Kerrigan (Dublin: Dolmen, 1966), pp. 129–51. The leading scholar currently working in this area is Masaru Sekine, the author of 'Noh, Fenollosa, Pound and Yeats – Have East and West Met?', *Yeats Annual*, 13 (1998), 176–96.

4 Yeats, *The Collected Works of W.B. Yeats: Volume II: The Plays*, ed. by David R. Clark and Rosalind E. Clark, 14 vols (Houndmills: Palgrave, 2001), II, 310. Further references to this edition will be given after quotations in the text. Padraic Pearse, *Collected Works: Political Writings and Speeches*, p. 216.

5 Padraic Pearse, *Collected Works: Plays, Stories, Poems*, p. 339.

6 Yeats quoted Pádraic Pearse's poetry in his address to the 1922 Irish Race Congress in Paris, and in his 1932 lecture 'Modern Ireland'. See Foster, *Yeats: A Life*, II, 207, 445. 'The Rebel' was even scrawled on the walls of Kilmainham jail during the Civil War.

7 Pádraic Pearse's words may also have influenced Yeats's 'Easter 1916', as suggested by Patrick Keane, *Terrible Beauty: Yeats, Joyce, Ireland, and the Myth of the Devouring Female* (Columbia: University of Missouri Press, 1988), p. 7; John Wilson Foster, *Colonial Consequences: Essays in Irish Literature and Culture* (Dublin: Lilliput, 1991), pp. 139–40; and Edna Longley, 'Helicon and ni Houlihan: *Michael Robartes and the Dancer*', in *Yeats's Political Identities: Selected Essays*, ed. by Jonathan Allison (Ann Arbor: University of Michigan Press, 1996), pp. 203–20 (p. 212).

8   Yeats, *Letters*, ed. by Wade, p. 788.
9   See F.X. Martin, 'Diarmait Mac Murchada and the Coming of the Anglo–Normans', in *A New History of Ireland: II: Medieval Ireland 1169–1534*, ed. by Art Cosgrove (Oxford: Clarendon Press, 1987), pp. 43–66; and Katharine Simms 'The Norman Invasion and the Gaelic Recovery', in *The Oxford History of Ireland*, ed. by R.F. Foster (Oxford: Oxford University Press, 1989), pp. 44–87.
10 *Speeches from the Dock: Or Protests of Irish Patriotism*, ed. by T.D. Sullivan, A.M. Sullivan, D.B. Sullivan, and Seán Ua Ceallaigh, rev. edn (Dublin: Gill, 1945), pp. xi–xii.
11 Yeats, *Letters*, ed. by Wade, p. 613.
12 Ure, *Yeats the Playwright: A Commentary on Character and Design in the Major Plays* (London: Routledge, 1963), pp. 95–6.
13 NLI, *The Dreaming of the Bones* Draft, MS 8775 (1).
14 The name 'MacDermot' may also have recalled Seán MacDermott, the executed IRB leader and signatory of the 1916 proclamation.
15 NLI, *The Dreaming of the Bones* Drafts, MS 8775 (1), fol.6.
16 Chadwick, 'Family Romance as National Allegory in Yeats's *Cathleen ni Houlihan* and *The Dreaming of the Bones*', *Twentieth Century Literature*, 32:2 (1986), 155–68 (pp. 161–2).
17 Before the first Abbey performance Yeats gave a private reading of the play to a group of friends, at Gogarty's house in July 1917. The group included James Stephens, who found the play 'marvellous' but disliked the 'artifice' of the Noh form. See Liam Miller, *The Noble Drama of W.B. Yeats* (Dublin: Dolmen, 1977), p. 235; and Richard J. Finneran, *The Olympian and the Leprechaun: W.B. Yeats and James Stephens* (Dublin: Dolmen, 1978), p. 15.
18 Quoted by Daniel J. Kevles, *In the Name of Eugenics: Genetics and the Uses of Human Heredity* (Cambridge, MA: Harvard University Press, 1995), p. 117.
19 Yeats, *Collected Works*, rev. edn, I, 101.
20 See Susan Cannon Harris, 'More Than a Morbid, Unhealthy Mind: Public Health and the *Playboy* Riots', in *A Century of Irish Drama: Widening the Stage*, ed. by Stephen Watt, Eileen Morgan, and Shakir Mustafa (Bloomington: Indiana University Press, 2000), pp. 72–94 (pp. 79–81).
21 Pound and Fenollosa, *Certain Noble Plays of Japan: From the Manuscripts of Ernest Fenollosa, Chosen and Finished by Ezra Pound, with an Introduction by William Butler Yeats* (Churchtown: Cuala Press, 1916), p. xi.
22 Pound and Fenollosa, p. ix, p. xi.
23 Yeats, 'An Acre of Grass', *Collected Works*, rev. edn, I, 301.
24 Donoghue, *Yeats* (London: Fontana, 1971), pp. 118–19. Yeats, 'In the Seven Woods', *Collected Works*, rev. edn, I, 77. Stanfield, *Yeats and Politics in the 1930s* (London: Macmillan, 1988), pp. 145–83.
25 Yeats, *Essays and Introductions* (London: Macmillan, 1961), p. 253.
26 An excellent introduction to Yeats's race philosophy is given by Marjorie Howes, pp. 166–7.
27 Grant, *The Passing of the Great Race: or The Racial Basis of European History* (London: Bell, 1917), pp. 7–8.
28 Yeats, *Memoirs*, ed. by Denis Donoghue (London: Macmillan, 1972), p. 156.
29 Yeats, *Explorations* (New York: Macmillan, 1962), p. 414.
30 Yeats, *Essays and Introductions*, p. 526.
31 Yeats, *Collected Works*, rev. edn, I, 307–8. A. Norman Jeffares, *A Commentary on the Collected Poems of W.B. Yeats* (London: Macmillan, 1968), p. 471.
32 Yeats, *Collected Works*, rev. edn, I, 307.
33 Yeats, *Collected Works*, rev. edn, I, 337.
34 Yeats, 'Easter 1916', *Collected Works*, rev. edn, I, 181.
35 Yeats, *Explorations*, p. 413.
36 Yeats, *Letters*, ed. by Wade, p. 614.
37 At the time of the Rising Yeats was staying in the Gloucestershire home of the painter

William Rothenstein, who recounts Yeats's worries about the rebellion in E.H. Mikhail, ed., *W.B. Yeats, Interviews and Recollections*, 2 vols (London: Macmillan, 1977), II, 282. The only point at which Yeats does not endorse the Rising as an aristocratic event is in a letter to Gregory written immediately after the rebellion, in which Yeats laments that 'all the work of years has been overturned, all the bringing together of classes, all the freeing of Irish literature and criticism from politics'. But, as David Cairns and Shaun Richards have shown, this statement was somewhat disingenuous. Yeats's most recent poetry had involved an explicit assertion of class identity and repudiation of the middle class. Yeats, *Letters*, ed. by Wade, p. 613. Cairns and Richards, *Writing Ireland* (Manchester: Manchester University Press, 1988), p. 112.

38 Pound and Fenollosa, p. ii, p. 51.
39 Yeats, *Collected Works*, rev. edn, I, 148–9.
40 Yeats, *Explorations*, p. 112.
41 'Episcopal Opinion', *Irish Independent*, 9 May 1916, p. 3. See also Tim Pat Coogan, *Ireland in the Twentieth Century* (London: Hutchinson, 2003), p. 60.
42 Coogan, *Ireland in the Twentieth Century*, p. 60.
43 Maud Gonne and W.B. Yeats, *The Gonne–Yeats Letters 1893–1938: Always Your Friend*, ed. by Anna MacBride White and A. Norman Jeffares (London: Hutchinson, 1992), p. 73.
44 Yeats, *Essays and Introductions*, p. 372, and *The Variorum Edition of the Poems of W.B. Yeats*, ed. by Peter Allt and Russell K. Alspach (London: Macmillan, 1956), p. 837.
45 Yeats, *Four Plays for Dancers* (New York: Macmillan, 1921), p. 105.
46 Yeats, *Four Plays for Dancers*, p. 105, p. 86.
47 Yeats, *Four Plays for Dancers*, p. v.
48 Pound and Fenollosa, p. iv.
49 O'Casey, *Autobiographies*, II, 232–3. O'Casey also described the evening to Denis Johnston, who in turn described the 'great embarrassment' felt by Yeats's audience. Johnston, *Orders and Desecrations*, p. 197.
50 Craig (under the pseudonym John Balance), 'A Note on Masks', in *The Mask*, 1:1 (1908), 9–12.
51 Lloyd, *Anomalous States: Irish Writing and the Post-Colonial Moment* (Dublin: Lilliput, 1993), p. 59.
52 Pound and Fenollosa, p. ii. James P. McGarry, *Place Names in the Writings of William Butler Yeats*, ed. by Edward Mallins (Gerrards Cross: Colin Smythe, 1976), p. 15.
53 The Dublin wags even had a ballad about the Abbey's previous role: 'It had many a life before it was a Theatre/It was once a Savings Bank and a Morgue sometime later'. Thomas MacAnna, 'Nationalism from the Abbey stage', in *Theatre and Nationalism in Twentieth Century Ireland*, ed. by Robert O'Driscoll (London: Oxford University Press, 1971), pp. 89–101 (p. 90).
54 Yeats, *Four Plays for Dancers*, p. 85.
55 For a full selection of Easter-week postcards see Sarah Rouse, *Into the Light: an Illustrated Guide to the Photographic Collections in the National Library of Ireland* (Dublin: NLI, 1998); and NLI, Frank Martin Papers, Scrapbooks, 2 vols, MS 32,695. The *Irish Independent* attests to the popularity of these images in the article 'Rebellion Anniversary', 23 April 1917, p. 3.
56 One such 1916 poster appears in *The Dawn*. Dir. Tom Cooper. Hibernia Films. 1936. Another can be seen in *Cal*. Dir. Pat O'Connor. Warner Brothers. 1984.
57 Yeats, 'Parnell's Funeral', *Collected Works*, rev. edn, I, 280.
58 See Coogan, *De Valera*, p. 296.
59 Quoted by Foster, *Yeats: A Life*, II, 470.
60 Yeats wrote these words in his private journal after meeting the Blueshirt leader Eoin O'Duffy. See Foster, *Yeats: A Life*, II, 474.
61 Yeats, *Letters*, ed. by Wade, p. 612.
62 Yeats, *Uncollected Prose*, II, 486–8.
63 See Coogan, *De Valera*, p. 315.

64 'Mr. de Valera on the Removal of Oath', *Irish Press*, 7 December 1931, p. 5.

65 O'Kelly, *Three Plays* (Dublin: Gill, 1912). O'Kelly's play, dating from 1908, was produced to mark the Rising by Aoife Taaffe at Easter 1935, see NLI, Easter Week Commemoration 1935, ILB 300 P14.

66 McCormack, *From Burke to Beckett: Ascendancy, Tradition and Betrayal in Literary History* (Cork: Cork University Press, 1994), p. 311. Vendler, *Yeats's Vision and the Later Plays* (London: Oxford University Press, 1963), p. 187. Vendler was contesting the reading of the play offered by F.A.C. Wilson in *Yeats's Iconography* (London: Gollancz, 1960), p. 205.

67 Yeats, *The Secret Rose* (London: Lawrence and Bullen, 1897), pp. 174–84.

68 At one point the rebel was to declare 'I have fought at Vinegar Hill. I have hell at my feet', rather than 'I was in the Post Office, and if taken/I shall be put against a wall and shot'. NLI, *The Dreaming of the Bones* Drafts, MS 8775 (1), fol.6. Yeats, *Collected Works*, II, 309.

69 Yeats, *Letters*, ed. by Wade, p. 626, p. 654.

70 Clarke, p. 76.

71 Sexton, *Ireland and the Crown, 1922–1936: The Governor-Generalship of the Irish Free State* (Dublin: Irish Academic Press, 1989), p. 112.

72 'Mr. de Valera Outlines His Party's Policy', *Irish Times*, 28 October 1931, p. 7.

73 Kuch, '"For Poetry Makes Nothing Happen": The Poetry of Yeats and the Politics of Ireland', in *Yeats: An Annual of Critical and Textual Studies*, 8 (1990), 188–205 (p. 203).

4. Fianna Fáil's Easter Rising

1   This song, 'Invisible Women', was written by Brian Moore, and is printed by Taillon, p. vii.

2   Anne Devlin, *Ourselves Alone* (London: Faber, 1990), p. 30.

3   Joyce, *Ulysses*, ed. by Declan Kiberd (London: Penguin, 1992), p. 206.

4   David Officer, 'For God and for Ulster', in *History and Memory in Modern Ireland*, ed. by Ian McBride (Cambridge: Cambridge University Press, 2001), pp. 160–83 (pp. 177–8).

5   NAI, Department of the Taoiseach, General Post Office Rebuilding, Note of 5 July 1929, S1966.

6   NAI, Department of the Taoiseach, General Post Office Rebuilding, 'Speech by President 11.7.29', S1966.

7   See William Rothenstein, *Since Fifty: Men and Memories 1922–1938* (London: Faber, 1939), p. 305.

8   Coogan, *De Valera*, pp. 67–70. Other historians have also indicated that de Valera was temporarily deranged during the battle: see Kostick and Collins, pp. 67–8, and Max Caulfield, *The Easter Rebellion: Dublin 1916*, 2nd edn (Boulder: Roberts Rinehart, 1995), p. 120, p. 216.

9   David Hogan, 'At the G.P.O', *Irish Press*, 22 April 1935, p. 1.

10 David Hogan, p. 1.

11 'March of Easter Week Veterans in Dublin', *Irish Press*, 22 April 1935, p. 1. 'Mr. de Valera and the Republic', *Irish Independent*, 22 April 1935, p. 7.

12 NAI, Department of the Taoiseach, 1916 Memorial GPO, Letter of 15 April 1935 to de Valera from Oliver St John Gogarty, S6405C.

13 'President at Opening of '16 Pageant', *Irish Press*, 13 April 1966, p. 1.

14 Robert Leach, 'Revolutionary Theatre, 1917–1930', in *A History of Russian Theatre*, ed. by Robert Leach and Victor Borovsky (Cambridge: Cambridge University Press, 1999), pp. 302–24 (pp. 304–5).

15 Mona Ozouf, *Festivals and the French Revolution*, trans. by Alan Sheridan (Cambridge, MA: Harvard University Press, 1988), pp. 33–60.

16 Boal, *Legislative Theatre: Using Performance to Make Politics* (London: Routledge, 1998), p. 227.

17 Boal, p. 227.

18 Boal, pp. 227–8.
19 See Ward, *Unmanageable Revolutionaries*, p. 110.
20 See Kostick and Collins, p. 76.
21 'Easter Week Celebration in Dublin: Significance of 1916 Memorial', *Irish Times*, 22 April 1935, p. 8.
22 Quoted by Coogan, *Michael Collins*, p. 53.
23 This plaque was made in 1934, when Fianna Fáil gave no indication that it included only an edited version of the proclamation. The *Irish Press* claimed simply that it was 'inscribed [with] the Proclamation of 1916'. 'Easter Week Rising: Memorial to be Erected in the G.P.O.', *Irish Press*, 1 November 1934, p. 7.
24 Waters, p. 12.
25 The National Graves Association also endorsed selective editing, recommending the following inscription from Yeats's 'Easter 1916': 'We know their dream . . . they dreamed and are dead'. The elision served to obliterate Yeats's uncertainty about the rebellion. See Edna Longley, 'Northern Ireland: Commemoration, Elegy, Forgetting', in *History and Memory in Modern Ireland*, ed. by Ian McBride (Cambridge: Cambridge University Press, 2001), pp. 223–53 (p. 239).
26 See for instance: 'Impressive 1916 Commemoration', *Irish Independent*, 22 April 1935, p. 3; 'Firing Party of 1916 Men', *Irish Independent*, 23 April 1935, p. 10; 'Yesterday's Ceremonies', *Irish Times*, 22 April 1935, p. 9; 'Rehearsing for To-morrow's Ceremonies', *Irish Press*, 19–20 April 1935, p. 3; 'Yesterday's 1916 Ceremonies in Dublin', *Irish Press*, 22 April 1935, p. 14.
27 'Dublin G.P.O. Ceremony', *Irish Press*, 22 April 1935, p. 2.
28 'Procession to GPO', *Irish Independent*, 22 April 1935, p. 7.
29 Ward, *Unmanageable Revolutionaries*, p. 213.
30 'Scene at General Post Office', *Irish Times*, 22 April 1935, p. 7.
31 NAI, Department of the Taoiseach, 1916 Memorial GPO, 'Easter Week Memorial' note of 9 April 1935 to secretary, S6405B. David Hogan, p. 1.
32 Ozouf, p. 11.
33 '1916 Ceremony in Dublin GPO', *Irish Independent*, 18 April 1935, p. 11. 'Connolly's Anniversary', *Bottom Dog*, 11 May 1918, p. 1. 'Songs of Freedom', *Bottom Dog*, 16 March 1918, p. 3.
34 Ronan Fanning, 'The Rule of Order: Eamon de Valera and the IRA, 1923–40', in *De Valera and his Times*, ed. by John P. O'Carroll and John A. Murphy (Cork: Cork University Press, 1983), pp. 160–72 (p. 165).
35 Sean Cronin, *The McGarrity Papers: Revelations of the Irish Revolutionary Movement in Ireland and America 1900–1940* (Tralee: Anvil, 1972), p. 166.
36 Ward, *Unmanageable Revolutionaries*, p. 233.
37 Erskine H. Childers, 'Padraig Pearse', *Fianna Fáil Bulletin*, April 1936, pp. 5–7 (p. 5, p. 7).
38 Lance Pettitt, *Screening Ireland: Film and Television Representation* (Manchester: Manchester University Press, 2000), p. 58.
39 Speaking in the Dáil about the similarly-calculating decision to exclude the new Governor General from the commemoration, de Valera said, 'He was entitled to be there. He was entitled to be there as well as anybody who participated in it and he was not there [. . .] because he did not want to have public controversy on the matter or misrepresentation of the matter'. NLI, *Dáil Eireann: Díosbóireachtaí Páirliminte, Tuairisg Oifigiúil*, vol. 56, col. 2081.
40 'Dublin Post Office Ceremony', *Irish Times*, 15 April 1935, p. 7.
41 NLI, *Díosbóireachtaí Páirliminte*, vol. 55, col. 2314.
42 NLI, *Díosbóireachtaí Páirliminte*, vol. 55, cols 2315–16.
43 NAI, Department of the Taoiseach, Abbey Theatre Objectionable Productions, Letter of 17 April to Lennox Robinson from government, S8208.
44 Only *Juno and the Paycock* and George Shiels's comedy *Professor Tim* were performed by

the company with greater frequency between 1926 and 1935, each being revived by the Abbey in Ireland twenty times. I am indebted to Mairead Delaney for helping me to locate this information in the Abbey Theatre Archives.

45　Carroll, 'The Conspirators' in *Irish Stories and Plays* (New York: Devin-Adair, 1958), pp. 111–29 (p. 122).

46　Carroll, p. 124, p. 126.

47　Elena Cabezali, Matilde Cuevas, and Maria Teresa Chicote, 'Myth as Suppression: Motherhood and the Historical Consciousness of the Women of Madrid, 1936–9', in *The Myths We Live By*, ed. by Raphael Samuel and Paul Thompson (Routledge: London, 1990), pp. 161–73 (p. 162).

48　Clarke, p. 188.

49　Maura Cronin, 'Women and Fenianism', in *Ireland (Ulster) Scotland: Concepts, Contexts, Comparisons*, ed. by Edna Longley, Eamonn Hughes, and Des O'Rawe (Belfast: Queens University Press, 2003), pp. 206–12 (p. 210).

50　NAI, Department of the Taoiseach, 1916 Memorial GPO, 'Easter Week Memorial GPO' note of 12 April 1935, S6405B.

51　Dolan, 'Commemoration: "Shows and stunts are all that is the thing now" – the Revolution Remembered, 1923–52', in *The Irish Revolution 1913–1923*, ed. by Joost Augusteijn (Houndmills: Palgrave, 2002), pp. 186–202 (p. 199).

52　'President's Son', *Irish Independent*, 22 April 1935, p. 9.

53　See Coogan, *De Valera*, p. 361.

54　In fact, the government was unlikely to demand that this republican blood price be anything other than symbolic. After the election victory in 1932 de Valera's administration consistently repressed any actual military attempts to reclaim the North.

55　Dermot Keogh, *Twentieth Century Ireland: Nation and State* (Dublin: Gill and Macmillan, 1994), p. 69.

56　Keogh, p. 70.

57　For more on Oliver Sheppard's statue 'The Death of Cuchulainn' see: John Turpin, *Oliver Sheppard 1865–1941: Symbolist Sculptor of the Irish Cultural Revival* (Dublin: Four Courts, 2000), pp. 134–42; Turpin, 'Cuchulainn Lives On', *CIRCA*, 69 (1994), 26–31; and Turpin, 'National Romanticism and the Sculpture of Oliver Sheppard' in *CIRCA*, 92 (2000) <http://www.recirca.com/backissues/c92/supplement/21.shtml> [accessed 1 May 2003].

58　'Bunreacht na hÉireann, Constitution of Ireland', <http://www.taoiseach.gov.ie/upload/publications/297.htm> [accessed 23 August 2003] (article 41 of 50).

59　For Justice Brian Walsh's opinion see Finola Kennedy, *Cottage to Crèche: Family Change in Ireland* (Dublin: Institute of Public Administration, 2001), p. 86.

60　Quoted by Clarke, p. 218.

61　Table of Female TDs, *Centre for Advancement of Women in Politics* <http://www.qub.ac.uk/cawp/Irish%20htmls/TD2.htm> [accessed 1 May 2003].

62　*The Dubliners 40 Years* CD. The Dubliners. 2002. The song was popularised by the superb versions sung by Jim McCann in the 1980s and 1990s.

63　Grace Gifford was part of the group of women who protested against a 'Loyal Address' from Dublin Corporation to King George V in 1911, was a member of the Sinn Féin executive in 1917, and was imprisoned in Kilmainham in 1923. Marie O'Neill, *Grace Gifford Plunkett and Irish Freedom: Tragic Bride of 1916* (Dublin: Irish Academic Press, 2000), p. 12, p. 53, p. 71.

64　Ryan, *The Rising: The Complete Story of Easter Week*, 3rd edn (Dublin: Golden Eagle, 1957), pp. 150–1.

65　Katie Donovan, 'Comrade as Mother', *Irish Times*, 4 April 1994, p. 10.

66　'104,000 see the Tattoo', *Irish Press*, 23 September 1935, p. 3.

67　'Varied Music at the Tattoo', *Irish Independent*, 18 September 1935, p. 8.

68　'Impressive Opening of Military Tattoo', *Irish Independent*, 18 September 1935, p. 10.

69　'104,000 see the Tattoo', p. 3.

70 'President Hopes for Resurgence', *Irish Independent*, 11 April 1966, p. 7.
71 Beckett, *Murphy* (London: Calder, 1993), p. 28.
72 For a discussion of the homoerotic implications of Ferdia's death see Phillip A. Bernhardt-House 'Youth, Warriors, and Homoerotic Reproduction: Queer and Celtic in Irish Studies as Strange Bedfellows', *Foilsiú*, 4:1 (2004), 85–93 (pp. 87–9).
73 Beckett, p. 36.
74 Kiberd, 'Eamon de Valera: The Image and the Achievement', in *Taking the Long View: Seventy Years of Fianna Fáil*, ed. by Philip Hannon and Jackie Gallagher (Dublin: Blackwater Press, 1996), pp. 21–8.
75 Spivak, 'Can the Subaltern Speak?' in *Marxism and the Interpretation of Culture*, ed. by Cary Nelson and Lawrence Grossberg (Urbana: University of Illinois Press, 1988), pp. 271–313 (p. 287).
76 Fitzpatrick, 'De Valera in 1917: the Undoing of the Easter Rising', in *De Valera and His Times*, ed. by John P. Carroll and John A. Murphy (Cork: Cork University Press, 1983), pp. 101–13 (p. 111).

5. *Saint Joan* and Hollywood

1 Brendan Behan, *Borstal Boy* (London: Arrow, 1990), p. 6.
2 James Joyce, *Finnegans Wake*, ed. by Seamus Deane (London: Penguin, 1993), p. 535.
3 The pomp of Casement's reburial is recorded by McDiarmid, p. 148.
4 For more information on Casement's re-interment see Wesley Hutchinson, 'Roger Casement et les Reliques de la Republique', *Études Irlandaises*, 26:1 (2001), 117–29.
5 Mosse, *Nationalism and Sexuality: Middle-Class Morality and Sexual Norms in Modern Europe* (Madison: University of Wisconsin Press, 1985), pp. 66–89.
6 Yeats, *A Vision* (New York: Macmillan, 1937), p. 143.
7 Further biographical information about Klein can be found in NLI, Roger McHugh Papers, Elmer Gertz's information for Chicago's 1956 G.B.S. Day, MS 31,732. See also 'Major General Julius Klein: His Life and His Work', *National Museum of American Jewish Military History* <http://www.nmajmh.org/exhibition/permanent.html> [accessed 15 August 2002].
8 Boucicault, p. 270.
9 BL, The Lord Chamberlain's Collection, *The Ulster Hero*, 1905/19N, fol.71.
10 Watt, p. 85.
11 The *Evening Post* is quoted by Mary Colum, *Life and the Dream*, rev. edn (Dublin: Dolmen, 1966), p. 207. Holloway, p. 186.
12 *Whom the Gods Destroy*. Dir. William P.S. Earle. Vitagraph Pictures. 1916. Information about the film is given by Anthony Slide, in *The Cinema and Ireland* (Jefferson: McFarland, 1988), pp. 104–6; and by Louisa Burns-Bisogno, in *Censoring Irish Nationalism: the British, Irish, and American Suppression of Republican Images in Film and Television, 1909–1995* (Jefferson: McFarland, 1997), pp. 33–34.
13 NLI, Frank Martin Papers, Scrapbooks, MS 32,695, I, 57.
14 'Roger Casement', in Fitzhenry, p. 75. 'A Longing: Eire to R.C.', in NLI, Frank Martin Papers, Scrapbooks, MS 32,695, I, 61.
15 *1916 Song Book*, p. 12.
16 This song, 'O Lordly Roger Casement', is printed by Brian Inglis, *Roger Casement* (London: Penguin, 2002), p. 376.
17 Indeed, when the Public Record Office released Casement's diaries in 1994 the *Irish Times* published the most pornographic excerpts during Holy Week. Rachel Borrill, 'Roger Casement's Numerous Homosexual Encounters Chronicled', *Irish Times*, 29 March 1994, p. 6.
18 Geoffrey Parmiter, *Roger Casement* (London: Barker, 1936). 'Roger Casement: A Tragic Failure', *Times Literary Supplement* (11 April 1936), 307. Shane Leslie, 'Roger Casement', *Times Literary Supplement* (18 April 1936), 336.

19 'Bernard Shaw on Casement Diaries', *Irish Press*, 11 February 1937, p. 9.

20 'Irish Novelist Replies to Mr. Shaw', *Irish Press*, 13 February 1937, p. 8.

21 For a detailed examination of Maloney's book and Noyes's recantation see W.J. McCormack, *Roger Casement in Death*, especially pp. 67–72.

22 Yeats's poem had read: 'Come Alfred Noyes and all the troop/That cried it far and wide,/Come from the forger and his desk,/Desert the perjurer's side'. It reappeared as: 'No matter what the names they wear!/A dog must have his day,/And whether a man be rich or poor/He takes the devil's pay'. 'Irish Poet's Striking Challenge', *Irish Press*, 2 February 1937, p. 6. 'Mr. Yeats Revises Song', *Irish Press*, 13 February 1937, p. 8.

23 Yeats reverted to the original verse, but changed the line that mentioned Noyes to 'Come Tom and Dick, come all the troop'. Yeats, *Complete Works*, rev. edn, I, 306.

24 See Roger Casement, *The Amazon Journal of Roger Casement*, ed. by Angus Mitchell (Dublin: Lilliput, 1997), p. 21.

25 NAI, Department of the Taoiseach, Sir Roger Casement Film and Book of Life, Letter of 4 August 1934 to Dorothy Hungerford from Gertrude Parry, S7804A.

26 NAI, Department of the Taoiseach, Sir Roger Casement Film and Book of Life, Letter of 4 August 1934 to Margaret Gavan Duffy from Gertrude Parry, S7804A.

27 NAI, Department of the Taoiseach, Sir Roger Casement Film and Book of Life, Note of 10 August 1934 from Chicago Consul to Department of External Affairs, S7804A.

28 NAI, Department of the Taoiseach, Sir Roger Casement Film and Book of Life, Letter of 10 September 1934 from Julius Klein to de Valera, S7804A.

29 Norris, p.31.

30 Turner, *Film as Social Practice*, 2nd edn (London: Routledge, 1993), p. 137.

31 'Film Notes', *Irish Times*, 18 December 1934, p. 4, similar comments are made in 'Film Notes', *Irish Times*, 4 December 1934, p. 4.

32 Klein, 'Skeleton of Story on Sir Roger Casement', now in the possession of Roger Sawyer, fol. 9.

33 NAI, Department of the Taoiseach, Sir Roger Casement Film and Book of Life, Letter of 11 October 1934 to Julius Klein from de Valera's private secretary, S7804A.

34 Casement was also Hibernicised by the Peacock theatre in 1937, where a play by John MacDonagh about Casement was only produced after it was translated into Irish by Seamus Ó Dubhda. 'Three Plays in Irish', *Irish Times*, 15 April 1936, p. 8.

35 Hanna's opinion is quoted by Brian McIlroy, *World Cinema 4: Ireland* (Trowbridge: Flicks, 1989), p. 31. The cost of Britain's military expenditure is estimated by Brian Moynahan, *The British Century: A Photographic History of the Last Hundred Years* (London: Weidenfeld and Nicolson, 1997), p. 164.

36 NLI, Roger McHugh Papers, Letter of 31 October 1934 to Julius Klein from BBFC, MS 31,732.

37 NAI, Department of the Taoiseach, Sir Roger Casement Film and Book of Life, Letter of 12 October 1934 to government from J. Deignan, S7804A. However, paradoxically, some members of the IRA wrote to Julius Klein, warning him to cease writing about Casement. I am grateful to Roger Sawyer for this information.

38 G.B. Shaw, *Bernard Shaw on Cinema*, ed. by Bernard F. Dukore (Carbondale: Southern Illinois University Press, 1997), p. 90.

39 Michael Holroyd, *Bernard Shaw: The One-Volume Definitive Edition* (London: Vintage, 1998), p. 377.

40 Quoted by Bernard F. Dukore, 'GBS, MGM, RKO: Shaw in Hollywood', *Shaw*, 5 (1985), 271–8 (p. 272).

41 NLI, Roger McHugh Papers, Letter of 19 December 1934 to Julius Klein from Shaw, MS 31,732.

42 BL, G.B. Shaw Papers, Letter of 3 December 1934 to Shaw from Julius Klein, Add. 50,520, fol. 257.

43 BL, G.B. Shaw Papers, Statement of 19 December 1934 to Julius Klein from Shaw,

Add. 50,678, fols 278–81.

44 Casement's copy of *John Bull's Other Island* was destroyed by the Home Office after his arrest, to the dismay of Gertrude Parry who wrote, 'I cannot describe the rage I feel when I think we were none of us allowed to see what he had written [. . .] To my mind more harm will be done to their cause by letting the fact of the <u>suppression</u> be known, than by any thing he could have written'. BL, Charlotte Shaw Papers, Letter of 30 October 1916 to Charlotte Shaw from Gertrude Parry, Add. 56,491, fols 230–1v (230v). Casement's praise for Shaw's journalism is related by Henry Nevinson, BL, G.B. Shaw Papers, Letter of 20 June 1916 to Shaw from Henry Nevinson, Add. 50,517, fol. 418.

45 For instance, Shaw received letters from 'A Bereaved Mother' and Mabel FitzGerald, both of whom had relatives in jail after the rebellion. BL, G.B. Shaw Papers, Letter of 12 May 1916 to Shaw from 'A. Bereaved Mother', Add. 50,517, fols 386–8. BL, G.B. Shaw Papers, Letter of 23 May 1916 to Shaw from Mabel FitzGerald, Add. 50,517, fols 396–9.

46 See Holroyd, p. 470.

47 Webb, *Beatrice Webb's Diaries 1912–1924*, ed. by Margaret I. Cole (London: Longmans, 1952), pp. 62–3. A more kindly interpretation of Shaw's intervention was offered by Henry Nevinson, who said, 'his highest value has always been the passionate and indignant seriousness with which he has thrown himself into all the most controversial questions of the time, always, in my view, on the right side [. . .] I may here mention [. . .] his share in our vain attempt to save his compatriot Roger Casement from the gallows'. Nevinson, 'Article in *Spectator*', in *George Bernard Shaw: The Critical Heritage*, ed. by T.F. Evans, rev. edn (London: Routledge, 1997), pp. 329–31 (pp. 330–1).

48 See Holroyd, p. 470.

49 BL, G.B. Shaw Papers, Roger Casement's notes on G.B. Shaw's 'Rex v. Casement' 1916, Add. 50,678, fols 246–54 (fol. 248).

50 BL, G.B. Shaw Papers, Roger Casement's notes on G.B. Shaw's 'Rex v. Casement' 1916, Add. 50,678, fols 246–54 (fol. 253).

51 Holroyd, p. 471.

52 G.B. Shaw's letters appeared in the *Manchester Guardian* and *Daily News*, and were rejected by *The Times*. His anonymously drafted petition to Asquith warned that to hang Casement would create a martyr.

53 Holroyd, p. 520.

54 Holroyd, p. 468.

55 For details of where and when the play was written see Brian Tyson, *The Story of Shaw's Saint Joan* (Kingston: McGill, 1982), pp. 6–8.

56 Kiberd, *Inventing Ireland*, p. 438.

57 G.B. Shaw, *The Bodley Head Bernard Shaw: Collected Plays with their Prefaces*, ed. by Dan H. Laurence, 7 vols (London: Bodley Head, 1973), VI, 45, 46. Further references to this edition will be given after quotations in the text.

58 An excellent study of Casement's impact on *Finnegans Wake* is offered by Robert L. Caserio, 'Casement, Joyce, and Pound: Some New Meanings of Treason', in *Quare Joyce*, ed. by Joseph Valente (Ann Arbor: University of Michigan Press, 1998), pp. 139–55.

59 Spoo, '"Nestor" and the Nightmare: The Presence of the Great War in *Ulysses*', *Twentieth Century Literature*, 32:2 (1986), 137–54. Joyce's dual time frame was too subtle for some: at the 1934 Congress of Soviet Writers Radek gave a paper that described Joyce's work as a heap of dung teeming with worms, and accused *Ulysses* of historical untruthfulness since it made no reference to the Easter Rising. Terry Eagleton, *Marxism and Literary Criticism* (London: Methuen, 1976), p. 38.

60 Walkley, 'A.B. Walkley, Unsigned Notice, *The Times*', in *George Bernard Shaw: The Critical Heritage*, ed. by T.F. Evans, rev. edn (London: Routledge, 1997), pp. 285–7

(p. 286). The *Christian Science Monitor* is quoted by Alice Griffin, 'The New York Critics and *Saint Joan*' in *Bernard Shaw's Plays: A Norton Critical Edition*, ed. by Warren S. Smith (London: Norton, 1970), pp. 451–7 (p. 452).

61 Weintraub, *Shaw's People: Victoria to Churchill* (University Park: Pennsylvania State University Press, 1996), p. 167. Thompson, p. xiii.

62 Tim Pat Coogan illustrates the ragbag nature of Casement's brigade most vividly, in *1916: The Easter Rising* (London: Cassell, 2001), p. 77.

63 Casement's words are reprinted by Mac Lochlainn, p. 203.

64 Gregory, *The Collected Plays*, ed. by Ann Saddlemyer, 4 vols (Gerrards Cross: Colin Smythe, 1970), III, 310.

65 G.B. Shaw, *The Matter with Ireland*, p. 133.

66 G.B. Shaw, *The Matter with Ireland*, p. 131.

67 Quoted by Angus Mitchell, *Casement* (London: Haus, 2003), p. 79.

68 Maxwell, 'Roberta Maxwell', *Playing Joan: Actresses on the Challenge of Shaw's* Saint Joan, ed. by Holly Hill (New York: Theatre Communications, 1987), pp. 201–9 (p. 205).

69 John Bowman, 'Cruise O'Brien Advised on how to Deal with the Casement Diaries', *Irish Times*, 3 January 2003 <http://www.ireland.com/newspaper/ireland/2003/0103/pf3575028827HM9SPCASEMENT.html> [accessed 29 May 2003] (para. 11 of 32).

70 NAI, Sir Roger Casement Film and Book of Life, Letter of 26 March 1935 to de Valera from Julius Klein, S7804A.

71 Monteith, *Casement's Last Adventure* (Chicago: Privately printed, 1932). 'Will Play Casement in Film', *Sunday Press*, 21 February 1954, p. 4.

72 McIlroy, p. 104.

73 I am indebted to Angus Mitchell for this information.

74 *The Lost World*. Dir. Irwin Allen. Fox. 1960. *Ryan's Daughter.* Dir. David Lean. MGM. 1970.

75 MacNeice, *Autumn Journal* (London, Faber, 1939), p. 61.

76 McDiarmid, p. 131.

77 Sawyer renounced his original belief that the diaries were forgeries whereas Mitchell's belief in the forgery theory was confirmed. In 1997 Mitchell published *The Amazon Journal of Roger Casement* and Sawyer published *Roger Casement's Diaries: 1910: the Black and the White* (London: Pimlico, 1997).

78 *New York Times*, 17 March 1992, p. A25.

79 McGuckian, *Drawing Ballerinas* (Oldcastle: Gallery, 2001), pp. 23–4.

80 I am grateful to Medbh McGuckian for this information.

81 McGuckian, *Selected Poems: 1978–1994* (Oldcastle: Gallery, 1997), p. 11.

82 NLI, *The Prisoner of the Crown*, MS 29,513.

83 McDonagh, *The Lieutenant of Inishmore* (London: Methuen, 2001), pp. 64–5.

84 McDonagh, *The Pillowman* (London: Faber, 2003), pp. 67–72.

85 See Sean O'Hagan, 'The Wild West', *Guardian*, 24 March 2001 <http://www.guardian.co.uk/weekend/story/0,461983,00.html> [accessed 12 July 2005] (para. 3 of 29).

6. Later Representations

1 'Zombie'. *No Need to Argue.* CD. The Cranberries. 1994.

2 Salman Rushdie, *Midnight's Children* (London: Vintage, 1995), p. 211.

3 Julia Carlson, ed., *Banned in Ireland: Censorship and the Irish Writer* (London: Routledge, 1990), p. 10.

4 For more details of Noyes's accusations see Inglis, pp. 376–80.

5 Noyes and McHugh's play is based on Noyes's repentant book that castigates the British for forging the 'black diaries', *The Accusing Ghost, or Justice for Casement* (London: Gollancz, 1957). The play was originally written for the radio.

6   NLI, *Roger Casement*, MS 31,748, fol. 2.

7   O'Flaherty, *Insurrection* (Dublin: Wolfhound, 1998), p. 28.

8   O'Flaherty, p. 29.

9   Ferriter, p. 147. Frank O'Connor, *The Big Fellow* (Dublin: Poolbeg, 1991), p. 41.

10 NLI, *Easter Christening*, MS 33,720, fol. 3. Further references to this manuscript will be given after quotations in the text.

11 Yeats, *Collected Works*, II, 314.

12 Farren, 'Lost Light: A Poetic Play about 1916', in *Rime, Gentlemen, Please*, ed. by Robert Farren (London: Sheed and Ward, 1945), pp. 78–112 (p. 104).

13 Farren, p. 109.

14 Blythe joined the IRB before the Rising, under the influence of Sean O'Casey, but was repeatedly arrested and spent Easter week in an Oxford jail cell.

15 I am grateful to Mairead Delaney for helping me to trace Mooney's career in the Abbey Theatre Archives.

16 *Mein Leben Für Irland*. Dir. Max Kimmich. Tobis-Filmkunst. 1941. The Tobis-Filmkunst company had a penchant for using Ireland as a setting in wartime propaganda films. They also produced *Der Fuchs von Glenarvon* ('The Fox from Glenarvon') in 1940, which tells the story of an English judge who betrays the Irish underground movement during the War of Independence.

17 Mac Lochlainn, p. 95.

18 Maynell and Gifford's poetry is reprinted by Marie O'Neill, pp. 48–9.

19 *The Dubliners 40 Years* CD.

20 Details of Gifford's pregnancy are given in the unpublished memoirs of her sister-in-law Geraldine Dillon. See Marie O'Neill, p. 45.

21 'Take me', she murmured. She added, 'for a long while'. Queneau, *On est toujours trop bon avec les femmes* (Paris: Gallimard, 2001), p. 123.

22 'But, I assure you, with a woman that is not the way to do it. But you are stupid. You think you are doing it with a man. But I tell you it is not like that.' Queneau, pp. 216–17.

23 Alan Simpson's version of Tennessee Williams's *The Rose Tattoo* at the Pike was prosecuted for obscenity in 1957. See Morash, p. 219.

24 Mary Maher, 'A Lovely Day for the Marching Men', *Irish Times*, 11 April 1966, p. 1. 'Nation Honours Men of 1916', *Irish Independent*, 11 April 1966, p. 1.

25 '"A Nation of Brothers" was Ultimate Goal of the Seven Signatories', *Irish Times*, 11 April 1966, p. 12. '16 Athletes Represent the Leaders', *Irish Independent*, 11 April 1966, p. 7. Just like the celebration of masculinity at the Kilkenny celebrations, in the 1970s Ulick O'Connor described Pearse as having the body of a 'world champion boxer'. NLI, *Padraic Pearse: A One Man Show*, MS 29,414, fol. 21.

26 Jack Cruise's *Easter Parade* combined Pearse's poems and a depiction of the Rising with parodic sketches about the mod craze and Gay Byrne's *Late Late Show*. See '"Late Late" Parody is a Real Gem', *Irish Independent*, 12 April 1966, p. 4. For information about McCabe's play, *Pull Down a Horseman*, see Colm Cronin, 'Playing Pearse', *Irish Press*, 8/9 April 1966, p. 9.

27 Like *The Dreaming of the Bones*, *Dervorgilla* features a wandering stranger who encounters a disguised Dervorgilla, and when her identity is revealed at the end of the play she is again refused the forgiveness that she craves. Gregory, *Collected Plays*, II, 93–112.

28 Colm Cronin, 'Abbey Captures Spirit of 1916 in Play Series', *Irish Press*, 12 April 1966, p. 8.

29 Ferriter, p. 564.

30 'President at Opening of '16 Pageant', *Irish Press*, 13 April 1966, p. 1.

31 Much has been written about the origins of revisionism, but two of the best accounts are Luke Gibbons's 'Challenging the Canon: Revisionism and Cultural Criticism', in *Field Day*, III, 561–8, and Stephen Howes's *Ireland and Empire: Colonial Legacies in Irish History and Culture* (Oxford: Oxford University Press, 2002), pp. 76–95.

32 Lyons, *Culture and Anarchy in Ireland 1890–1939* (Oxford: Clarendon Press, 1979), p. 1.
33 Francis Shaw, 'The Canon of Irish History – A Challenge', *Studies*, 242 (1972), 117–53.
34 Krause, p. 16, p. 5.
35 Kavanagh, *Selected Poems*, ed. by Antoinette Quinn (Harmondsworth: Penguin, 1996), pp. 18–44.
36 Thompson, pp. 123–4.
37 Murdoch, *The Red and the Green* (London: Vintage, 2002), p. 209.
38 For the jokes about Casement see McDiarmid, p. 146. For information about Mac Liammoir see Walshe, p. 151.
39 I am grateful to Mairead Delaney for helping me find this information in the Abbey Theatre Archives.
40 Brien, 'O'Casey for Today', *Sunday Telegraph*, 7 October 1962, p. 10. See also Bernice Schrank, *Sean O'Casey: A Research and Production Sourcebook* (Westport: Greenwood, 1996), p. 53.
41 Seamus Deane was dismayed by those who found parallels between the situation in the North and O'Casey's Dublin trilogy. He wrote, 'it would be wrong, especially in present conditions, to take him [O'Casey] as our paradigm of a dramatist who made political preoccupation central to his work'. Deane later reprinted these thoughts with some interesting alterations and excisions in his book *Celtic Revivals*. Deane, 'Irish Politics and O'Casey's Theatre', pp. 11–12; and *Celtic Revivals: Essays in Modern Irish Literature, 1880–1980* (London: Faber, 1985), pp. 108–22 (p. 122).
42 See 'Ploughing Twice', *Irish Independent*, 8 May 1991, p. 8; and 'O'Casey Given the Hynes Treatment: Stars Come Out to See New Plough', *Irish Press*, 8 May 1991, p. 3.
43 Quoted by Joseph Ronsley, 'A Humane and Well-Intentioned Piece of Gallantry: Denis Johnston's *The Scythe and the Sunset*', in *Denis Johnston: A Retrospective*, ed. by Joseph Ronsley (Gerrards Cross: Colin Smythe, 1981), pp. 133–56 (p. 133).
44 Behan, *The Dubbalin Man*, p. 75.
45 Behan, *An Giall and the Hostage*, trans. by Richard Wall (Gerrards Cross: Colin Smythe, 1987), p. 38.
46 Behan, *An Giall and the Hostage*, pp. 139–41.
47 Johnston, *The Dramatic Works of Denis Johnston*, 2 vols (Gerrards Cross: Colin Smythe, 1977), I, 107. Further references to this edition will be given after quotations in the text.
48 Leonard, *Home Before Night* (Harmondsworth: Penguin, 1981), p. 159.
49 *Insurrection*. Dir. Louis Lentin. RTÉ. 1966.
50 Declan Kiberd writes that few Northern homes could actually receive the RTÉ transmission in 1966. 'The Elephant of Revolutionary Forgetfulness', in Ní Dhonnchadha and Dorgan, pp. 1–20 (p. 2).
51 The characters of *The Patrick Pearse Motel* invite a cabinet minister to unveil a bust in the 'De Valera Snackery', a bishop to bless their 'Kitchen Garden of Remembrance', and a guard of honour to fire a salute over their swimming pool. Leonard, *Selected Plays of Hugh Leonard*, ed. by S.F. Gallagher (Gerrards Cross: Colin Smythe, 1992), p. 158.
52 Leonard, *Selected Plays*, p. 140.
53 Leonard, *Selected Plays*, p. 124.
54 Leonard, *Selected Plays*, p. 100.
55 D'Arcy and Arden, *The Non-Stop Connolly Show*, 5 vols (London: Pluto Press, 1977), I, v.
56 D'Arcy and Arden, V, 79.
57 D'Arcy and Arden, I, 14.
58 D'Arcy and Arden, V, 54, 22.
59 *Young Indiana Jones, Chapter 7: 'Love's Sweet Song'*. Dir. Gilles MacKinnon and Carl Schultz. ABC. 1992.
60 See Nicholas Wroe, 'Britain's Brecht', *Guardian*, 3 January 2004, <http://www.guardian.co.uk/arts/features/story/0,11710,1115212,00.html#article_continue> [accessed 16 July 2005] (para. 27 of 30).
61 O'Flynn, *A Man Called Pearse* (Dublin: FNT, 1980), p. 14.

62   NLI, *The Prisoner of the Crown*, MS 29,513, fols 11–12.

63   Rudkin, p. 25.

64   McGuinness, *Innocence: the Life and Death of Michelangelo Merisi, Caravaggio* (London: Faber, 1987). Friel, *The Gentle Island* (Oldcastle: Gallery, 1993). Kilroy, *The Death and Resurrection of Mr Roche: A Comedy in Three Acts* (London: Faber, 1969).

65   Kilfeather, 'Contesting Ireland: The Erosion of Heterosexual Consensus, 1940–2001', in *Field Day*, IV, 1039–41 (p. 1040).

66   O'Neill, *At Swim Two Boys* (London: Scribner, 2001), p. 512.

67   'Sex, Lies and the Black Diaries', *Irish Times*, 2 March 2002, Weekend section, p. 4. Colm Tóibín, *Love in a Dark Time* (London: Picador, 2002).

68   See Fiachre Gibbons, 'Casement Painting goes on Display', *Guardian*, 2 July 2003 <http://www.guardian.co.uk/uk_news/story/0,,989276,00.html> [accessed 16 July 2005].

69   Angus Mitchell, 'The Casement "Black Diaries" Debate: the Story So Far', *History Ireland* (Summer 2001), 42–5 (p. 43).

70   *Secrets of the Black Diaries*. Prod. Paul Tilzey. BBC 4. 15 March 2002.

71   *The Ghost of Roger Casement*. Prod. Alan Gilsenan. RTÉ 1. 14 March 2002.

72   *Michael Collins*. Dir. Neil Jordan. Warner Bros. 1996. Something similar happens in the 1992 Irish episode of *Young Indiana Jones*. Indy tries to seduce Maggie Lemass, but is thwarted by the third person in their relationship, her rebel brother Seán (the future Taoiseach), whose company Indy comes to enjoy more than that of Maggie herself.

73   See Cullingford, *Ireland's Others*, p. 94.

74   Ferriter, p. 666.

75   Tom Dunne, 'New Histories: beyond "Revisionism"', *Irish Review*, 12 (1992), 1–12.

76   Smyth, ed., *Wildish Things: An Anthology of New Irish Women's Writing* (Dublin: Attic, 1989). Ní Dhuibhne, ed., *Voices on the Wind: Women Poets of the Celtic Twilight* (Dundrum: New Island, 1995).

77   For more about the Field Day controversy see Marilynn J. Richtarik, *Acting Between the Lines: The Field Day Theatre Company and Irish Cultural Politics 1980–1984* (Oxford: Clarendon Press, 1994), pp. 266–9.

78   *Ferocious Humanism: An Anthology of Irish Poetry from Before Swift to Yeats and After*, ed. by W.J. McCormack (London: Dent, 2000). Marreco, *The Rebel Countess: The Life and Times of Constance Markievicz*, rev. edn (London: Phoenix, 2000).

79   Roddy Doyle, *A Star Called Henry* (London: Jonathan Cape, 1999), p. 132.

80   Roddy Doyle, p. 231.

81   *Rebel Heart*. Prod. Kevin Jackson, Robert Cooper, and Malcolm Craddock. BBC 1. 2000.

82   Charabanc staged eighteen new plays between its inception in 1983 and its termination in 1995. Claudia W. Harris, 'Reinventing Women: Charabanc Theatre Company: Recasting Northern Ireland's Story', in *The State of Play: Irish Theatre in the Nineties*, ed. by Eberhard Bort (Trier: Wissenschaftlicher Verlag Trier, 1996), pp. 104–23 (p. 105).

83   *The Witness* is described by Jean Sheridan, 'A Noble Evocation of 1916 Sung and Acted', *Irish Press*, 12 April 1966, p. 9.

84   Murphy, *Plays: One* (London: Methuen, 1992), p. 133.

85   McGuinness, *Plays I* (London: Faber, 1996), p. 175.

86   Tóibín, *Beauty in a Broken Place* (Dublin: Lilliput, 2004), p. 56.

87   MacIntyre, 'Good Evening, Mr Collins', in *The Dazzling Dark: New Irish Plays*, ed. by Frank McGuinness (London: Faber, 1996), pp. 173–234 (pp. 232–3).

88   Nuala Haughey, 'Shop to appeal corporation order to close down', *Irish Times*, 2 October 1999 <http://www.ireland.com/newspaper/front/1999/1002/archive.99100200002.html> [accessed 16 July 2005]. Matt Doyle, 'A Name for the Spike', *Irish Times*, 22 November 2002 <http://www.ireland.com/newspaper/letters/2002/1122/index.html#1036708355694> [accessed 16 July 2005] (letter 8 of 15).

Works Cited

Bibliography of Published Sources

Arblaster, Anthony, *Viva la Libertà!: Politics in Opera* (London: Verso, 1992)

Babbage, Frances, *Augusto Boal* (London: Routledge, 2004)

Ballagh, Bobby, '1916 – Goodbye to All That?', *Irish Reporter*, 2 (1991), 6–8

Barnes, Ben, 'Vision and Revision', in *The Page and the Stage: The Plough and the Stars*, ed. by Martin Drury (Dublin: Abbey Theatre, 2003), pp. 47–9

Beckett, Samuel, *Murphy* (London: Calder, 1993)

Behan, Brendan, *Borstal Boy* (London: Arrow, 1990)

——, *An Giall and the Hostage*, trans. by Richard Wall (Gerrards Cross: Colin Smythe, 1987)

——, *The Dubbalin Man: A New Selection of his Irish Press Columns* (Dublin: A & A Farmar, 1997)

Benjamin, Walter, 'Unpacking My Library: A Talk about Book Collecting', in *Illuminations*, ed. by Hannah Arendt, trans. by Harry Zorn (London: Pimlico, 1999), pp. 61–9

Beresford, David, *Ten Men Dead: The Story of the 1981 Hunger Strike* (London: Grafton, 1987)

Bernhardt-House, Phillip A., 'Youth, Warriors, and Homoerotic Reproduction: Queer and Celtic in Irish Studies as Strange Bedfellows', *Foilsiú*, 4:1 (2004), 85–93

Bew, Paul, 'The Easter Rising: Lost Leader and Lost Opportunities', *The Irish Review*, 11 (1991/2), 9–13

Boal, Augusto, *Legislative Theatre: Using Performance to Make Politics* (London: Routledge, 1998)

Boucicault, Dion, 'Robert Emmet', in *Forbidden Fruit and Other Plays*, ed. by Allardyce Nicoll and F. Theodore Cloak (Bloomington: Indiana Press, 1963), pp. 263–313

Bourke, Angela, Siobhán Kilfeather, Maria Luddy, Margaret Mac Curtain, Gerardine Meaney, Máirín Ní Dhonnchadha, Mary O'Dowd, and Clair Wills, eds, *The Field Day Anthology of Irish Writing: Irish Women's Writing and Traditions*, 2 vols (Cork: Cork University Press, 2002)

Bourke, Patrick, 'For the Land She Loved', in *For the Land They Loved: Irish Political Melodramas, 1890–1925*, ed. by Cheryl Herr (Syracuse: Syracuse University Press, 1991), pp. 311–59

Boyce, D. George, '1916, Interpreting the Rising', in *The Making of Modern Irish History: Revisionism and the Revisionist Controversy*, ed. by D. George Boyce and Alan O'Day (London: Routledge, 1996), pp. 163–87

Buckland, Patrick, *'Ireland in Schools': Irish History in Song 2: Some Notes* (Liverpool: Ireland in Schools, 2002)

'Bunreacht na hÉireann, Constitution of Ireland',
<http://www.taoiseach.gov.ie/upload/publications/297.htm> [accessed 23 August
2003]

Burns-Bisogno, Louisa, *Censoring Irish Nationalism: the British, Irish, and American
Suppression of Republican Images in Film and Television, 1909–1995* (Jefferson: McFarland, 1997)

Cabezali, Elena, Matilde Cuevas, and Maria Teresa Chicote, 'Myth as Suppression: Motherhood and the Historical Consciousness of the Women of Madrid, 1936–9', in *The
Myths We Live By*, ed. by Raphael Samuel and Paul Thompson (Routledge: London,
1990), pp. 161–73

Cairns, David and Shaun Richards, *Writing Ireland* (Manchester: Manchester University
Press, 1988)

Carlson, Julia, ed., *Banned in Ireland: Censorship and the Irish Writer* (London: Routledge,
1990)

Carlson, Marvin, *Performance: A Critical Introduction* (London: Routledge, 1996)

Carroll, Paul Vincent, 'The Conspirators', in *Irish Stories and Plays* (New York: Devin-Adair, 1958), pp. 111–29

Casement, Roger, *Roger Casement's Diaries: 1910: the Black and the White*, ed. by Roger
Sawyer (London: Pimlico, 1997)

——, *The Amazon Journal of Roger Casement* ed. by Angus Mitchell (Dublin: Lilliput,
1997)

Caserio, Robert L., 'Casement, Joyce, and Pound: Some New Meanings of Treason', in
Quare Joyce, ed. by Joseph Valente (Ann Arbor: University of Michigan Press, 1998),
pp. 139–55

Caulfield, Max, *The Easter Rebellion: Dublin 1916*, 2nd edn (Boulder: Roberts Rinehart,
1995)

Chadwick, Joseph, 'Family Romance as National Allegory in Yeats's *Cathleen ni Houlihan* and *The Dreaming of the Bones*', *Twentieth Century Literature*, 32:2 (1986),
155–68

Clark, David R., 'Nishikigi and Yeats's *The Dreaming of the Bones*', *Modern Drama*, 7:2
(1964), 111–25

Clarke, Kathleen, *Revolutionary Woman: My Fight for Ireland's Freedom*, ed. by Helen
Litton (Dublin: O'Brien, 1991)

Colum, Mary, *Life and the Dream*, rev. edn (Dublin: Dolmen, 1966)

Colum, Padraic and Edward J. O'Brien, eds, *Poems of the Irish Revolutionary Brotherhood*,
rev. edn (Boston: Small, Maynard & Co., 1916)

Connolly, James, *James Connolly: Selected Writings*, ed. by Peter Beresford Ellis (London:
Pluto Press, 1997)

Coogan, Tim Pat, 'The Exile', in *The World of Sean O'Casey*, ed. by Sean McCann
(London: Four Square, 1966), pp. 106–28

——, *Michael Collins: A Biography* (London: Hutchinson, 1990)

——, *De Valera: Long Fellow, Long Shadow* (London: Hutchinson, 1993)

——, *1916: The Easter Rising* (London: Cassell, 2001)

——, *Ireland in the Twentieth Century* (London: Hutchinson, 2003)

Corkery, Daniel, *The Labour Leader* (Dublin: Talbot, 1920)

——, 'Resurrection', *Theatre Arts Monthly*, 8:4 (1924), 259–72

——, *Synge and Anglo-Irish Literature* (Cork: Mercier, 1966)

Craig, Edward Gordon (under the pseudonym John Balance), 'A Note on Masks', *The
Mask*, 1:1 (1908), 9–12

Cronin, Maura, 'Women and Fenianism', in *Ireland (Ulster) Scotland: Concepts, Contexts, Comparisons*, ed. by Edna Longley, Eamonn Hughes, and Des O'Rawe (Belfast: Queens University Press, 2003), pp. 206–12

Cronin, Sean, *The McGarrity Papers: Revelations of the Irish Revolutionary Movement in Ireland and America 1900–1940* (Tralee: Anvil, 1972)

Cullingford, Elizabeth Butler, '"Thinking of Her . . . as . . . Ireland": Yeats, Pearse and Heaney', *Textual Practice*, 4:1 (1990), 1–21

——, *Ireland's Others: Gender and Ethnicity in Irish Literature and Popular Culture* (Cork: Cork University Press, 2001)

Dalton, Maurice, *Sable and Gold* (Dublin: Maunsel, 1922)

D'Arcy, Margaretta and John Arden, *The Non-Stop Connolly Show*, 5 vols (London: Pluto Press, 1977)

Davies, R.G., 'Guerrilla Theatre', *Tulane Drama Review*, 10:4 (1966), 130–6

Deane, Seamus, 'Irish Politics and O'Casey's Theatre', *Threshold*, 24 (1973), 5–16

——, *Celtic Revivals: Essays in Modern Irish Literature, 1880–1980* (London: Faber, 1985)

——, *Strange Country* (Oxford: Clarendon Press, 1997)

Deane, Seamus, Andrew Carpenter, and Jonathan Williams, eds, *The Field Day Anthology of Irish Writing*, 3 vols (Derry: Field Day, 1991)

Deputies of Dáil Éireann, *Tuairisg Oifigiúil: Díosbóireacht ar an gConnradh Idir Éire Agus Sasana*, ed. by Dáil Éireann staff (Dublin: Talbot, 1922)

De Rosa, Peter, *Rebels: The Irish Rising of 1916* (New York: Fawcett Columbine, 1990)

Devlin, Anne, *Ourselves Alone* (London: Faber, 1990)

Dolan, Anne, 'Commemoration: "Shows and stunts are all that is the thing now" – the Revolution Remembered, 1923–52', in *The Irish Revolution 1913–1923* , ed. by Joost Augusteijn (Houndmills: Palgrave, 2002), pp. 186–202

Donoghue, Denis, *Yeats* (London: Fontana, 1971)

Doyle, Roddy, *A Star Called Henry* (London: Jonathan Cape, 1999)

The Dubliners, *More Dubliners Songs* (London: Wise, 1979)

Dudgeon, Jeff, *Roger Casement: the Black Diaries: With a Study of His Background, Sexuality and Irish Political Life* (Belfast: Belfast Press, 2002)

Dudley Edwards, Ruth, *Patrick Pearse: The Triumph of Failure* (London: Gollancz, 1977)

Dukore, Bernard F., 'GBS, MGM, RKO: Shaw in Hollywood', *Shaw*, 5 (1985), 271–78

Dunne, Tom, 'New Histories: beyond "Revisionism"', *Irish Review*, 12 (1992), 1–12

Eagleton, Terry, *Marxism and Literary Criticism* (London: Methuen, 1976)

Esslin, Martin, *An Anatomy of Drama* (London: Temple Smith, 1978)

Fallon, Gabriel, 'The House on the North Circular Road: Fragments from a Biography', *Modern Drama*, 4 (1961), 223–33

Fanning, Ronan, 'The Rule of Order: Eamon de Valera and the IRA, 1923–40', in *De Valera and his Times*, ed. by John P. O'Carroll and John A. Murphy (Cork: Cork University Press, 1983), pp. 160–72

Farren, Robert, 'Lost Light: A Poetic Play about 1916', in *Rime, Gentlemen, Please*, ed. by Robert Farren (London: Sheed and Ward, 1945), pp. 78–112

Ferriter, Diarmaid, *The Transformation of Ireland 1900–2000* (London: Profile, 2004)

Finneran, Richard J., *The Olympian and the Leprechaun: W.B. Yeats and James Stephens* (Dublin: Dolmen, 1978)

Fitzhenry, Edna C., ed., *Nineteen-Sixteen: An Anthology* (Dublin: Browne and Nolan, 1935)

Fitzpatrick, David, 'De Valera in 1917: the Undoing of the Easter Rising', in *De Valera and His Times*, ed. by John P. O'Carroll and John A. Murphy (Cork: Cork University Press, 1983), pp. 101–12

Foster, John Wilson, *Colonial Consequences: Essays in Irish Literature and Culture* (Dublin: Lilliput, 1991)

Foster, R.F., *W.B. Yeats: A Life: 1, The Apprentice Mage* (Oxford: Oxford University Press, 1997)

——, *W.B. Yeats: A Life: II, The Arch-Poet* (Oxford: Oxford University Press, 2003)

Foy, Michael and Brian Barton, *The Easter Rising* (Phoenix Mill: Sutton, 1999)

Friel, Brian, *The Gentle Island* (Oldcastle: Gallery, 1993)

Galsworthy, John, *Strife*, ed. by Non Worral (London: Methuen, 1984)

Gaynor, J.P., 'A.O.H. and Rebellion: A Reply to Critics of Our Organisation', *Hibernian Journal*, 6:3 (1916), 271

Gibbons, Luke, 'Challenging the Canon: Revisionism and Cultural Criticism', in *The Field Day Anthology of Irish Writing*, ed. by Seamus Deane, Andrew Carpenter, and Jonathan Williams, 3 vols (London: Faber, 1991), III, 561–8

——, 'The Camel in the Koran: Rumour in Irish Politics', *Irish Reporter*, 5 (1992), 12–15

Gillis, Father, *Irish Rosary* (September 1935), 651

Girard, René, *Deceit, Desire and the Novel: Self and Other in Literary Structure*, trans. by Yvonne Freccero (London: John Hopkins University Press, 1976)

Glenny, Misha, *The Balkans 1804–1999: Nationalism, War and the Great Powers* (London: Granta, 2000)

Gonne, Maud and W.B. Yeats, *The Gonne–Yeats Letters 1893–1938: Always Your Friend*, ed. by Anna MacBride White and A. Norman Jeffares (London: Hutchinson, 1992)

Gorman, Declan, 'Prejudice on Parade', *Irish Reporter*, 2 (1991), 9–11

Grant, Madison, *The Passing of the Great Race: or The Racial Basis of European History* (London: Bell, 1917)

Greaves, Desmond, *Sean O'Casey, Politics and Art* (London: Lawrence and Wishart, 1979)

Gregory, Augusta, *The Collected Plays*, ed. by Ann Saddlemyer, 4 vols (Gerrards Cross: Colin Smythe, 1970)

——, *Seventy Years, Being the Autobiography of Lady Gregory* (Gerrards Cross: Colin Smythe, 1974)

——, *Lady Gregory's Journals*, ed. by Daniel J. Murphy, 2 vols (New York: Oxford University Press, 1987)

Grene, Nicholas, *The Politics of Irish Drama: Plays in Context from Boucicault to Friel* (Cambridge: Cambridge University Press, 1999)

——, 'The Class of the Clitheroes: O'Casey's Revisions to *The Plough and the Stars* Promptbook', *Bullán: An Irish Studies Journal*, 4:2 (1999/2000), 57–66

Griffin, Alice, 'The New York Critics and *Saint Joan*', in *Bernard Shaw's Plays: A Norton Critical Edition*, ed. by Warren S. Smith (London: Norton, 1970), pp. 451–7

'Guerrilla Girls Bare All', <http://www.guerrillagirls.com/interview/index.shtml> [accessed 22 January 2005]

Harris, Claudia W., 'Reinventing Women: Charabanc Theatre Company: Recasting Northern Ireland's Story', in *State of Play: Irish Theatre in the Nineties*, ed. by Eberhard Bort (Trier: Wissenschaftlicher Verlag Trier, 1996), pp. 104–23

Harris, Susan Cannon, 'Watch Yourself: Performance, Sexual Difference, and National Identity in the Irish Plays of Frank McGuinness', *Genders*, 28 (1998) <http://www.genders.org/g28/g28_watchyourself.html> [accessed 12 December 2002]

——, 'More Than a Morbid, Unhealthy Mind: Public Health and the *Playboy* Riots', in *A Century of Irish Drama: Widening the Stage*, ed. by Stephen Watt, Eileen Morgan, and Shakir Mustafa (Bloomington: Indiana University Press, 2000), pp. 72–94

——, *Gender and Modern Irish Drama* (Bloomington: Indiana University Press, 2002)

Herr, Cheryl, *For the Land They Loved: Irish Political Melodramas, 1890–1925* (Syracuse: Syracuse University Press, 1991)

Hogan, Robert, James Kilroy, Richard Burnham, and Daniel P. Poteet, eds, *The Modern Irish Drama: A Documentary History*, 6 vols (Dublin: Dolmen, 1975–1984 and Gerrards Cross: Colin Smythe, 1992)

Holloway, Joseph, *Joseph Holloway's Abbey Theatre: A Selection from his Unpublished Journal, Impressions of a Dublin Playgoer*, ed. by Robert Hogan and Michael J. O'Neill (London: Southern Illinois University Press, 1967)

Holroyd, Michael, *Bernard Shaw: The One-Volume Definitive Edition* (London: Vintage, 1998)

Howes, Marjorie, *Yeats's Nations: Gender, Class and Irishness* (Cambridge: Cambridge University Press, 1996)

Howes, Stephen, *Ireland and Empire: Colonial Legacies in Irish History and Culture* (Oxford: Oxford University Press, 2002)

Hutchinson, Wesley, 'Roger Casement et les Reliques de la Republique', *Études Irlandaises*, 26:1 (2001), 117–29

Inglis, Brian, *Roger Casement* (London: Penguin, 2002)

Ishibashi, Hiro, *Yeats and the Noh: Types of Japanese Beauty and their Reflection in Yeats's Plays*, ed. by Anthony Kerrigan (Dublin: Dolmen, 1966)

Jeffares, A. Norman, *A Commentary on the Collected Poems of W.B. Yeats* (London: Macmillan, 1968)

Johnston, Denis, *The Dramatic Works of Denis Johnston*, 2 vols (Gerrards Cross: Colin Smythe, 1977)

——, *Orders and Desecrations: The Life of the Playwright Denis Johnston*, ed. by Rory Johnston (Dublin: Lilliput, 1992)

Joyce, James, *Ulysses*, ed. by Declan Kiberd (London: Penguin, 1992)

——, *Finnegans Wake*, ed. by Seamus Deane (London: Penguin, 1993)

Jung, Carl, *The Collected Works of C.G. Jung: Civilization in Transition*, trans. by R.F.C. Hull, 2nd edn (London: Routledge, 1970)

Kavanagh, Patrick, *Selected Poems*, ed. by Antoinette Quinn (Harmondsworth: Penguin, 1996)

Keane, Patrick, *Terrible Beauty: Yeats, Joyce, Ireland, and the Myth of the Devouring Female* (Columbia: University of Missouri Press, 1988)

Kennedy, Finola, *Cottage to Crèche: Family Change in Ireland* (Dublin: Institute of Public Administration, 2001)

Keogh, Dermot, *Twentieth Century Ireland: Nation and State* (Dublin: Gill and Macmillan, 1994)

Kevles, Daniel J., *In the Name of Eugenics: Genetics and the Uses of Human Heredity* (Cambridge, MA: Harvard University Press, 1995)

Kiberd, Declan, 'The Elephant of Revolutionary Forgetfulness', in *Revising the Rising*, ed. by Máirín Ní Dhonnchadha and Theo Dorgan (Derry: Field Day, 1991), pp. 1–20

——, 'Eamon de Valera: The Image and the Achievement', in *Taking the Long View: Seventy Years of Fianna Fáil*, ed. by Philip Hannon and Jackie Gallagher (Dublin: Blackwater Press, 1996), pp. 21–8

——, *Inventing Ireland: The Literature of the Modern Nation* (London: Vintage, 1996)

Kilfeather, Siobhán, 'Contesting Ireland: The Erosion of Heterosexual Consensus, 1940–2001', in *The Field Day Anthology of Irish Writing: Irish Women's Writing and Traditions*, ed. by Angela Bourke, Siobhán Kilfeather, Maria Luddy, Margaret Mac

Curtain, Gerardine Meaney, Máirín Ní Dhonnchadha, Mary O'Dowd, and Clair Wills, 2 vols (Cork: Cork University Press, 2002), IV, 1039–41

Kilroy, Thomas, *The Death and Resurrection of Mr. Roche: A Comedy in Three Acts* (London: Faber, 1969)

Kostick, Conor and Lorcan Collins, *The Easter Rising: A Guide to Dublin in 1916* (Dublin: O'Brien, 2000)

Kowsan, Tadeusz, *Littérature et spectacle*, rev. edn (Paris: Mouton, 1975)

Krause, David, 'Some Truths and Jokes about the Easter Rising', *Sean O'Casey Review*, 3:1 (1976), 3–23

Kuch, Peter, '"For Poetry Makes Nothing Happen": The Poetry of Yeats and the Politics of Ireland', in *Yeats: An Annual of Critical and Textual Studies*, 8 (1990), 188–205

Leach, Robert, 'Revolutionary Theatre, 1917–1930', in *A History of Russian Theatre*, ed. by Robert Leach and Victor Borovsky (Cambridge: Cambridge University Press, 1999)

Lee, J.J., *Ireland 1912–1985: Politics and Society* (Cambridge: Cambridge University Press, 1989)

Lenin, V.I., 'The Irish Rebellion of 1916', in *1916: The Easter Rising*, ed. by O. Dudley Edwards and Fergus Pyle (London: MacGibbon and Kee, 1968), pp. 191–5

Leonard, Hugh, *Home Before Night* (Harmondsworth: Penguin, 1981)

——, *Selected Plays of Hugh Leonard*, ed. by S.F. Gallagher (Gerrards Cross: Colin Smythe, 1992)

Leslie, Shane, 'Roger Casement', *Times Literary Supplement* (18 April 1936), 336

Levitas, Ben, *The Theatre of Nation: Irish Drama and Cultural Nationalism 1890–1916* (Oxford: Clarendon Press, 2002)

Lloyd, David, *Anomalous States: Irish Writing and the Post-Colonial Moment* (Dublin: Lilliput, 1993)

——, *Ireland After History* (Cork: Cork University Press, 1999)

Longley, Edna, 'Helicon and ni Houlihan: *Michael Robartes and the Dancer*', in *Yeats's Political Identities: Selected Essays*, ed. by Jonathan Allison (Ann Arbor: University of Michigan Press, 1996), pp. 203–20

——, 'Northern Ireland: Commemoration, Elegy, Forgetting', in *History and Memory in Modern Ireland*, ed. by Ian McBride (Cambridge: Cambridge University Press, 2001), pp. 223–53

Lowery, Robert G., 'Prelude to Year One: Sean O'Casey Before 1916', *Sean O'Casey Review*, 2:2 (1976), 92–103

——, ed., *A Whirlwind in Dublin:* The Plough and the Stars *Riots* (Westport: Greenwood Press, 1984)

Lyons, F.S.L., *Culture and Anarchy in Ireland 1890–1939* (Oxford: Clarendon Press, 1979)

MacAnna, Thomas, 'Nationalism from the Abbey stage', in *Theatre and Nationalism in Twentieth Century Ireland*, ed. by Robert O'Driscoll (London: Oxford University Press, 1971), pp. 89–101

McCormack, W.J., *From Burke to Beckett: Ascendancy, Tradition and Betrayal in Literary History* (Cork: Cork University Press, 1994)

——, ed., *Ferocious Humanism: An Anthology of Irish Poetry from Before Swift to Yeats and After* (London: Dent, 2000)

——, *Fool of the Family: A Life of J.M. Synge* (London: Weidenfeld and Nicolson, 2000)

——, *Roger Casement in Death: Or Haunting the Free State* (Dublin: University College Dublin Press, 2002)

McDiarmid, Lucy, 'The Posthumous Life of Roger Casement', in *Gender and Sexuality in Modern Ireland*, ed. by Anthony Bradley and Maryann Valiulis (Amherst: University of Massachusetts Press, 1997), pp. 127–58

McDonagh, Martin, *The Lieutenant of Inishmore* (London: Methuen, 2001)

——, *The Pillowman* (London: Faber, 2003)

MacDonagh, Thomas, *When the Dawn is Come: A Tragedy in Three Acts* (Dublin: Maunsel, 1908)

——, *Pagans: A Modern Play in Two Conversations* (Dublin: Talbot, 1920)

McDonald, Ronan, *Tragedy and Irish Literature: Synge, O'Casey, Beckett* (Basingstoke: Palgrave, 2002)

McGarry, James P., *Place Names in the Writings of William Butler Yeats*, ed. by Edward Mallins (Gerrards Cross: Colin Smythe, 1976)

McGuckian, Medbh, *Selected Poems: 1978–1994* (Oldcastle: Gallery, 1997)

——, *Drawing Ballerinas* (Oldcastle: Gallery, 2001)

McGuinness, Frank, *Innocence: the Life and Death of Michelangelo Merisi, Caravaggio* (London: Faber, 1987)

——, *Plays I* (London: Faber, 1996)

McHugh, Roger, '"Always Complainin'": The Politics of Young Sean', *Irish University Review*, 10:1 (1980), 91–7

McIlroy, Brian, *World Cinema 4: Ireland* (Trowbridge: Flicks, 1989)

MacIntyre, Tom, 'Good Evening, Mr Collins', in *The Dazzling Dark: New Irish Plays*, ed. by Frank McGuinness (London: Faber, 1996), pp. 173–234

MacLaverty, Bernard, *Cal* (London: Vintage, 1998)

Mac Lochlainn, Piaras F., ed., *Last Words* (Dublin: Stationery Office, 1990)

MacNeice, Louis, *Autumn Journal* (London, Faber, 1939)

'Major General Julius Klein: His Life and His Work', *National Museum of American Jewish Military History* <http://www.nmajmh.org/exhibition/permanent.html> [accessed 15 August 2002]

Marreco, Anne, *The Rebel Countess: The Life and Times of Constance Markievicz*, rev. edn (London: Phoenix, 2000)

Martin, F.X., 'Eoin MacNeill on the 1916 Rising', *Irish Historical Studies*, 12:47 (1961), 226–71

——, '1916; Myth, Fact, and Mystery', *Studia Hibernica*, 7 (1967), 7–126

——, 'Diarmait Mac Murchada and the Coming of the Anglo-Normans', in *A New History of Ireland: II: Medieval Ireland 1169–1534*, ed. by Art Cosgrove (Oxford: Clarendon Press, 1987), pp. 43–66

Maxwell, Roberta, 'Roberta Maxwell', in *Playing Joan: Actresses on the Challenge of Shaw's Saint Joan*, ed. by Holly Hill (New York: Theatre Communications, 1987), pp. 201–9

Mikhail, E.H., ed., *W.B. Yeats, Interviews and Recollections*, 2 vols (London: Macmillan, 1977)

Miller, Liam, *The Noble Drama of W.B. Yeats* (Dublin: Dolmen, 1977)

Mitchell, Angus, 'The Casement "Black Diaries" Debate: the Story So Far', *History Ireland* (Summer 2001), 42–5

——, *Casement* (London: Haus, 2003)

Mitchell, Jack, 'Desmond Greaves *contra* Sean O'Casey', *O'Casey Annual*, 1 (1982), 195–211

Monteith, Robert, *Casement's Last Adventure* (Chicago: Privately printed, 1932)

Mooney, Ria, 'Playing Rosie Redmond', *Journal of Irish Literature*, 6:2 (1977), 21–7

Morash, Christopher, *A History of the Irish Theatre 1601–2000* (Cambridge: Cambridge University Press, 2002)

Mosse, George, *Nationalism and Sexuality: Middle-Class Morality and Sexual Norms in Modern Europe* (Madison: University of Wisconsin Press, 1985)

Moynahan, Brian, *The British Century: A Photographic History of the Last Hundred Years* (London: Weidenfeld and Nicolson, 1997)

Murdoch, Iris, *The Red and the Green* (London: Vintage, 2002)

Murphy, Tom, *Plays: One* (London: Methuen, 1992)

Murray, Christopher, *Twentieth-Century Irish Drama: Mirror up to Nation* (Manchester: Manchester University Press, 1997)

Nandy, Ashis, *The Intimate Enemy: Loss and Recovery of Self Under Colonialism* (Delhi: Oxford University Press, 1988)

Nevinson, Henry, 'Article in *Spectator*', in *George Bernard Shaw: The Critical Heritage*, ed. by T.F. Evans, rev. edn (London: Routledge, 1997), pp. 329–31

Nic Shiubhlaigh, Maire and Edward Kenny, *The Splendid Years: Recollections of Maire Nic Shiubhlaigh as Told to Edward Kenny* (Dublin: Duffy, 1955)

Ní Dhonnchadha, Máirín and Theo Dorgan, eds, *Revising the Rising* (Derry: Field Day, 1991)

Ní Dhuibhne, Eilís, ed., *Voices on the Wind: Women Poets of the Celtic Twilight* (Dundrum: New Island, 1995)

Norman, Diana, *Terrible Beauty: A Life of Constance Markievicz 1868–1927* (London: Hodder and Stoughton, 1987)

Norris, David, 'Homosexual People and the Christian Churches in Ireland: A Minority and its Oppressors', *Crane Bag*, 5:1 (1981), 31–37

Norstedt, Johann A., *Thomas MacDonagh: A Critical Biography* (Charlottesville: University of Virginia Press, 1980)

Noyes, Alfred, *The Accusing Ghost, or Justice for Casement* (London: Gollancz, 1957)

O'Brien, Conor Cruise, 'The Embers of Easter 1916–1966', in *1916: The Easter Rising*, ed. by O. Dudley Edwards and Fergus Pyle (Dublin: MacGibbon and Kee, 1968), pp. 223–40

——, *Ancestral Voices: Religion and Nationalism in Ireland* (Chicago: University of Chicago Press, 1995)

——, *Memoir: My Life and Themes* (London: Profile, 1998)

O'Casey, Sean (Sean Ó Cathasaigh), *The Story of Thomas Ashe* (Dublin: O'Connor, 1918)

——, *Songs of the Wren* (Dublin: O'Connor, 1918)

—— (P. Ó Cathasaigh), *The Story of the Irish Citizen Army* (Dublin: Maunsel, 1919)

——, *The Letters of Sean O'Casey*, ed. by David Krause, 4 vols (London: Macmillan, 1975, 1980 and Washington: Catholic University of America Press, 1989, 1992)

——, *Autobiographies*, 2 vols (London: Macmillan, 1981)

——, *The Complete Plays of Sean O'Casey*, 5 vols (London: Macmillan, 1984)

O'Connor, Frank, *The Big Fellow* (Dublin: Poolbeg, 1991)

O'Connor, Garry, *Sean O'Casey: A Life* (London: Hodder and Stoughton, 1988)

O'Connor, John, *The Story of the 1916 Proclamation* (Dublin: Abbey, [1986?])

Ó Crualaoich, Gearóid, 'Responding to the Rising', in *Revising the Rising*, ed. by Máirín Ní Dhonnchadha and Theo Dorgan (Derry: Field Day, 1991), pp. 50–70

Officer, David, 'For God and for Ulster', in *History and Memory in Modern Ireland* ed. by Ian McBride (Cambridge: Cambridge University Press, 2001), pp. 160–83

O'Flaherty, Liam, *Insurrection* (Dublin: Wolfhound, 1998)

O'Flynn, Criostoir, *A Man Called Pearse* (Dublin: FNT, 1980)

O'Hegarty, P.S. 'A Dramatist of New-born Ireland', in *Sean O'Casey: Modern Judgements*, ed. by Ronald Ayling (London: Macmillan, 1969), pp. 60–7

O'Kelly, Seumas, *Three Plays* (Dublin: Gill, 1912)

O'Neill, Jamie, *At Swim Two Boys* (London: Scribner, 2001)

O'Neill, Marie, *Grace Gifford Plunkett and Irish Freedom: Tragic Bride of 1916* (Dublin: Irish Academic Press, 2000)

Oshima, Shotaro, *W.B. Yeats and Japan* (Tokyo: Hokuseido, 1965)

Ozouf, Mona, *Festivals and the French Revolution*, trans. by Alan Sheridan (Cambridge, MA: Harvard University Press, 1988)

Parmiter, Geoffrey, *Roger Casement* (London: Barker, 1936)

Pearse, Margaret Mary, 'Patrick and Willie Pearse', *Capuchin Annual* (1943), 86–8

Pearse, P.H., *The Mother and Other Tales*, trans. by T.A. Fitzgerald (Dundalk: Dundalgan, 1916)

——, *Collected Works of Padraic H. Pearse: Plays, Stories, Poems* (Dublin: Maunsel, 1917)

——, *The Story of a Success: Being a Record of St. Enda's College, September, 1908, to Easter, 1916*, ed. by Desmond Ryan (Dublin: Maunsel, 1917)

——, *Collected Works of Padraic H. Pearse: Political Writings and Speeches* (Dublin: Maunsel, 1922)

——, *The Home-Life of Pádraig Pearse: As Told By Himself, His Family and Friends*, ed. by Mary Brigid Pearse (Dublin: Browne and Nolan, 1934)

Pearse, Padraic and M.H. Gaffney, *Stories of Padraic H. Pearse: Dramatised by M.H. Gaffney, O.P.* (Dublin: Talbot, 1935)

Pettitt, Lance, *Screening Ireland: Film and Television Representation* (Manchester: Manchester University Press, 2000)

Pfister, Manfred, *The Theory and Analysis of Drama*, trans. by John Halliday (Cambridge: Cambridge University Press, 1988)

Pilkington, Lionel, *Theatre and the State in Twentieth-Century Ireland: Cultivating the People* (London: Routledge, 2001)

Pound, Ezra and Ernest Fenollosa, *Certain Noble Plays of Japan: From the Manuscripts of Ernest Fenollosa, Chosen and Finished by Ezra Pound, with an Introduction by William Butler Yeats* (Churchtown: Cuala Press, 1916)

Queneau, Raymond, *On est toujours trop bon avec les femmes* (Paris: Gallimard, 2001)

Richtarik, Marilynn J., *Acting Between the Lines: The Field Day Theatre Company and Irish Cultural Politics 1980–1984* (Oxford: Clarendon Press, 1994)

Robins, Elizabeth, 'Votes for Women!', in *The New Woman and Other Emancipated Woman Plays*, ed. by Jean Chothia (Oxford: Oxford University Press, 1998), pp. 135–210

'Roger Casement: A Tragic Failure', *Times Literary Supplement* (11 April 1936), 307

Ronsley, Joseph, 'A Humane and Well-Intentioned Piece of Gallantry: Denis Johnston's *The Scythe and the Sunset*', in *Denis Johnston: A Retrospective*, ed. by Joseph Ronsley (Gerrards Cross: Colin Smythe, 1981), pp. 133–56

Rothenstein, William, *Since Fifty: Men and Memories 1922–1938* (London: Faber, 1939)

Rouse, Sarah, *Into the Light: an Illustrated Guide to the Photographic Collections in the National Library of Ireland* (Dublin: NLI, 1998)

Rudkin, David, *Cries From Casement As His Bones Are Brought To Dublin* (London: BBC, 1974)

Rushdie, Salman, *Midnight's Children* (London: Vintage, 1995)

Ryan, Desmond, *The Rising: The Complete Story of Easter Week*, 3rd edn (Dublin: Golden Eagle, 1957)

Said, Edward, *Yeats and Decolonization* (Derry: Field Day, 1988)

——, *Culture and Imperialism* (London: Chatto and Windus, 1993)

Schechner, Richard, 'Approaches to Theory/Criticism', *The Drama Review*, 10:4 (1966), 20–53

——, 'Guerrilla Theatre: May 1970', *Tulane Drama Review*, 14:3 (1970), 163–8

Schrank, Bernice, *Sean O'Casey: A Research and Production Sourcebook* (Westport: Greenwood, 1996)

Sekine, Masaru, 'Noh, Fenollosa, Pound and Yeats – Have East and West Met?', *Yeats Annual*, 13 (1998), 176–96

Sexton, Brendan, *Ireland and the Crown, 1922–1936: The Governor-Generalship of the Irish Free State* (Dublin: Irish Academic Press, 1989)

Shaw, G.B., *The Bodley Head Bernard Shaw: Collected Plays with their Prefaces*, ed. by Dan H. Laurence, 7 vols (London: Bodley Head, 1973)

——, *Bernard Shaw on Cinema*, ed. by Bernard F. Dukore (Carbondale: Southern Illinois University Press, 1997)

——, *The Matter With Ireland*, ed. by Dan H. Laurence and David H. Greene, 2nd edn (Florida: University Press of Florida, 2001)

Shaw, Francis, 'The Canon of Irish History – A Challenge', *Studies*, 242 (1972), 117–53

Simms, Katharine, 'The Norman Invasion and the Gaelic Recovery', in *The Oxford History of Ireland*, ed. by R.F. Foster (Oxford: Oxford University Press, 1989), pp. 44–87

Simpson, Alan, 'O'Casey and the East Wall Area in Dublin', *Irish University Review*, 10:1 (1980), 41–51

Slide, Anthony, *The Cinema and Ireland* (Jefferson: McFarland, 1988)

Smyth, Ailbhe, ed., *Wildish Things: An Anthology of New Irish Women's Writing* (Dublin: Attic, 1989)

The 1916 Song Book, 9d edn (Dublin: Irish Book Bureau, [1938?])

Spivak, Gayatri, 'Can the Subaltern Speak?', in *Marxism and the Interpretation of Culture*, ed. by Cary Nelson and Lawrence Grossberg (Urbana: University of Illinois Press, 1988), pp. 271–313

Spoo, Robert, '"Nestor" and the Nightmare: The Presence of the Great War in *Ulysses*', *Twentieth Century Literature*, 32 (1986), 137–54

Stanfield, Paul Scott, *Yeats and Politics in the 1930s* (London: Macmillan, 1988)

Stanislavski, Konstantin, *My Life in Art*, trans. by J.J. Robbins (London: Methuen, 1948)

Stephens, James, *The Insurrection in Dublin* (Dublin: Maunsel, 1916)

Sullivan, T.D., A.M. Sullivan, D.B. Sullivan, and Sean Ua Ceallaigh, eds, *Speeches from the Dock: Or Protests of Irish Patriotism*, rev. edn (Dublin: Gill, 1945)

Table of Female TDs, *Centre for Advancement of Women in Politics* <http://www.qub.ac.uk/cawp/Irish%20htmls/TD2.htm> [accessed 1 May 2003]

Taillon, Ruth, *When History was Made: The Women of 1916* (Belfast: Beyond the Pale, 1996)

Thompson, William Irwin, *The Imagination of an Insurrection: Dublin, Easter 1916: A Study of an Ideological Movement*, 2nd edn (West Stockbridge: Lindisfarne Press, 1982)

Tifft, Stephen, 'The Parricidal Phantasm: Irish Nationalism and the *Playboy* Riots', in *Nationalisms and Sexualities*, ed. by Andrew Parker, Mary Russo, Doris Sommer, and Patricia Yaeger (New York: Routledge, 1992)

Tóibín, Colm, *Love in a Dark Time* (London: Picador, 2002)

——, *Beauty in a Broken Place* (Dublin: Lilliput, 2004)

Trimble, David, *The Easter Rebellion of 1916* (Lurgan: Ulster Society, 1992)

Trotter, Mary, *Ireland's National Theaters* (Syracuse: Syracuse University Press, 2001)

Turner, Graeme, *Film as Social Practice*, 2nd edn (London: Routledge, 1993)

Turpin, John, *Oliver Sheppard 1865–1941: Symbolist Sculptor of the Irish Cultural Revival* (Dublin: Four Courts, 2000)

——, 'Cuchulainn Lives On', *CIRCA*, 69 (1994), 26–31

——, 'National Romanticism and the Sculpture of Oliver Sheppard' in *CIRCA*, 92 (2000) <http://www.recirca.com/backissues/c92/supplement/21.shtml> [accessed 1 May 2003]

Tyson, Brian, *The Story of Shaw's Saint Joan* (Kingston: McGill, 1982)

Ure, Peter, *Yeats the Playwright: A Commentary on Character and Design in the Major Plays* (London: Routledge, 1963)

Vendler, Helen, *Yeats's Vision and the Later Plays* (London: Oxford University Press, 1963)

Walkley, A.B., 'A.B. Walkley, Unsigned Notice, *The Times*', in T.F. Evans, *George Bernard Shaw: The Critical Heritage*, rev. edn (London: Routledge, 1997), pp. 285–7

Wall, Maureen, 'The Background to the Rising, from 1914 until the Issue of the Countermanding Order on Easter Saturday, 1916/The Plan and the Countermand: the Country and Dublin', in *The Making of 1916: Studies in the History of the Rising*, ed. by Kevin B. Nowlan (Dublin: Stationery Office, 1969), pp. 157–251

Walshe, Éibhear, ed., *Sex, Nation and Dissent in Irish Writing* (Cork: Cork University Press, 1997)

Ward, Margaret, *Unmanageable Revolutionaries: Women and Irish Nationalism* (London: Pluto, 1983)

——, 'Gender: Gendering the Irish Revolution', in *The Irish Revolution 1913–1923*, ed. by Joost Augusteijn (Houndmills: Palgrave, 2002), pp. 168–85

Warschausky, Sidney, 'Yeats's Purgatorial Plays', *Modern Drama*, 7:3 (1963), 278–86

Watt, Stephen, *Joyce, O'Casey, and the Irish Popular Theater* (Syracuse: Syracuse University Press, 1991)

Webb, Beatrice, *Beatrice Webb's Diaries 1912–1924*, ed. by Margaret I. Cole (London: Longmans, 1952)

Weintraub, Stanley, *Shaw's People: Victoria to Churchill* (University Park: Pennsylvania State University Press, 1996)

Welch, Robert Welch, ed., *The Oxford Companion to Irish Literature* (Oxford: Oxford University Press, 1996)

——, *The Abbey Theatre, 1899–1999: Form and Pressure* (Oxford: Oxford University Press, 1999)

Whitbread, J.W., 'Wolfe Tone', in *For the Land They Loved: Irish Political Melodramas, 1890–1925*, ed. by Cheryl Herr (Syracuse: Syracuse University Press, 1991), pp. 171–257

Williams, Raymond, *The Long Revolution* (London: Chatto and Windus, 1961)

Wilson, F.A.C., *Yeats's Iconography* (London: Gollancz, 1960)

Yeats, William Butler, *The Secret Rose* (London: Lawrence and Bullen, 1897)

——, *Four Plays for Dancers* (New York: Macmillan, 1921)

——, *A Vision* (New York: Macmillan, 1937)

——, *The Letters of W.B. Yeats*, ed. by Allan Wade (London: Hart–Davis, 1954)

——, *The Variorum Edition of the Poems of W.B. Yeats*, ed. by Peter Allt and Russell K. Alspach (London: Macmillan, 1956)

——, *Essays and Introductions* (London: Macmillan, 1961)

——, *Explorations* (New York: Macmillan, 1962)

——, *Memoirs*, ed. by Denis Donoghue (London: Macmillan, 1972)

——, *Uncollected Prose*, ed. by John P. Frayne and Colton Johnson, 2 vols (New York: Macmillan, 1975)

——, *The Collected Works of W.B. Yeats: Volume I: The Poems*, ed. by Richard J. Finneran, part of 14 vol. collected works, rev. edn (Houndmills: Macmillan, 1991)

——, *The Collected Letters of W.B. Yeats: Volume Two, 1896–1900*, ed. by Warwick Gould, John Kelly, and Deirdre Toomey, part of 3 vol. collected letters (Oxford: Clarendon Press, 1997)

——, *The Collected Works of W.B. Yeats: Volume II: The Plays*, ed. by David R. Clark and Rosalind E. Clark, part of 14 vol. collected works (Houndmills: Palgrave, 2001)

Newspaper sources

'Abbey Theatre Scene', *Irish Times*, 12 February 1926, p. 7

'16 Athletes Represent the Leaders', *Irish Independent*, 11 April 1966, p. 7

Borrill, Rachel, 'Roger Casement's Numerous Homosexual Encounters Chronicled', *Irish Times*, 29 March 1994, p. 6

Bowman, John, 'Cruise O'Brien Advised on how to Deal with the Casement Diaries', *Irish Times*, 3 January 2003
<http://www.ireland.com/newspaper/ireland/2003/0103/pf3575028827HM9SPCA SEMENT.html> [accessed 29 May 2003]

Brien, Alan, 'O'Casey for Today', *Sunday Telegraph*, 7 October 1962, p. 10

'1916 Ceremony in Dublin GPO', *Irish Independent*, 18 April 1935, p. 11

Childers, Erskine H., 'Padraig Pearse', *Fianna Fáil Bulletin*, April 1936, pp. 5–7

'Connolly's Anniversary', *Bottom Dog*, 11 May 1918, p. 1

Croft, Mordaunt, 'Ireland – the Weak Spot in the Empire', *The Times*, 16 October 1916, p. 9

Cronin, Colm, 'Playing Pearse', *Irish Press*, 8/9 April 1966, p. 9

——, 'Abbey Captures Spirit of 1916 in Play Series', *Irish Press*, 12 April 1966, p. 8

Donovan, Katie, 'Comrade as Mother', *Irish Times*, 4 April 1994, p. 10

Doyle, Matt, 'A Name for the Spike', *Irish Times*, 22 November 2002
<http://www.ireland.com/newspaper/letters/2002/1122/index.html#1036708355694> [accessed 16 July 2005]

'Dublin G.P.O. Ceremony', *Irish Press*, 22 April 1935, p. 2

'Dublin Post Office Ceremony', *Irish Times*, 15 April 1935, p. 7

'Easter Week Celebration in Dublin: Significance of 1916 Memorial', *Irish Times*, 22 April 1935, p. 8

'Easter Week Rising: Memorial to be Erected in the G.P.O.', *Irish Press*, 1 November 1934, p. 7

'Episcopal Opinion', *Irish Independent*, 9 May 1916, pp. 2–3

'Film Notes', *Irish Times*, 4 December 1934, p. 4

'Film Notes', *Irish Times*, 18 December 1934, p. 4

'Firing Party of 1916 Men', *Irish Independent*, 23 April 1935, p. 10

Gaffney, M.H., 'Readers' Views: "The Silver Tassie"', *Irish Press*, 12 September 1935, p. 6

Gibbons, Fiachre, 'Casement Painting goes on Display', *Guardian*, 2 July 2003
<http://www.guardian.co.uk/uk_news/story/0,,989276,00.html> [accessed 16 July 2005]

Haughey, Nuala, 'Shop to Appeal Corporation Order to Close Down', *Irish Times*, 2 October 1999
<http://www.ireland.com/newspaper/front/1999/1002/archive.99100200002.html> [accessed 16 July 2005].

Hogan, David, 'At the GPO', *Irish Press*, 22 April 1935, p. 1

'Impressive 1916 Commemoration', *Irish Independent*, 22 April 1935, p. 3

'Impressive Opening of Military Tattoo', *Irish Independent*, 18 September 1935, p. 10

'Irish Poet's Striking Challenge', *Irish Press*, 2 February 1937, p. 6

'"Late Late" Parody is a Real Gem', *Irish Independent*, 12 April 1966, p. 4

Maher, Mary, 'A Lovely Day for the Marching Men', *Irish Times*, 11 April 1966, p. 1

'March of Easter Week Veterans in Dublin', *Irish Press*, 22 April 1935, p. 1

'Mr. de Valera and the Republic', *Irish Independent*, 22 April 1935, p. 7

'Mr. de Valera on the Removal of Oath', *Irish Press*, 7 December 1931, p. 5

'Mr. de Valera Outlines His Party's Policy', *Irish Times*, 28 October 1931, p. 7

'Mrs. Margaret Pearse Dies at St. Enda's', *Irish Press*, 23 April 1932, p. 1

'Mr. Yeats Revises Song', *Irish Press*, 13 February 1937, p. 8

Muldoon, Paul, 'A Clear Signal', *New York Times*, 17 March 1992, p. A25

'Nation Honours Men of 1916', *Irish Independent*, 11 April 1966, p. 1

'"A Nation of Brothers" was Ultimate Goal of the Seven Signatories', *Irish Times*, 11 April 1966, p. 12

Ní Chathain, Nora, 'The Old Woman of the House', *Irish Freedom/Saoirse na hÉireann*, December 1926, p. 7

'No Opposition', *Irish Independent*, 15 February 1926, p. 8

O'Casey, Sean, 'Mr. O'Casey and the Abbey Theatre: "Defensive Words" on *The Silver Tassie*', 11 September 1935, p. 8

'O'Casey Given the Hynes Treatment: Stars Come Out to See New Plough', *Irish Press*, 8 May 1991, p. 3

O'Hagan, Sean, 'The Wild West', *Guardian*, 24 March 2001 <http://www.guardian.co.uk/weekend/story/0,,461983,00.html> [accessed 12 July 2005]

Pearse, P.H., 'The Coming Revolution', *An Claidheamh Soluis*, 8 November 1913, p. 6

——, 'Peace and the Gael', *The Spark*, December 1915, pp. 1–2

'Ploughing Twice', *Irish Independent*, 8 May 1991, p. 3

'President at Opening of '16 Pageant', *Irish Press*, 13 April 1966, p. 1

'President Hopes for Resurgence', *Irish Independent*, 11 April 1966, p. 7

'President's Son', *Irish Independent*, 22 April 1935, p. 9

'Procession to GPO', *Irish Independent*, 22 April 1935, p. 7

'Public Meetings in Dublin: Mansion House Meetings Postponed', *Irish Times*, 23 April 1917, p. 4

'Rebellion Anniversary', *Irish Independent*, 23 April 1917, p. 3

'Rehearsing for To-morrow's Ceremonies', *Irish Press*, 19–20 April 1935, p. 3

Roddy the Rover, 'Poems of Easter Week', *Irish Press*, 22 April 1935, p. 6

Rushe, Desmond, 'The Abbey Presents Works on the Rising', *Irish Independent*, 12 April 1966, p. 4

'Scene at General Post Office', *Irish Times*, 22 April 1935, p. 7

'104,000 see the Tattoo', *Irish Press*, 23 September 1935, p. 3

'Sex, Lies and the Black Diaries', *Irish Times*, 2 March 2002, Weekend section, p. 4

Shaw, G.B., 'Bernard Shaw on Casement Diaries', *Irish Press*, 11 February 1937, p. 9

Sheehy Skeffington, Francis, '"Under Which Flag?": James Connolly's Patriotic Play', *The Workers' Republic*, 6 April 1916, p. 6

Sheridan, Jean, 'A Noble Evocation of 1916 Sung and Acted', *Irish Press*, 12 April 1966, p. 9

'Songs of Freedom', *Bottom Dog*, 16 March 1918, p. 3

Southwoman, 'To the Young Women of Ireland', *Irish Freedom/Saoirse na hÉireann*, November 1913, p. 2

Stuart, Francis, 'Irish Novelist Replies to Mr. Shaw', *Irish Press*, 13 February 1937, p. 8

'Three Plays in Irish', *Irish Times*, 15 April 1936, p. 7

'Varied Music at the Tattoo', *Irish Independent*, 18 September 1935, p. 8

Waters, John, 'Giving the Memory of 1916 more than a Ritual Nod', *Irish Times*, 17 May 1994, p. 12

Walsh, Sheila, 'A Mother's Letter', *Irish Press*, 27 April 1966, p. 12

'Will Play Casement in Film', *Sunday Press*, 21 February 1954, p. 4

Wroe, Nicholas, 'Britain's Brecht', *Guardian*, 3 January 2004<http://www.guardian.co.uk/arts/features/story/0,11710,1115212,00.html#article_continue> [accessed 16 July 2005]

'Yesterday's Ceremonies', *Irish Times*, 22 April 1935, p. 9

'Yesterday's 1916 Ceremonies in Dublin', *Irish Press*, 22 April 1935, p. 14

Film, television, and CD sources

Cal. Dir. Pat O'Connor. Warner Brothers. 1984.

The Dawn. Dir. Tom Cooper. Hibernia Films. 1936.

The Dubliners 40 Years. CD. The Dubliners. 2002.

Endgame in Ireland. Prod. Brian Lapping and Norma Percy. BBC 2. 2001.

The Ghost of Roger Casement. Prod. Alan Gilsenan. RTÉ 1. 2002.

Insurrection. Dir. Louis Lentin. RTÉ. 1966.

The Lost World. Dir. Irwin Allen. Fox. 1960.

Mein Leben Für Irland. Dir. Max Kimmich. Tobis-Filmkunst. 1941.

Michael Collins. Dir. Neil Jordan. Warner Brothers. 1996.

No Need to Argue. CD. The Cranberries. 1994.

Rebel Heart. Prod. Kevin Jackson, Robert Cooper, and Malcolm Craddock. BBC 1. 2000.

Ryan's Daughter. Dir. David Lean. MGM. 1970.

Secrets of the Black Diaries. Prod. Paul Tilzey. BBC 4. 2002.

Young Indiana Jones, Chapter 7: 'Love's Sweet Song'. Dir. Gilles MacKinnon and Carl Schultz. ABC. 1992.

Unpublished sources

A. Bereaved Mother, BL, G.B. Shaw Papers, Letter of 12 May 1916 to Shaw from 'A. Bereaved Mother', Add. 50,517, fols 386–8

Abbey Directorate, Abbey Theatre Archives, Abbey Theatre Papers, vol. 17, P8134

Ashbee, Charles Robert, King's College Cambridge, Ashbee Journals

British Board of Film Censors, NLI, Roger McHugh Papers, Letter of 31 October 1934 to Julius Klein from BBFC, MS 31,732

Casement, Roger, BL, G.B. Shaw Papers, Roger Casement's notes on G.B. Shaw's 'Rex v. Casement' 1916, Add. 50,678, fols 246–54

Chicago Consul, NAI, Department of the Taoiseach, Sir Roger Casement Film and Book of Life, Note of 10 August 1934 from Chicago Consul to Department of External Affairs, S7804A

1935 Commemoration Organisers, NLI, Easter Week Commemoration 1935, ILB 300 P14

Connolly, James, NLI, William O'Brien Papers, *Under Which Flag?*, MS 13,945

Cosgrave, William, NAI, Department of the Taoiseach, General Post Office Rebuilding, 'Speech by President 11.7.29', S1966

Countryman, John Coddington, 'Life Imitates Art: The Drama of the 1916 Easter Uprising in Ireland' (unpublished doctoral thesis, Bowling Green State University, 1977)

Deignan, J., NAI, Department of the Taoiseach, Sir Roger Casement Film and Book of Life, Letter of 12 October 1934 to government from J. Deignan, S7804A

Department of the Taoiseach, NAI, Department of the Taoiseach, General Post Office Rebuilding, Note of 5 July 1929, S1966

——, NAI, Department of the Taoiseach, Abbey Theatre Objectionable Productions, Draft document of April 1933 to Abbey from government, S8208

——, NAI, Department of the Taoiseach, Abbey Theatre Objectionable Productions, Letter of 17 April 1934 to Lennox Robinson from government, S8208

——, NAI, Department of the Taoiseach, 1916 Memorial GPO, 'Easter Week Memorial' note of 9 April 1935 to secretary, S6405B

——, NAI, Department of the Taoiseach, 1916 Memorial GPO, 'Easter Week Memorial GPO' note of 12 April 1935, S6405B

Deputies of Dáil Éireann, NLI, *Dáil Eireann: Díosbóireachtaí Páirliminte, Tuairisg Oifigiúil*, vols 55 and 56

De Valera, Éamon (through private secretary), NAI, Department of the Taoiseach, Sir Roger Casement Film and Book of Life, Letter of 11 October 1934 to Julius Klein from de Valera's private secretary, S7804A

Devine, John, NAI, Department of the Taoiseach, Abbey Theatre Objectionable Productions, Letter of 24 September 1934 to de Valera from John Devine, S8208

FitzGerald, Mabel, BL, G.B. Shaw Papers, Letter of 23 May 1916 to Shaw from Mabel FitzGerald, Add. 50,517, fols 396–9

Gertz, Elmer, NLI, Roger McHugh Papers, Elmer Gertz's information for Chicago's 1956 G.B.S. Day, MS 31,732

Gogarty, Oliver St John, NAI, Department of the Taoiseach, 1916 Memorial GPO, Letter of 15 April 1935 to de Valera from Oliver St John Gogarty, S6405C

Klein, Julius, NAI, Department of the Taoiseach, Sir Roger Casement Film and Book of Life, Letter of 10 September 1934 to de Valera from Julius Klein, S7804A

——, NAI, Sir Roger Casement Film and Book of Life, Letter of 26 March 1935 to de Valera from Julius Klein, S7804A

——, BL, G.B. Shaw Papers, Letter of 3 December 1934 to Shaw from Julius Klein, Add. 50,520, fol.257

——, 'Skeleton of Story on Sir Roger Casement', now in the possession of Roger Sawyer

MacDonagh, Donagh, NLI, *Easter Christening*, MS 33,720

McHugh, Roger and Alfred Noyes, NLI, *Roger Casement*, MS 31,748

Martin, Frank, NLI, Frank Martin Papers, Scrapbooks, 2 vols, MS 32,695

Molony, Helena, NLI, Ernán de Blaghd Papers, Letter of 22 August 1916 from Helena Molony, MS 20,702

Nevinson, Henry, BL, G.B. Shaw Papers, Letter of 20 June 1916 to Shaw from Henry Nevinson, Add. 50,517, fol.418

O'Casey, Sean, NLI, *The Plough and the Stars* Typescript with MS Annotations, MS 29,407

——, Abbey Theatre Archives, *The Plough and the Stars* Promptbook, 1926/A/6

O'Connor, Ulick, NLI, *Padraic Pearse: A One Man Show*, MS 29,414

Parry, Gertrude, BL, Charlotte Shaw Papers, Letter of 30 October 1916 to Charlotte Shaw from Gertrude Parry, Add. 56,491, fols 230–1v

——, NAI, Department of the Taoiseach, Sir Roger Casement Film and Book of Life, Letter of 4 August 1934 to Dorothy Hungerford from Gertrude Parry, S7804A

——, NAI, Department of the Taoiseach, Sir Roger Casement Film and Book of Life,

Letter of 4 August 1934 to Margaret Gavan Duffy from Gertrude Parry, S7804A
Pearse, Mary Brigid, Pearse Museum Rathfarnham, Oration manuscript, MB108
Shaw, G.B., BL, G.B. Shaw Papers, Statement of 19 December 1934 to Julius Klein from
    Shaw, Add. 50,678, fols 278–81
——, NLI, Roger McHugh Papers, Letter of 19 December 1934 to Julius Klein from Shaw,
    MS 31,732
Stockton, Richard, NLI, *The Prisoner of the Crown*, MS 29,513
Whitbread, J.W., BL, The Lord Chamberlain's Collection, *The Ulster Hero*, 1905/19N
Yeats, W.B., NLI, *The Dreaming of the Bones* Drafts, MS 8775 (1)

Index